THE CAPITAL REGION

TOURING NORTH AMERICA

SERIES EDITOR
Anthony R. de Souza, *National Geographic Society*

MANAGING EDITOR
Winfield Swanson, *National Geographic Society*

THE CAPITAL REGION

Day Trips in Maryland, Virginia, Pennsylvania, and Washington, D.C.

EDITED BY

ANTHONY R. DE SOUZA

RUTGERS UNIVERSITY PRESS • NEW BRUNSWICK, NEW JERSEY

This book is published in cooperation with the 27th International Geographical Congress, which is the sole sponsor of *Touring North America*. The book has been brought to publication with the generous assistance of a grant from the National Science Foundation/Education and Human Resources, Washington, D.C.

Rutgers University Press
109 Church Street
New Brunswick, New Jersey 08901

The paper used in this book meets the minimum requirements of American National Standard for Information Sciences—Permanence of Paper for Printed Library Materials, ANSI Z39.48-1984.

Library of Congress Cataloging-in-Publication Data

The Capital region: day trips in Maryland, Virginia, Pennsylvania, and Washington, D.C.
 / edited by Anthony R. de Souza
    p.   cm.—(Touring North America)
  Includes bibliographical references and index.
  ISBN 0-8135-1870-9 (cloth)—ISBN 0-8135-1871-7 (paper)
  1. Washington Region—Tours. 2. Middle Atlantic States—Tours. 3.Virginia—
Tours. I. De Souza, Anthony R. II. Series.
F192.3.C24 1992
917.9704′43—dc20   92-10412
                                             CIP

First Edition

Frontispiece: "Grant's rear guard": (left to right) Mifflin W. Gibbs, municipal judge who served in Little Rock, Ark.; P.B.S. Pinchbeck, elected lieutenant governor of Louisiana, later acting governor, elected senator but never served; Col. James Lewis, who organized First Louisiana Volunteers in the Civil War, later Apted Collector, Port of New Orleans. LeDroit Park, c. 1915. Photograph by Scurlock Studio.

Series design by John Romer

Typeset by Peter Strupp/Princeton Editorial Associates

△ Contents

PART TWO

RESOURCES

△ Foreword

Touring North America is a series of field guides by leading professional authorities under the auspices of the 1992 International Geographical Congress. These meetings of the International Geographical Union (IGU) have convened every four years for over a century. Field guides of the IGU have become established as significant scholarly contributions to the literature of field analysis. Their significance is that they relate field facts to conceptual frameworks.

Unlike the last Congress in the United States in 1952, which had only four field seminars all in the United States, the 1992 IGC entails 13 field guides ranging from the low latitudes of the Caribbean to the polar regions of Canada, and from the prehistoric relics of pre-Columbian Mexico to the contemporary megalopolitan eastern United States. This series also continues the tradition of a transcontinental traverse from the nation's capital to the California coast.

Nine great day-trips provide the rich physical, historical, and cultural character of the nation's capital region—monumental Washington including L'Enfant's plan, historic Georgetown, District of Columbia neighborhoods, high-tech corridors, edge cities, George Washington's Mount Vernon, Tidewater Maryland and Virginia, the renowned Amish settlement of Lancaster County, the earliest sites of colonial America in Virginia, famous battle sites of the Civil War, scenic landforms of the Piedmont and Blue Ridge. The authors all have in common an intimate knowledge of and affection for this densely textured region. Each author has a broad background in a specialized aspect of the geography of this region and has a college or federal government affiliation.

Anthony R. de Souza
BETHESDA, MARYLAND

⚠ Acknowledgments

We acknowledge the dedicated work of the following cartographic interns at the National Geographic Society, who were responsible for producing the maps that appear in this book: Nikolas H. Huffman, cartographic designer for the 27th IGC; Patrick Gaul, GIS specialist at COMSIS in Sacramento, California; Scott Oglesby, who was responsible for the relief artwork; Lynda Barker, Michael B. Shirreffs, and Alisa Pengue Solomon. Assistance was provided by the staff at the National Geographic Society, especially the Map Library and Book Collection, the Cartographic Division, the Illustrations Library, Computer Applications, and Typographic Services. Special thanks go to Susie Friedman of Computer Applications for procuring the hardware needed to complete this project on schedule.

We thank Lynda Sterling, public relations manager and executive assistant to Anthony R. de Souza, the series editor; Richard Walker, editorial assistant of the 27th International Geographical Congress; Cynthia Suchman; and National Geographic Society interns Natalie Jacobus, who proofread the volume, and Tod Sukontarak, who served as photo researcher. They were major players behind the scenes. Many thanks, also, to all those at Rutgers University Press who had a hand in the making of this book—especially Kenneth Arnold, Karen Reeds, Marilyn Campbell, and Barbara Kopel.

Errors of fact, omission, or interpretation are entirely the responsibility of the author or authors of each field trip; the opinions and interpretations are not necessarily those of the 27th International Geographical Congress, which is the sponsor of this field guide and the *Touring North America* series.

Two of the field guide's authors also wish to make their own acknowledgments. Joseph Thornton thanks the following people for information: Ada G. Piper, Margaret A. Dodson (Mrs. George Dodson), Mr. and Mrs. William Mayo, Irven E. Washington, Mildred B. Tyson, the people in the Washington Room at the Martin Luther King Library, the *Washington Post,* the *Washington Star,* the *Washington News,* and the *Afro-American News.*

Harold Winters wrote two of the field trips. His chapter on the geography of the Civil War is derived, in part, from an ongoing comprehensive study of military geography with Brigadier General Gerald E. Galloway, Jr., of the United States Military Academy, and Colonel William J. Reynolds, U.S.M.A. retired. He thanks them both for their astute insights and good advice on military geography and the Civil War. He also thanks George F. Thompson for assistance in the field and in the presentation of his text, and John M. Morgan III, of Towson State University, and Stephen Bockmiller, of the National Park Service, for sharing much useful information on the battlefield and surrounding area of Gettysburg. The Department of Geography and the College of Social Science at Michigan State University provided funds to support Winters's efforts on behalf of the 27th IGC.

With respect to Professor Winters's day trip on the scenic geomorphology of Maryland's Piedmont and Blue Ridge, he wishes to thank Jim O'Connor as well as John M. Morgan, of Towson State University, for information on certain aspects of the geology and geomorphology of eastern Maryland. He expresses gratitude to the Henry Strong Foundation for permitting public access to Sugar Loaf Mountain, the management of Pier One Imports in Frederick, Maryland, for generously permitting access to geologic exposures on its property, and to George F. Thompson who offered valuable advice that enhanced the excursion.

PART ONE

Introductions and Itineraries

The Capital Region

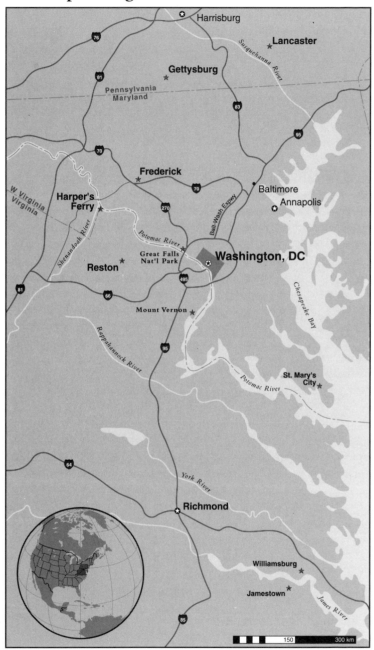

◢ Day One

L'ENFANT'S WASHINGTON— TWO CENTURIES OF CHANGE

by Ralph E. Ehrenberg and Richard W. Stephenson,
Library of Congress

On 26 August 1991, the nation celebrated the bicentennial anniversary of Pierre-Charles L'Enfant's bold design for the city of Washington, the world's first planned capital city. George Washington (b. 1732; d. 1799) selected for this assignment a French-born (b. 1754; d. 1825) military engineer, artist, and architect who served with the Continental Army during the American Revolutionary War. The President was captivated by the Frenchman's vision for a capital city "magnificent enough to grace a great nation." L'Enfant's plan expresses not only the optimism of Washington and the Founding Fathers in the idea of the survival and expansion of the new nation; it also reflects the basic transformation of a society to a republican form of government. The imprint of L'Enfant's vision on the landscape has survived two centuries and today forms the core of the Washington, D.C., metropolitan region.

The selection of the present site for the new capital city was not preordained. Prior to its establishment on the Potomac River, the Continental and Federal governments met in eight different towns and cities along the eastern seaboard. This experience demonstrated that a permanent site should be selected and that on it an

L'Enfant's Washington

Map of L'Enfant's Washington showing major landmarks including Union Station, The U.S. Capitol, Library of Congress, Capitol Hill, The White House, The National Mall, The Smithsonian, Lincoln Memorial, Jefferson Memorial, Tidal Basin, West Potomac Park, The Ellipse, Judiciary Square, Dupont Circle, Logan Circle, and the Potomac River. Notable streets include Florida Ave, New York Ave, New Jersey Ave, Massachusetts Ave, Rhode Island Ave, Connecticut Ave, Pennsylvania Ave, Constitution Ave, Independence Ave, Virginia Ave, New Hampshire Ave, Wisconsin Ave, and various lettered and numbered streets. Bridges shown include Key Bridge, T. Roosevelt Memorial Bridge, and Arlington Memorial Bridge. Also shown are Rock Creek Parkway, G. Washington Parkway, Georgetown, Arlington Cemetery, Reservoir Rd, To National Cathedral, and To Naval Observatory.

entirely new city should be built that would provide proper accommodations for congressional delegates. At the same time, it was hoped the construction of a new city would reduce the influence of commercial interests to which the delegates had been exposed in the larger urban centers. This idea also reflected the contemporary ideals of rural values and distrust of big cities shared by Washington, Jefferson, and others of the political elite.

Six sites were seriously considered for the new federal city, all inland on rivers or bays—Germantown, Pennsylvania, and another site below the falls on the Delaware River near Trenton, New Jersey; Annapolis and Baltimore on Chesapeake Bay; the banks of the Susquehanna, near present Columbia/Wrightsville, Pennsylvania; and the Potomac River in Maryland.

The process of selecting the Potomac River site had geographical, economic, and political overtones. Congress decreed in 1789 that the federal city should be located "as near the centre of wealth, population, and extent of territory, as may be consistent with convenience to navigation of the Atlantic Ocean, and having due regard to the particular situation of the Western country." In the 1790s, the Potomac site was roughly midway between the northern and southern states. It was also easily accessible to major northern cities via the main post route connecting New York City, Philadelphia, Baltimore, and Alexandria and to foreign ports by way of the Potomac River and Chesapeake Bay. Finally, it was believed that the Potomac River would serve as the country's main route to the Ohio River Valley hinterland, an idea George Washington strongly promoted.

In the final analysis, however, the selection of the Potomac River site was the result of geopolitical compromises between sectional interests. In a scheme engineered by Secretary of the Treasury Alexander Hamilton (b. 1757; d. 1804), southern delegates agreed to have the federal government assume debts contracted by the states during the Revolutionary War. In exchange northerners would support establishing the permanent seat of government on the Potomac River south of the Mason–Dixon Line, but leaving the determination of the actual site to President Washington.

Territory of Columbia

After inspecting numerous sites along the Potomac River in 1790, President Washington chose a ten-mile square, diamond-shaped parcel of land straddling the Potomac River. The parcel included land in both Maryland (now comprising the District of Columbia) and Virginia. The federal territory and capital city were named the Territory of Columbia (later District of Columbia) and the City of Washington after Christopher Columbus (whose tercentenary the nation was about to celebrate) and George Washington, respectively. In 1846 that part of the District of Columbia south of the Potomac River was retroceded back to the Commonwealth of Virginia.

The landscape of the District of Columbia embodies two distinct physiographic provinces. The northern half is part of the Piedmont Plateau, a rolling, hilly upland underlain by hard metamorphic and igneous rocks. South of Arlington Memorial Bridge and Rock Creek lies the Atlantic Coastal Plain, consisting of easily eroded sands, clays, gravel, and marine deposits laid down by prehistoric streams and encroaching seas during the past 100 million years.

Dominating the physical geography of the center of the diamond is the confluence of the Potomac River and its Eastern Branch (renamed by Thomas Jefferson [b. 1743; d.1826] the Anacostia River). Forming a Y, the Potomac and Anacostia rivers mark the southwestern and southeastern boundaries of L'Enfant's capital.

The Potomac River, whose headwaters lie deep in the Appalachian Mountains, is the second largest river on the Atlantic seaboard, draining some 12,000 square miles in Maryland, Pennsylvania, Virginia, and West Virginia. The river is navigable for 108 miles, from its mouth at Point Lookout on Chesapeake Bay to just below Georgetown at the Fall Line, the geologic boundary marking the place where the river drops from the upland plateau to the Tidewater plain. Below the Fall Line the Potomac estuary occupies an ancient "drowned" valley gouged out of the softer sediments of the Atlantic Coastal Plain when the sea level stood much lower and then flooded as the sea rose to its present level.

Captain John Smith (b. 1580; d. 1631), who reconnoitered the region in the spring of 1608, was the first European to describe and map the Potomac River. He recorded its name as *Patawomeck flu,* an Algonquin Indian name. The English explorer found several riparian settlements along the Potomac and Anacostia rivers, situated to take advantage of two major trade routes that crossed the Potomac River at the Fall Line. Within the present city of Washington, Greenleaf Point (now home to Fort McNair) served as a council gathering place and James Creek at the foot of Capitol Hill was used as a fishing ground. Along Rock Creek in the northern section of the city were significant quarrys for soapstone and pigment used to make vessels and paints, which were both traded.

Permanent European settlement of the Potomac estuary began about 1690 and was closely associated with the tobacco and Tidewater plantation culture. By the time President Washington chose the Territory of Columbia, it contained two colonial seaports, George Town and Alexandria. George Town, on a bluff at the head of navigation on the Potomac, was formerly the site of an ancient Indian village. It was incorporated in 1751. Alexandria, about 6 miles south of Washington on the west bank of the Potomac, was laid out and surveyed in 1749 by John West, Jr., assisted by George Washington. These two towns, situated at strategic sites at the eastern and southern ends of tobacco-rolling roads, were among the greatest tobacco markets in the United States. They serviced a vast hinterland that ultimately stretched west and north to the Blue Ridge Mountains, the Shenandoah Valley in Virginia, and northern Maryland. By the 1770s, various grains such as wheat and corn supplanted tobacco as the dominant crop of the region. These grains were processed in flour and grist mills near George Town and other sites along the Potomac, such as George Washington's mill near his plantation at Mount Vernon south of Alexandria. Tobacco, grain, and other farm produce were exchanged for rum, molasses, and other luxuries. This trade was usually managed by Scottish-born merchants representing large firms in London and Glasgow.

During the early eighteenth century, a fishing industry flourished along the Potomac, and George Town shipped large quantities of

Potomac shad and herring inland to Maryland, Pennsylvania, and Virginia. George Town also boasted one of America's finest gun foundries. An act of Congress in 1871 abolished the separate government of George Town, making it part of the District of Columbia; thereafter it was known as Georgetown.

The Anacostia River drains the Tidewater plain of Maryland to the east. Its deep channels made it the area's most desirable shipping route in the 1790s. For this reason the original boundaries of the territory were modified to include the lower part of the Anacostia River. Soundings taken in 1797 showed depths of twenty to thirty-five feet. Tobacco was shipped downstream during the last half of the eighteenth century from the port town of Bladensburg, Maryland, just north of the present District of Columbia boundary line. A fishing industry also prospered during this period. Soil erosion associated with tobacco culture and discharge of the District's sewage into the Anacostia progressively decreased the width and depth of the river during the nineteenth century so that Bladensburg, like many other southern port settlements, could no longer function as a seaport. From 1902 to the 1950s, the U.S. Army Corps of Engineers undertook a program of dredging and reclamation, reclaiming some 460 acres on the south bank of the river where the U.S. Naval Station is now located. Farther north, land was reclaimed for the Kenilworth Aquatic Gardens, Kingman Lake, and Anacostia Park.

Following the selection of the Potomac River site, President Washington appointed three commissioners to define, limit, and survey the new territorial district "by proper metes and bounds." The survey of the ten-mile square tract was conducted from 1791 to 1793 by Andrew Ellicott, one of the nation's leading surveyors and mapmakers. Ellicott was assisted for a short period by Benjamin Banneker, a free black, who helped make astronomical observations and calculations to establish the initial point of the survey at Jones Point on the Potomac River in the southeastern corner of Alexandria. Ellicott's final manuscript map of the Territory of Columbia was completed 25 June 1793 and published in 1794. Now housed in the Library of Congress, the map depicts general topography, waterways, and settlements as well as L'Enfant's proposed plan for the Capital City.

L'Enfant's Vision of the Capital City, 1791

While Ellicott undertook the surveying and mapping of the district boundaries, L'Enfant began the "delineation of the grand plan" that would organize the allotted space in a rational pattern. His vision was based upon four considerations: the constraints imposed by geographic and topographic features, the constitutional requirements of three equal branches of republican government, commercial interests, and aesthetics.

Playing a crucial role in L'Enfant's conception of his plan was the lay of the land. Washington City is on a peninsula encircled by a range of hills rising some 400 feet above sea level. Most of the landscape features of the original federal city tract have been obliterated through time, but architectural historian Don Alexander Hawkins has re-created the city's topography as it appeared to L'Enfant in 1791. Using a set of large-scale street and canal grading maps prepared in 1794 by city surveyor Nicholas King, Hawkins has identified four distinct physiographic regions: a low river terrace in the southwest, bounded by Tiber Creek on the north and the Potomac and Anacostia rivers on the west and southeast; a high rounded hill on the east, known as Jenkins's (now the site of the U.S. Capitol building); a set of irregular terraces rising toward the northwest, bounded by Rock Creek, the Potomac River, and Tiber Creek; and the shallow upper valley of Tiber Creek.

Rock Creek forms the boundary of Washington City and Georgetown. A lush, picturesque valley, Rock Creek originates in the Piedmont Plateau of Maryland and flows southwestward to the Potomac River. The lower valley of Rock Creek marks the demarcation line between the Piedmont Plateau and the Coastal Plain. Two hundred years ago, its mouth formed a large bay that served as the major harbor for George Town. During the early nineteenth century, Rock Creek was a source of herring and other fish for export and it provided waterpower for grist mills, mostly wheat and rye. The only reminder today of nineteenth-century industry along its banks is the Godey lime kilns near the Whitehurst Freeway. The dumping of sewage and other trash during the late nineteenth century nearly destroyed the natural beauty of the river.

In response to public reaction, Congress converted the valley to park-land in 1890. Today Rock Creek Park forms the largest recreation area in the National Capital Parks system. A roadway (Rock Creek Parkway) carries commuter and tourist traffic along the valley floor.

Tiber Creek (originally Goose Creek) drained about half of the proposed city in 1791. Beginning in a range of hills about 3.5 miles north of the Capitol, it flowed southward and then westward through marsh and swamps, entering the Potomac River in an elongated embayment where Seventeenth Street N.W. and Constitution Avenue now intersect. Its banks were covered with large trees. Fish such as shad, herring, eel, and catfish were abundant as far upstream as the Capitol. Tiber Creek, eastward to the base of the Capitol, was converted to a canal in the 1820s. By 1870, the canal had become an open cesspool from sedimentation and waste disposal. Shortly thereafter it was converted to a underground sewer concealed today by Constitution Avenue.

The third major waterway was St. James (James) Creek, which drained the area south of the Capitol. This stream, originating in a spring two blocks southwest of the Capitol near Maryland Avenue and Third Street S.W., flowed southwestward through a marshy area until it emptied into the Anacostia River. During the nineteenth century, James Creek also was converted to a canal in accordance with L'Enfant's plan. Between 1916 and 1930 this canal was transformed into a sewer. Today it flows beneath Washington Avenue (formerly Canal Street).

When L'Enfant first reconnoitered the 6,111-acre site set aside for the new Federal City, he found some thirty tracts of land owned or occupied by nineteen proprietors. This land was originally part of a royal charter granted by King Charles I (b. 1600; d. 1649) in 1632 to George Calvert, Lord Baltimore (b. 1850?; d. 1632). In 1715 it became part of Rock Creek Hundred, an administrative division of Prince George's County, which now borders the southeastern boundary of the District of Columbia. Planters in southern Maryland began buying land within the future boundaries of the Federal City in 1664, in anticipation of the depletion of the fertility of their tobacco lands. The first patentees claimed land along the

Potomac and Anacostia rivers in southwestern Washington. In 1714, fifty acres near Buzzard's Point was leased for fourteen years at an annual rent of 500 pounds of tobacco and another fifty acres near the Washington Monument grounds was leased, initiating settlement in the area.

Some of the original tracts—ranging from one acre to 1,400 acres—were owned by George Town and Maryland land speculators who purchased their holdings in anticipation that the Potomac River site would be chosen for the new capital. Most of the proprietors, however, were planters and slaveholders who raised tobacco, corn, wheat, and cattle. The largest plantation was owned by Daniel Carroll (b. 1730; d. 1796) of Duddington and included Capitol Hill. His manor house was four blocks south of the Library of Congress at the present site of Duddington Place.

Included within the boundaries of the future city were two communities that were planned, but never built. Hamburg was a 130-acre tract on the terraces north of Tiber Creek, which was later occupied by the State Department. It was platted and recorded in 1771 by a German immigrant named Jacob Funk, who probably named it after his home town. In 1791 Hamburg was apparently uninhabited; many of the lots were owned by absentee landlords. Carrollsburg, the second "paper" community, was a 160-acre tract surveyed in 1770 and named for its developer, Charles Carroll (b. 1737; d.1832). It was between James Creek and the Anacostia River, now known as Buzzard Point. The name is derived from Turkey Bussard Point, the oldest English place-name within the Federal City; it dates from 1650.

L'Enfant's original grand plan, submitted to President Washington about 26 August 1791, has been reproduced by the Library of Congress in two formats—as a full-size facsimile and as a computer-generated image. The focal points of the plan are the two public reservations designated as the Congress House (renamed "Capitol" by Jefferson), centrally located on Jenkins's Hill—"A pedestal waiting for a monument"—and the President's House, 1.5 miles to the northwest on a terrace above Tiber Creek. A large unidentified square (Judiciary Square), also northwest of the Congress House on the Tiber Creek terrace, was reserved for the

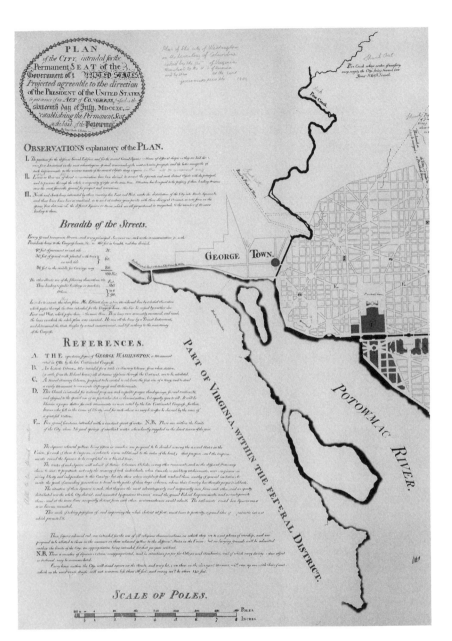

"Plan of the City, intended for the Permanent Seat of the Government of the United States. Projected agreeable to the direction of the President of the United States in pursuance of an Act of Congress, passed on the

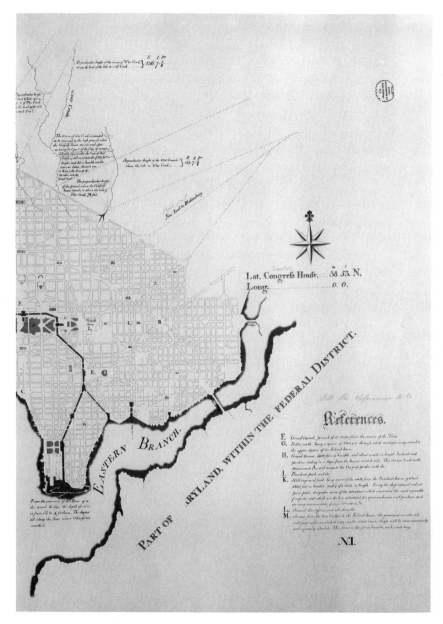

sixteenth day of July, MDCCXC, 'establishing the Permanent Seat on the bank of the Potomac.' By Peter Charles L'Enfant." Photograph courtesy of the Library of Congress.

Supreme Court and now houses the U.S. District Court for the District of Columbia. In placing these buildings on elevated sites "commanding the most extensive prospects," L'Enfant used the natural setting to enhance his plan.

The geographic arrangement of these primary institutions of republican government symbolize in spatial terms the separate but equal dynamics of the balance of power inherent in the constitution. Contemporary observers believed that the great distances between these buildings would be impractical and that their arrangement reflected the commercial interests of land speculators. President Washington later wrote that the public buildings were dispersed to provide separate accommodations for federal officials and employees and to facilitate the work of the separate branches of government. Today, the executive departments (State, Treasury, Federal Triangle) and congressional offices (House, Senate, Government Printing Office, Library of Congress) are clustered around the White House and Capitol, respectively.

Framing the plan is the traditional American gridiron street pattern. Superimposed on this grid are L'Enfant's architectural and urban design elements. Diagonal avenues, 160 feet wide, radiate from open squares and reservations distributed evenly over the plan. L'Enfant envisioned that the fifteen largest squares would serve as the focal points for small settlements, each supported by a different state of the Union. As the city grew, these settlement nodes would gradually coalesce, providing the commercial and social base for a developing urban complex. Smaller, secondary squares were designed as public space for places of worship, libraries, academies, and fraternal organizations. The avenues, designed to connect these open spaces physically and visually, were conceived by L'Enfant to be tree-lined promenades and carriageways.

The names of the streets and avenues do not appear on L'Enfant's original plan of 26 August 1791, since that decision was not made until September of that year at a meeting of Jefferson, James Madison, and the commissioners. The streets are designated by letters (north–south) and numbers (east–west) starting at the Capitol; the avenues are named after the states. The locations of the avenues within the city, L'Enfant scholar Pamela Scott notes, reflect each state's geographic location within the country and the lengths of the avenues mirror their contributions in the Revolutionary War.

Central to L'Enfant's plan is the Grand Avenue (now the Mall), which is depicted as 1 mile long and 1,200 feet wide. Designed to take advantage of a low-lying parcel of land stretching from the Potomac flats to Jenkins's Hill, it connects two public gardens—one south of the President's House, the other west of the Congress House. One historian, Sibley Jennings, has suggested that L'Enfant envisioned that it would be lined with rows of trees with shops housed beneath, similar to the Avenue des Tuileries in Paris, the city of L'Enfant's birth. At the intersection of two lines drawn due west from the Congress House and due south from the President's House, L'Enfant marked a place for an equestrian statue of George Washington in response to the 1783 Congressional resolution to honor General Washington's leadership in the Revolutionary War. President Washington's objection to this project delayed its implementation during his lifetime. Not until 1848 were sufficient funds raised to begin the construction of the Washington Monument, which was not completed until 1884.

A dominant feature of the plan is the canal, which L'Enfant, with President Washington's support, designed for both commercial and aesthetic purposes. Connecting the deep, well-sheltered natural harbors of the Anacostia River with the Potomac River, it was conceived as a major transportation artery through the center of the city. The route of the Washington City Canal, completed in 1815, follows L'Enfant's plan, except for the southwest branch of James Creek. The canal served the City of Washington until 1871, providing inexpensive transportation for boats carrying firewood, lumber, and stone to wharves at Twelfth and Seventeenth streets, N.W. and farm produce to Market Square (now National Archives) at Seventh Street, N.W. In the early 1830s, the Washington City Canal was extended to George Town, connecting it with the famous Chesapeake and Ohio Canal, which reached the town of Cumberland, 186 miles up the Potomac River, in western Maryland.

McMillan Commission

L'Enfant's plan guided the development of the Federal City until the 1830s. The placement of the Treasury Building on Pennsylvania Avenue by President Andrew Jackson (b.1767; d.1845; pres. 1828 to 1836), just east of the White House, obstructed L'Enfant's reciprocal vistas of the White House and Capitol along that famous avenue.

By mid-century, L'Enfant's Grand Avenue was virtually destroyed. The advent of the railroad in 1835 resulted in the construction of tracks across the Mall and the erection of Pennsylvania Railroad Station on the east end of the Mall. The site of the Washington Monument was shifted several hundred feet, changing the point of intersection of the two major axes between the Capitol and the White House. In 1851, landscape designer Andrew Jackson Downing (b. 1815; d. 1852) proposed an informal landscape treatment for the Mall, which was partially implemented later in the century.

During the 1880s and 1890s, the U.S. Army Corps of Engineers resculptured the western boundary of the city, extending its shoreline out to what in 1791 was the center of the Potomac River. In L'Enfant's day, the Potomac's eastern shoreline generally followed the eastern edge of the Tidal Basin and then turned south along Maine Avenue to the tip of Greenleaf Point. At that time the Potomac was 1 mile wide at this point. Through dredging and reclamation, the malarial swamplands and two large shoal areas that had formed at Tiber Bay (mouth of Tiber Creek) and Long Bridge (now the Fourteenth Street Bridge) were transformed into what are now West and East Potomac parks and the Tidal Basin, comprising 721 acres.

L'Enfant's plan was revitalized in 1901 when Congress adopted the McMillan plan (named after Senator James McMillan, chairman of the Senate's District Committee). The plan authorized the appointment of an advisory committee of prominent architects and landscape architects to recommend plans for the development and improvements of the park system of the District of Columbia. The resulting Park Commission report in 1902 was initially dismissed

Streamlines and River Shorelines

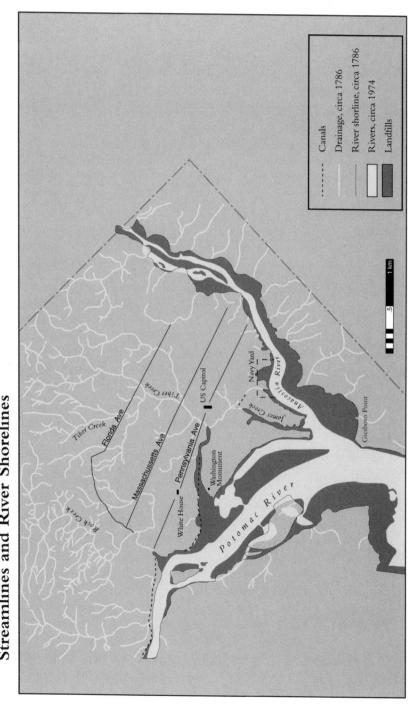

Canals
Drainage, circa 1786
River shoreline, circa 1786
Rivers, circa 1974
Landfills

1 km
.5

Rock Creek
Tiber Creek
Florida Ave
Tiber Creek
Massachussetts Ave
Pennsylvania Ave
White House
Washington Monument
US Capitol
Navy Yard
James Creek
Anacostia River
Giesboro Point
Potomac River

as too visionary, but during the next thirty years many of its proposals were implemented, restoring the basic aesthetic concepts and central themes of the L'Enfant plan.

The major alteration imposed on the L'Enfant plan was the McMillan Commission's incorporation of the reclaimed land along the eastern shore of the Potomac. L'Enfant's basic design of a Grand Avenue was extended beyond the Washington Monument to include West Potomac Park and the recently proposed site for the Lincoln Memorial (completed in 1922). Land south of the Washington Monument was set aside for a future commemorative building or monument and the Jefferson Memorial was subsequently built there.

When the role of the federal government greatly expanded during the first half of the century, the City of Washington pushed beyond the geographic boundaries of L'Enfant's original plan, extending far into the surrounding states of Maryland and Virginia. The heart of the nation's capital, however, is L'Enfant's visionary design, which is expressed most dramatically by "Monumental Washington"—the White House, the Capitol, and the Mall with its monuments to Washington, Jefferson, Lincoln, and, most recently, the Vietnam War veterans.

Itinerary

The tour begins as we ascend Capitol Hill on Constitution Avenue at First Street, N.W., the *Capitol Grounds* on the right and the *Union Station Plaza* (actually an extension of the Capitol Grounds) on the left. Originally, the land now occupied by the plaza was a residential area. George Washington, for example, acquired lots on North Capitol Street in 1798 and constructed two houses to serve as rental properties. The houses were razed when the park was constructed. The plaza is a terraced, landscaped park that descends to Union Station. At the foot of the terrace is the plaza fountain. A fine view of the north side of the Capitol is available from this site, particularly at night when both the fountain and the Capitol dome are illuminated. To the northeast of the fountain, approximately

0.5 mile from the Capitol, is Union Station. Designed by Daniel H. Burnham, the Beaux Arts railroad station opened in 1907 to serve as the gateway to the city. Its completion permitted the elimination of several nineteenth-century railroad stations, particularly one at the foot of Capitol Hill whose tracks for decades had bisected and blighted the Mall. Recently restored to great acclaim (at a cost of 300 million dollars) and refurbished with shops, restaurants, and a food court containing numerous American and ethnic fast-food outlets, the station still serves as the terminal for all commuter passenger trains entering and departing the city. The concourse with its vaulted ceiling is one of the grand interior spaces in the nation's capital. Union Station is also a stop on Metro's Red Line.

At the top of Capitol Hill ("the Hill") on the northwest corner of Constitution Avenue and First Street, N.E., is the Russell Building. This building, the Dirksen Building on the northeast corner, and the Hart Building next to it are all office buildings of the U.S. Senate. Turn right on First Street. On the left at the northeast corner of East Capitol Street stands the U.S. Supreme Court, designed by Cass Gilbert (b. 1859; d. 1934) and built entirely of white marble. Across the street on the southeast corner is the Jefferson Building of the Library of Congress. The building was designed by John L. Smithmeyer and Paul J. Pelz and completed in 1897 under the direction of Brigadier General Thomas L. Casey, chief of engineers, U.S. Army. The French Renaissance style of architecture stands in marked contrast to the classical styles used for the Capitol building and the Supreme Court. The Jefferson Building was named to commemorate Thomas Jefferson's donation of his personal library after the British burned the Capitol. Now, just under 100 years after its construction, it is one of three buildings on Capitol Hill that now house the vast holdings of the *Library of Congress,* the world's largest library. The library's James Madison Memorial Building, one of the largest buildings in the city, is immediately south of the Jefferson Building on Independence Avenue, S.E., and the Adams Building is on Third Street, S.E., to the east.

L'Enfant did not plan for government buildings to face the Capitol; rather, he imagined a commercial district of arcaded buildings with shops facing onto the Capitol Grounds and extending down East Capitol Street ("M" on his plan). On this street, 1 mile from the Capitol building, he suggested "An historic Column— Also intended for a Mile or itinerary Column" be erected from which "all distances of places through the Continent, are to be calculated" ("B" on his plan). East Capitol Street did not become the commercial center that L'Enfant imagined, but rather a principal street in a large, middle-class residential neighborhood. The site L'Enfant selected for the itinerary column is now Lincoln Park, where the Emancipation Monument was erected in 1876.

The Capitol grounds to your right were designed in the 1870s by the extraordinary American landscape architect, Frederick Law Olmsted (b. 1822; d. 1903), the creator of New York City's famous Central Park and numerous other landscape gems. The grounds cover nearly sixty acres and feature curving walks and streets as well as some 800 trees of many species.

Physician and amateur architect William Thornton (b. 1759; d. 1828) designed the Capitol building in a classical style. It dominates the city both figuratively and literally. The cornerstone was laid in a public ceremony on 18 September 1793 by President George Washington. The building was constructed from Aquia Creek sandstone found along one of the tributaries of the Potomac River in Virginia. Burned by the British in August 1814, it was rebuilt and expanded several times. The present iron dome, completed in 1863 to replace an earlier and much smaller wooden dome, is 285 feet high from the eastern plaza and is topped by the "Statue of Freedom." Between 1958 and 1961, the East Front of the Capitol was extended eastward thirty-two and a half feet and faced with Georgia marble, a more weather-resistant stone that does not require periodic painting as did the soft sandstone it replaced.

Turn right on Independence Avenue. The three buildings on the left as we descend Capitol Hill are, in order, the Cannon, Longworth, and Rayburn House of Representatives office buildings. At the foot of the Hill on the southwest corner is a fountain designed by Frédéric Auguste Bartholdi (b. 1834; d. 1904), the sculptor of the Statue of Liberty in New York Harbor. Bartholdi created the fountain for the International Centennial Exhibition held in Philadelphia in 1876. One year later, Bartholdi sold the fountain to the U.S. government for erection in the nation's capital.

Turn right on First Street, S.W. The building to the left is the U.S. Botanical Garden. Founded in 1820, the present building dates from 1931. Included in its collections are many plants brought to the United States in 1842 from the Pacific Basin by the U.S. Exploring Expedition, led by Lieutenant Charles Wilkes.

CAPITOL GROUNDS

Follow the walk to the stairs, and ascend the stairs to the West Terrace of the Capitol. The *Capitol* sits on a hill eighty-eight feet above sea level. The site was originally called Jenkins's Hill, receiving its name from the Jenkins family that two centuries ago farmed rented land nearby. The land was owned by Daniel Carroll of Duddington, Maryland, the largest landholder in the area when the city was laid out in 1791.

The West Front of the Capitol was recently restored following many years of debate on how best to care for the only remaining original sandstone facade of the building. After many coats of paint were stripped away, the sandstone blocks were repaired, strengthened, and, in some instances, replaced. The last three presidential inaugurations have been held on the West Front rather than on the East Front of the Capitol where previous ceremonies had been held since the inauguration of Andrew Jackson (1829).

You are standing on the West Terrace or esplanade designed by Olmsted in the 1870s. Looking westward from this dramatic vantage point, a significant portion of monumental Washington is exposed to your view. At the reflecting pool at the foot of Capitol Hill begins the Mall, a large grass and tree-lined open space that has been called America's park. It extends to the Potomac River. Framing the Mall to the north is Constitution Avenue and to the south is Independence Avenue. On both sides of the Mall are the various buildings that comprise the Smithsonian Institution. The National Gallery of Art, designed by John Russell Pope (1941), is on the immediate right and the red sandstone main building ("the castle") of the Smithsonian, designed in the Gothic Revival style in

1851 by James Renwick, is in the middle distance on the left. L'Enfant noted on his plan that the lots along the Mall "are the best calculated for spacious houses and gardens, such as may accommodate foreign ministers, & c." On 22 June 1791, however, L'Enfant suggested to the President that along the walk between the Capitol and the President's House "may be placed [a] play house—room of assembly—accademies [sic] and all such sort of places as may be attractive to the l[e]arned and afford divertion [sic] to the idle."

Pennsylvania Avenue is the major boulevard that approaches Capitol Hill from the northwest. This is the city's (and the nation's) ceremonial avenue, down which all major parades, marches, and state funeral cortèges progress from the Capitol to the White House. Pennsylvania Avenue is representative of the fifteen broad boulevards that dominate L'Enfant's plan of the city, each named for a state in the union. In explaining the gridiron pattern of streets and diagonal avenues to President Washington in June 1791, L'Enfant said that after

having first determined some principal points to which I wished making the rest subordinate I next made the distribution regular with Streets at right angle north–south & East–West but afterwards I opened other[s] on various directions as avenues to & from Every principal place.

The city planner pointed out that the avenues will provide the citizens with "a variety of pleasant ride[s]" and also

insure a rapids Inter course with all the part[s] of the City to which they will Serve as doses [i.e. does] the main vains [sic] in the animal body to diffuse life through smaller vessells [sic] in quickening the active motion of the heart.

The land between Pennsylvania and Constitution avenues from Sixth to Fifteenth streets, N.W., is called the Federal Triangle. This large area consists of a series of government buildings beginning with the Federal Trade Commission at the apex of the triangle and concluding with the Department of Commerce at the base or the western edge at Fifteenth Street, N.W. As early as 1901, the Senate Park Commission (McMillan Commission) suggested that a mix of government buildings and parks be built in this area to replace the deteriorating neighborhood of shops, houses, and shanties. Not until 1926, however, did Congress authorize purchase of the land. The Great Depression that gripped the country in 1928 and for a few years thereafter prevented completion of the architectural and landscape plan.

The Mall you see was proposed by L'Enfant. He viewed it as an essential open space separating the legislative and executive branches of government, yet linking them by a broad promenade. Note that the Mall is laid out on an east–west axis and the "President's park" ("I" on the plan) and an adjoining "well improved field" ("K" in the "References" but inadvertently left off the plan) are on a north–south axis, creating a large T-shaped open space in the center of the city. Running the length of the Mall, L'Enfant suggested a "Grand Avenue, 400 feet in breadth, and about a mile in length, bordered with gardens, ending in a slope from the houses on each side" ("H" on the plan). At the point of intersection of the White House and Capitol axes, he proposed placing an equestrian figure of George Washington ("A" on his plan), a site near the one occupied today by the obelisk of the Washington Monument.

One feature absent from today's landscape, but conspicuously present on L'Enfant's plan, is a canal. L'Enfant proposed that a canal be constructed, using the waters of Tiber Creek that drained the area north and west of the Capitol and St. James Creek that drained the area to the south. In addition, the city planner suggested that the Tiber be diverted to create a forty-foot cascade down the south side of the Capitol Grounds, falling into a basin that would serve as a reservoir for the canal. The waterfall was never built, but the canal was constructed and for many years was marginally successful in transporting commodities and hauling building stones for the government buildings under construction. The city's Center Market was strategically situated on the canal between Seventh and Ninth streets, N.W., on grounds now occupied by the National Archives. By the time of the Civil War in 1861, however, the canal had become a health hazard, and shortly thereafter it was converted to sewers, over which streets ran. Today's Constitution Avenue, for example, from the foot of Capitol Hill to Seventeenth Street, N.W., is built on top of the old Washington Canal.

In the northwest quadrant of the Capitol Grounds is a grotto constructed by Olmsted to preserve one of the many natural springs that originally watered the area before the city was laid out. Aware of the possibilities that the many springs offered, L'Enfant proposed the erection of "Five grand fountains, intended with a constant spout of water" ("E" on the plan). L'Enfant explained that "There are within the limits of the City, above 25 good springs of excellent water, abundantly supplied in the driest season of the year." The natural spring in Capitol Grotto is now gone, having been replaced by municipal water some years ago.

Resume the tour by going north on First Street, N.W., to D Street, N.W. Turn left on D Street, N.W., and follow D Street three blocks to Judiciary Square.

JUDICIARY SQUARE

Judiciary Square rests on the second terrace formed by the Potomac River. You are standing at the fifty-foot contour line, the highest point between the Capitol and the White House. As you look southwestward down Indiana Avenue to the National Archives building and due south toward the Mall, note how the land slopes downward to the first, or twenty-five-foot, river terrace.

On this site, L'Enfant depicted a large open space with a semicircular row of trees to the north and rows of trees on the east and west. In the middle of the space he placed what appears to be a building. Although unidentified on the plan, more than likely it was intended for use by the courts. Judiciary Square is surrounded by buildings occupied by the United States and District of Columbia courts. The building facing D Street, N.W., designed by George Hadfield in 1820, however, had its beginning as City Hall. Considered to be an excellent example of Federal architecture, it was the first building erected to house the government of the District of Columbia. The building was subsequently used by the District courts. *The National Law Enforcement Officers Memorial* (architect, Davis Buckley; sculptor, Raymond Kaskey) now occupies the center of the square. Judiciary Square is also a stop on Metro's Red Line; subway riders emerge between large-than-life lions guarding the names of fallen officers.

Resume the tour by going west one-half block to Indiana Avenue. Turn left on Indiana Avenue and go one block to Sixth Street, N.W. Turn on Sixth Street, N.W., and proceed to Constitution Avenue. Turn right on Constitution Avenue and go one block to Seventh Street, N.W.

CENTER MARKET

You are standing on the site of what was the north shore of Tiber Creek and, later, the Washington Canal. Until the canal was constructed, this was a low, marshy area subject to periodic flooding. On the south side of Constitution Avenue stands the last remaining canal post. The Mall is adjacent to the avenue on the south side.

The large, classically styled building occupying the blocks from Seventh to Ninth streets, N.W., and Constitution to Pennsylvania avenues, N.W., is the *National Archives*. Designed by John Russell Pope (b.1874; d.1937) and opened in November 1935, this building and its records centers in other parts of the country house the official papers of the U.S. government. On permanent view in this building are the Declaration of Independence, the Constitution, and the Bill of Rights.

The National Archives is built on the site of the city's former *Center Market*. The principal product market for the city from 1801 until it was removed in 1931, its massive building (the second one on the site) contained indoor stalls for 1,000 vendors and space for many more out-of-doors. Its long life as the dominant market center for agricultural products derived not only from its central location between the canal on the south and Pennsylvania Avenue on the north, but also on Seventh Street, N.W., which was an important nineteenth-century thoroughfare leading from the many farms in Maryland to the north of the city.

Walk north on Seventh Street, N.W., to Pennsylvania Avenue, then turn left and walk to the middle of the block. To the north across the avenue is the recently completed *Navy Memorial*. This was one of the five locations that L'Enfant selected for a fountain ("E" on the plan). Included in the new memorial are pools of water and fountains, a 100-foot circular map made of inlaid granite, a statue called The Lone Sailor, and a visitor's center. L'Enfant suggested that a naval monument be built south of this location at the foot of Eighth Street, S.W. identified by the letter "C" on his plan. He proposed that "A Naval itinerary Column . . . be erected to celebrate the first rise of a navy, and to stand a ready monument to consecrate its progress and Atchievements [sic]."

The building sitting abreast Eighth Street, N.W., as you look north beyond the Navy Memorial, is the old *Patent Office Building* designed by William P. Elliot and constructed by Robert Mills, the city's architect of public buildings from 1836 to 1851. Formerly the nation's patent museum, it now houses the *National Museum of American Art* and the *National Portrait Gallery.* L'Enfant suggested for this site a nondenominational church "for national purposes, such as public prayer, thanksgivings, funeral orations, &c . . . It will be likewise a proper shelter for such monuments as were voted by the late Continental Congress, for those heroes who fell in the cause of liberty, and for such others as may hereafter be decreed by the voice of a grateful nation" ("D" on the plan).

Resume the tour by going west on Constitution Avenue, N.W., six blocks to the Washington Monument. Climb the hill to the west side of the Monument.

THE WASHINGTON MONUMENT TO THE WHITE HOUSE

You are standing near the spot that L'Enfant proposed for "The equestrian figure of George Washington, a Monument voted in 1783, by the late Continental Congress" ("A" on the plan). The monument actually erected to honor Washington was designed by American architect Robert Mills. Mills is not only famous for his numerous buildings, but also for his *Atlas of the State of South Carolina* (1825), the first published atlas of an American state. The unstable ground dictated that Mills construct the monument of 360 feet east and 120 feet south of the intersection of L'Enfant's Capitol and White House axes. Construction began in 1848, but work ceased six years later because of the lack of private funds (government funding was not used at that time for such public projects). A second effort to raise private support was undertaken in 1859 by Lieutenant Joseph L. Ives, U.S. Army Corps of Topographical Engineers, who was the first white man to explore and map the Colorado River and later served during the Civil War as aide-de-camp to Confederate president Jefferson Davis. Construction did not resume again until 1876, the centennial year of the nation, when Congress finally appropriated public funds to complete the project, which had become a public embarrassment and eyesore. Part way up the obelisk, the change in color of the stone still marks the two construction phases of the monument. Completed in 1884, the obelisk measures 555 feet, 5⅛ inches from its base to the top. (You can take the elevator to the top.)

Some 600 acres of land to the west and south of the *Washington Monument* were reclaimed in the 1880s and 1890s. The largest reclamation project in the history of the city, it resulted in a deeper Potomac River shipping channel and the creation of a protected harbor called Washington Channel, the Tidal Basin whose water is used to flush clean the Washington Channel, and the West and East Potomac parks. The present-day *Lincoln Memorial,* designed by Henry Bacon (b. 1866; d. 1924), and containing the seated statue of Abraham Lincoln by sculptor Daniel Chester French (b. 1850; d. 1931), the *Reflecting Pool,* the *Constitution Gardens,* and the *Vietnam Memorial* all lie on the reclaimed land of *West Potomac Park.* The Tidal Basin, ringed today with cherry trees the Japanese gave the American people, is a tourist favorite in the springtime. In East Potomac Park on the south side of the Basin stands the *Jefferson Memorial.* Built on the north–south axis of the White House, it was designed by the noted American architect John Russell Pope. Pope's classical design incorporates the dome so much admired by Thomas Jefferson.

About 0.5 mile north of the Washington Monument is the *White House.* Built on the second river terrace of the Potomac at approximately fifty feet above sea level, the building occupies a site selected by President Washington. On 22 June 1791, L'Enfant reminded the President of the site on "that ridge which attracted your attention at the first inspection of the ground on the west side of the tiber Entrance." The city planner remarked that the house will be visible from "10 or 12 miles down the potowmack front [i.e. from] the town and harbor of allexandria [i.e. Alexandria, Va.] and Stand to the view of the whole City." Built of Aquia Creek (Virginia) sandstone, the building was burned by the British when they invaded the city in August 1814. After it was rebuilt, the mansion was painted white to hide the scars left by the fire. From that time onward, the "President's House" has been known as the "White House."

Originally, the White House grounds sloped down to a low bluff overlooking the 1,000-foot-wide mouth of Tiber Creek. This was later filled in to create the *Ellipse*. During much of the nineteenth century, the White House was an unhealthy place to live because of the increasing pollution of the canal and the Potomac River. In 1867, a survey was made to relocate the White House in upper northwest Washington in what is today Rock Creek Park. Nothing came of this scheme. Improved sanitation, the filling-in of the canal, and the creation of new land west and south of the White House eventually solved the health problem. On the north side of the Ellipse is the zero milestone used by the U.S. Geological Survey to calculate road mileages for national highways passing through the city.

CONSTITUTION AVENUE TO ARLINGTON CEMETERY

Resume the tour by going west on Constitution Avenue, N.W. On the southwest corner at Seventeenth Street, N.W., stands the lockkeepers stone house, a remnant of when this was the entrance to the Washington Canal from the Potomac River. On the opposite corner is a gatehouse designed originally for the Capitol Grounds by Charles Bullfinch.

Continue west on Constitution Avenue for four blocks. On the south side of the avenue are *Constitution Gardens* and the *Vietnam Memorial,* inscribed with the name of each American who died in the war. On the north side of the avenue from east to west are the two buildings of the Organization of American States, the Department of the Interior South Building, the Federal Reserve Board, and the *National Academy of Sciences.* On the grounds of the academy is a seated statue of Albert Einstein, who, though known to many as the creator of $E = MC^2$, is known to others for his saying, "Imagination is more important than knowledge."

Turn left on Henry Bacon Drive to the Lincoln Memorial traffic circle. Continue around the circle to the third right. Cross the Potomac River on the Arlington Memorial Bridge. The 1901 Senate Park Commission (McMillan) plan proposed a bridge at this site. It was not until 1926, however, that public funds were available and construction began. It was completed in 1932. Immediately to the north of the bridge on the east bank of the Potomac River is the ceremonial *Watergate.* Consisting of 240 steps in a semicircle leading down to river's edge, Watergate was a popular place to hold summer bank concerts. In recent years it has fallen into disuse because of the noise created by jet aircraft that are required to fly over the Potomac on their way to and from nearby National Airport. The name is now more widely associated with the Watergate Apartments nearby and the scandal caused by the June 1972 break-in of the Democratic National Committee offices and an attempted cover-up of the event, which subsequently led to the resignation of President Richard M. Nixon and the incarceration of ranking Republican officials, among them Attorney General John Mitchell.

Continue partially around the traffic circle at the end of the bridge, cross the bridge into Virginia, and follow the road leading to the entrance to Arlington National Cemetery. Turn left into the parking lot.

ARLINGTON CEMETERY

In front of historic Arlington House (a twenty-minute walk), on a hill overlooking the city he designed, lie the remains of *Pierre Charles L'Enfant.* L'Enfant died virtually penniless on 14 June 1825. For more than three quarters of a century he was buried on the estate of William D. Digges at Green Hill, Maryland. (The Digges family had befriended L'Enfant in the later years of his life.) In 1909, his remains were exhumed and, after lying in state in the Rotunda of the United States Capitol, they were reinterred in

Arlington National Cemetery. At the foot of this hill are the graves of President *John F. Kennedy* and his brother, *Robert F. Kennedy,* both of whom were assassinated.

Arlington House provides a magnificent view of the city. The Anacostia Ridge in the distance dominates the city to the east. The Pentagon is to your right and occupies the former site of Washington, D.C.'s first airport. Visible along the Potomac River are the Kennedy Center for the Performing Arts and the Watergate Apartments. Other major buildings and monuments you can see include the Lincoln Memorial, the Jefferson Memorial, the Washington Monument, the Capitol, and the Library of Congress. In the foreground are some of the thousands of tombstones that cover the hills and valleys that make up this national cemetery.

Arlington House, designed by George Hadfield for George Washington Parke Custis (b. 1781; d. 1857), was begun in 1802 and completed in 1817. Custis was raised by his grandmother, Martha, and step-grandfather, George Washington. Arlington House and its 1,100 acres was inherited by Custis's daughter, Mary Anna Randolph Custis. For 30 years it was her home and that of her husband, Robert E. Lee. With the outbreak of the American Civil War in 1861, Lee was offered the command of the Union Army. He declined, accepting instead the command of the military forces of his native state of Virginia. The Arlington plantation was occupied by federal forces shortly thereafter and the plantation house became the headquarters of the Army of the Potomac. The estate was officially confiscated by the federal government in May 1864 and one month later, the first soldiers were buried on the property. By the end of the war, Arlington contained some 16,000 graves. Today, more than 200,000 military veterans and their dependents are buried here on 612 acres of land.

To the west of Arlington Cemetery is Arlington Heights, the present site of *Fort Myer,* a military reservation which was formerly part of the Custis-Lee plantation. The Fort Myer parade ground played an important role in the development of aviation and aerial photography. Following their experiments at Kitty Hawk, the Wright brothers did pioneering work for the U.S. Army at this site. During World War I, the U.S. Army devised procedures for aerial photography and tested cameras with flights over the region.

Freedman's Village was begun in June 1863 on the southern portion of Arlington Plantation. For more than thirty years, this village provided much-needed housing for former slaves who had made their way to the nation's capital.

Arlington House is a fine example of an imposing, early nineteenth-century southern mansion. A National Park Service ranger will give a brief introduction to the house before you tour the rooms on your own.

GEORGETOWN

Continue on the Virginia or western shore of the Potomac River via Route 50 to Rosslyn. Cross the Potomac River via the *Key Bridge* to *Georgetown*. Key Bridge is named for Francis Scott Key (b. 1779; d. 1843), author of the words to the national anthem, whose home once stood near the bridge on the District of Columbia side. It is the second bridge to have been constructed at this point across the Potomac. In 1791, L'Enfant suggested that a bridge be built at this location to connect the planned city with the American South. Turn right on M Street, N.W., and continue three blocks east to Wisconsin Avenue.

The town of Georgetown was authorized by the Maryland Provincial Assembly in 1751. Situated at the head of navigation on the Potomac River, the town quickly became the leading tobacco market in the colony. The merchants and landowners of Georgetown did much to encourage the First Congress to locate the nation's capital on the banks of the Potomac below Great Falls. The 10-mile Federal District selected by President Washington included the thriving river ports of Georgetown, Maryland, and Alexandria, Virginia, 6.5 miles downstream, as well as the largely undeveloped towns of Carrollsburg and Hamburg on the Maryland side. The *Forrest–Marbury House* on your right at 3350 M Street, N.W., was built about 1788. Recently restored, it is typical of merchants' houses of two centuries ago. This house was owned by the successful merchant and landowner General Uriah Forrest. George Washington dined here with the city commissioners on

29 March 1791, after having met with L'Enfant and the local landowners at Suter's Tavern.

At the corner of M Street, N.W., and Wisconsin Avenue, turn right and stop in midblock where the avenue crosses over the Chesapeake and Ohio Canal. On the east side of the street approximately where the Filomena Restaurant (1063 Wisconsin Avenue, N.W.) is today stood *Suter's Tavern.* For a time, L'Enfant had his rooms in this popular tavern and it was here on 29 March 1791 that George Washington and the city commissioners first met with the proprietors to discuss the proposed city. The next day, Washington noted in his diary that the proprietors

> having taken the matter into consideration saw the propriety of my observations; and that whilst they were contending for the shadow they might loose the substance; and therefore mutually agreed and entered into articles to surrender for public purposes, one half of the land they severally possessed within bounds which were designated as necessary for the City to stand with some other stipulations, which were inserted in the instruments which they respectively subscribed.

Looking westward you see one of the locks of the *Chesapeake and Ohio Canal.* The canal was chartered in 1823; work was begun five years later. Backers envisaged that the canal would link the Potomac River with the westward-flowing waters of the Ohio River, thereby tapping the resources of a vast interior hinterland. When work ceased in 1851, the canal extended from Georgetown below the falls of the Potomac to Cumberland, Maryland, 688 feet above sea level in the Appalachian Mountains, a distance of 186 miles, requiring seventy-six locks. Although the canal remained in operation from 1830 until 1923 largely hauling bulky, non-perishable cargo such as coal, its financial success was doomed by the Baltimore and Ohio Railroad which won the race to the Ohio country. Associate Justice William D. Douglas was largely responsible for making the C & D Canal a national park in 1972. Today it is highly valued as a recreational greenway for residents and tourists alike.

Continue south one block to the shore of the Potomac River. You are standing on the shore of the Georgetown Channel of the Potomac River. Directly across the channel is *Theodore Roosevelt Island National Park*. The island is a wildlife refuge today and contains a memorial to President Theodore Roosevelt (b. 1858; d. 1919; pres. 1901 to 1909). Known as Mason's Island in 1791, it was named after its owner George Mason (b. 1725; d. 1792), author of the Bill of Rights. For many years the Mason family operated an important ferry from near this spot. It is shown as a dotted line on L'Enfant's plan of the city.

In the eighteenth and early nineteenth centuries, Georgetown waterfront was bustling with activity. Ocean-going ships from all over the world filled the channel. As you can see, all this is gone. As the ships grew larger and the harbor gradually silted in, the port declined in importance. Today the character of the waterfront has changed as parks, restaurants, esplanades, and luxury hotels replace the decaying wharves, warehouses, and industrial buildings of the past.

WASHINGTON NATIONAL CATHEDRAL AND CLEVELAND PARK

Turn around and go north on Wisconsin Avenue. This avenue follows the early colonial road that entered Georgetown from Frederick, Maryland, some 43 miles to the northwest. Rather than crossing river terrace deposits found in L'Enfant's city, Wisconsin Avenue bisects an exposed portion of igneous rocks from the Piedmont Formation. Wisconsin Avenue leads to the Piedmont Plateau and the highest elevations in Washington, D.C. Reno Reservoir, two blocks east of Wisconsin Avenue at an elevation of about 420 feet above sea level, is the highest point of land within the city limits.

Travel approximately 2 miles north on Wisconsin Avenue to Massachusetts Avenue, N.W. The fifty-seven–acre close or grounds of the *Washington National Cathedral* (381 feet above sea level) begins on the northeast corner of Wisconsin and Massachusetts avenues, N.W. This beautifully designed Gothic cathedral is the seat of the bishop of the Episcopal diocese of Washington and of the presiding bishop of the U.S. Episcopal Church. In many ways, however, the cathedral serves as the national church that George Washington envisaged and L'Enfant depicted as "D" on his plan. In addition to its regular services, countless nondenominational services, celebrations, and funerals—many of national significance—are held here each year. Begun in 1907, the cathedral was completed in 1990. It is the sixth largest Gothic cathedral in the world. The top of the Gloria in Excelsis tower is 676 feet above sea level, the highest structure in Washington, D.C.

Docents give a brief introduction in the nave of the cathedral. Then take the elevator to the observation gallery for a 360-degree view of Washington, D.C. and the surrounding region. You can also explore the rest of the cathedral, including the shop, herb cottage, rose garden, and greenhouse.

Leave the cathedral, exiting onto Wisconsin Avenue; turn right on Woodley Road and right again at the next corner onto Thirty-fourth Street, N.W. This route passes through a small section of *Cleveland Park,* one of Washington, D.C.'s older but still fashionable subdivisions. This and many others like it were made possible by the extension of streetcar lines beyond the boundaries of the city designed by L'Enfant. Cleveland Park, begun in 1894, is named for President Grover Cleveland (b. 1837; d. 1908; pres. 1885 to 1889 and 1893 to 1897). Earlier, however, it had been the site of summer homes of the wealthy and famous. Grover Cleveland, for example, owned a house in this area called Oak View, which served as his summer White House during his first term as President.

MASSACHUSETTS AVENUE TO THE CAPITOL

Turn left onto Massachusetts Avenue. The grounds of the U.S. Naval Observatory are on the right. Originally located on high ground at Twenty-third and E streets, N.W., the observatory was moved to what was in 1893 a remote location. The Vice President of the United States occupies the white frame, Victorian-style house on the grounds.

As you descend Massachusetts Avenue, note the many nations that have their embassies here. For many years, this portion of Massachusetts Avenue has been called *Embassy Row.* Immediately after crossing Rock Creek, the building on the left is the *Islamic Center,* formerly the Iranian Embassy.

Proceed on Massachusetts Avenue to one block past Sheridan Circle. Turn left on Florida Avenue. The world-famous *Cosmos Club* at the corner at 2121 Massachusetts Avenue, N.W., was founded in 1878 by John Wesley Powell (b. 1834; d. 1902; the geologist and ethnographer who explored the Green and Colorado rivers, 1869 to 1874) and others as a private cultural and social club for geologists, geographers, and other scientists.

Florida Avenue follows the boundary of the city as planned in 1791 (and was known as Boundary Street until the city expanded). The long arc of the northwestern part of Florida Avenue follows the path of the colonial road that linked Georgetown and Bladensburg, Maryland. The original road followed this seemingly rambling route to avoid having to cross the higher terrace to the north. At Ninth Street, N.W., Florida Avenue departs from the path of the colonial road and heads southeastward where it ends at Fifteenth and H streets, N.W., a few blocks short of the Anacostia River.

North of Florida Avenue at Sixteenth Street, N.W., is the residential neighborhood of *Meridian Hill.* In 1867, this portion of the city was platted and lots were sold to the public for ten cents a square foot. Meridian Hill Park (also called Malcolm X Park in honor of the Black Muslim leader; b. 1925; d. 1965) is on the east side of Sixteenth Street north of Florida Avenue, N.W. At the turn of the century, when the canal downtown had become an open sewer, this site was considered for a new presidential mansion to replace the aging White House. Instead, in 1910, Congress authorized the creation of a park. Built on the edge of the 200-foot terrace, the formal, Italianate design of the park skillfully incorporates the natural topography of the site.

On the west side of Sixteenth Street across from Meridian Hill Park are the gateposts to all that remains of *Henderson Castle.* Built in 1888, it was the home of Senator and Mrs. John B. Henderson of Missouri. Mrs. Henderson became one of the driving forces behind the development of the area and did much to make Sixteenth Street, N.W., one of the preeminent residential streets in the city.

From Fifteenth Street east to North Capitol Street, Florida Avenue forms the northern boundary of *Shaw,* a portion of the city defined in 1966 as an urban renewal district. Actually consisting of several neighborhoods, the district takes its name from Shaw Junior High School. Much of this area was developed for middle-income housing in the years following the Civil War. By the turn of the twentieth century, the Shaw district had become the center of the city's growing black population. As the district became predominantly black, the number of black-owned businesses in the area also substantially increased. Black entertainment flourished here at such well-known places as the Howard Theater on T Street, N.W., at Florida Avenue. World-famous Edward "Duke" Ellington developed his extraordinary musical talents as a performer and composer in the Shaw district. Today, much of the Shaw district visible from Florida Avenue is economically depressed and in need of restoration and economic renewal.

The campus of *Howard University* begins on the northeast corner of Georgia and Florida avenues, N.W. The large building at this edge of the campus is the Howard University Hospital. The area south of Florida Avenue is *LeDroit Park,* a black residential neighborhood built in the late nineteenth century. Howard University is the largest black educational institution in the United States. Chartered in 1867 by the federal government, it is the only university that receives public funds directly in support of its operations. The university is named for Major General Oliver O. Howard (b. 1830; d. 1909), who was instrumental in its founding and served as its president from 1869 to 1874.

Turn right on North Capitol Street. At this point you have left the northern boundary of L'Enfant's city and are heading south toward the Capitol building, which concludes this tour.

△ Day Two

TWO WASHINGTON, D.C., NEIGHBORHOODS— SHAW AND LEDROIT PARK

by Joseph B. Thornton, Jr., *University of the District of Columbia*

Washington, D.C., is a mosaic of neighborhoods. This tour focuses on two of them, Shaw and LeDroit Park. Both are mostly poor and predominantly black neighborhoods that have seen better days and are now enjoying a resurgence. Despite drug-related violence and crime, they are attracting young middle-class professionals of all races, especially whites. The new Metro stop in Shaw has certainly boosted its popularity.

Georgetown

Let's first drive through the more affluent areas to form a basis for later comparison with Shaw and LeDroit Park. From Dupont Circle, drive west on P Street, N.W.; cross Rock Creek Park, and on the left at 2600 P Street is *Jerusalem Baptist Church,* one of three black churches in *Georgetown.* The other two are the *First Baptist Church of Georgetown* (Twenty-seventh and Dumbarton Avenue, N.W.) and *Mount Zion United Methodist Church* (1334 Twenty-

Washington's Neighborhoods

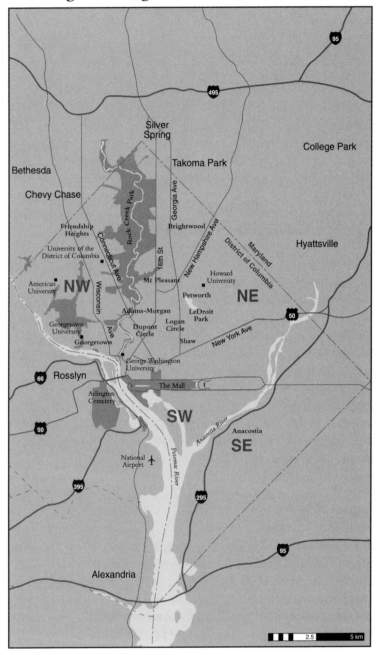

ninth Street, N.W.). Historic *Mount Zion Cemetery* lies on the north side of the 2700 block of Q Street.

The churches are still active, but few blacks live in Georgetown today. From the mid to late 1800s, most of the 1,000 black families in Georgetown lived south of P Street, N.W., between Rock Creek Park and Twenty-ninth Street. By the early part of this century Georgetown was no longer fashionable, however, and by the 1940s realtors were buying what had become inexpensive real estate. Most of the blacks sold and left. Interestingly, Georgetown is currently one of the wealthiest neighborhoods in the District.

Continue west on P Street to 3044, the residence of Emma V. Brown. Ms. Brown was educated at Oberlin College and devoted her life to educating black children. She opened a school for black children in her home in 1861, and in 1871 became principal of the *Sumner School* (Seventeenth and M Street, N.W.). Turn left (south) on Thirtieth Street, stopping at 1208, the residence of Dr. James Fleet, one of three black physicians in Washington before 1864. He bought his house for 800 dollars in 1843. Continue down Thirtieth to M Street and turn right. At 2906 M Street, Alfred and William H. Lee sold flour, grain, feed, and hay. Alfred earned enough to buy the mansion on H Street, N.W., that had housed the British delegation, and when he died in 1893, it was worth more than 300,000 dollars. He was one of the wealthy merchants who probably began by living above the loading docks along the Potomac when Georgetown was a port city. More recent members of the black community of Georgetown included the George Dodson family who lived at 2611 and 2613 Dumbarton Avenue, N.W.; George Dodson's brother, Dr. Joseph Dodson, and his family, who lived at 2709 P Street, N.W.; and Dr. Charles Marshall, a prominent black physician, and his family, who lived in the 2700 block of P Street, N.W. Dr. Marshall's son still lives in Georgetown on P Street, but Dr. Dodson's widow recently sold her home and moved out of the neighborhood. On 20 September 1991, about 500 people attended a "Black Georgetown Reunion."

Other notable residents of Georgetown were Olga S. Halsey and her sister Marion S. Halsey, originally from Unaddilla, New York, who lived at 2905 P Street, N.W. A cousin of Admiral "Bull"

Halsey of Antarctica fame, Olga Halsey served on the Civil Service Commission and President Franklin D. Roosevelt's Civil Rights Commission. The late Dr. Gordon Gray, former president of the Georgetown Association and a member of the Reynolds tobacco family, lived on Thirtieth Street. The late Dorothea de Schweinitz, as a force in the Georgetown renovation movement and a past president of the Georgetown Association, prevailed in the renovation efforts along M Street. Miss de Schweinitz came from a long line of German Quaker ministers from Bethlehem, Pennsylvania. She worked as a government economist and wrote four books. Former Governor Endicott and Mrs. Peabody of Massachusetts bought her house (it has since been sold to the syndicated columnist George Will). The home of the late Averell Harriman served as a temporary residence for former first lady Jacqueline B. Kennedy and her children after the assassination of her husband, President John F. Kennedy. A drive through Georgetown would not be complete without recognizing Mrs. Buchanan Tyson. In 1991, she was ninety-nine years old. Her grandfather, William Windom, served as the secretary of the treasury, and one of her nephews appears as a regular on the TV series, "Murder She Wrote."

Continue west on M Street. Turn right on Wisconsin Avenue (about four blocks) and take the first left onto Prospect Street. Our main reason for visiting Georgetown and the other neighborhoods west of Rock Creek Park is to contrast affluent and less affluent neighborhoods of Washington, D.C. Those interested in historic Georgetown should stop at the *Georgetown Visitors' Center* at 3251 Prospect Street, N.W. It is open seven days a week: Monday through Friday, 9:00 a.m. to 5:00 p.m.; Saturday and Sunday, 11:00 a.m. to 4:00 p.m.

Continue on Prospect until you must turn right on Thirty-seventh Street. *Georgetown University* lies directly ahead. In the Jesuit cemetery there is the grave of Father Patrick Healy, S.J., the first black Jesuit. Dedicated to turning a small college into a major educational and spiritual center, he died in 1908. Follow Thirty-seventh, turn right on P, left on Thirty-fifth, and left on Reservoir Road.

Reservoir Road to Upper Northwest and Adams Morgan

One of the most unusual embassies is the *French Embassy* at 4101 Reservoir Road, N.W., across from Georgetown University Hospital (3800 Reservoir Road, N.W.). Constructed of white marble with black streaks, the embassy appears to be built partially underground and into the hill behind it. Next to it is an upper-income townhouse development called *Hillandale.* The gatehouse is a remnant of more graceful living in the past. (Compare this with the *Cloisters,* another townhouse development, at Fifteenth Street just a few blocks south of U Street, N.W. The Cloisters is more convenient to downtown than the Hillandale.) The *German Embassy* is just west of Foxhall Road on Reservoir Road. Turn north on Foxhall Road, and drive by some of the mansions of Washington's elite.

Along Chain Bridge, N.W., is an affluent neighborhood, but at the turn of the twentieth century it housed a large black community. Dr. Daniel G. Hill, former dean of the School of Religion at Howard University, lived here. The frame house next to the Hill house is the former home of the late Clayton Bannister who taught science at Garnet Patterson Junior High School. He tried, without success, to attract professional blacks here when the area was still truck farms before World War II. The neighborhood began to attract the affluent after the construction of the new British Chancery and the British ambassador's residence in 1928. This was an ethnically mixed neighborhood in the early 1900s. Around 1917 Mrs. Ada G. Piper purchased some land in what is now called the *Kent* neighborhood. There is still a black graveyard and the site of the former black schoolhouse where the teacher had to arrive early enough in winter to start the fire. It was sold at auction and is now a residence.

Turn on MacArthur Boulevard. Take the first right on Elk Ridge Terrace, then the first right on University Terrace, N.W. Then turn right on Loughboro, which becomes Nebraska Avenue. We will stop in front of the homes of Mrs. Ada G. Piper and her brother and his wife, Dr. and Mrs. James Gray. She taught geography at the Miner Teachers College and D.C. Teachers College. The sister-in-law of Dr. Ralph Bunche, the first black to receive the Nobel Peace Prize, which he won for bringing a negotiated peace to the Middle East, lived in this area. Dr. Bunche and his sister-in-law's husband taught at Howard University. Several houses in this area cost over one million dollars even though they are on very small lots with little or no surrounding land.

While driving to the campus of the *University of the District of Columbia,* stay on Nebraska Avenue, pass the *American University* campus on the left, the *National Presbyterian Church and Center* on the right, and the *Naval Chapel.* Turn right on Van Ness, pass the *Israeli Embassy* (at Reno Road), and turn left onto the university campus.

After leaving the campus, return on Van Ness to Reno Road. Turn left on Reno, which becomes Thirty-fourth Street, N.W. Proceed to the *Naval Observatory* at the intersection of Massachusetts Avenue and Thirty-fourth, and turn left. Notice along Massachusetts Avenue—*Embassy Row*—the British Embassy, the Brazilian Embassy, the South African Embassy, and the former Embassy of Iran and its ambassador's residence. The old *Vanderbilt Mansion* was recently purchased for about 3 million dollars, and several million dollars were spent literally rebuilding it. It houses a virtual treasure in paintings.

Continue on Massachusetts Avenue (past more embassies) to Dupont Circle (also a Metro Stop). Go clockwise around the circle 300 degrees to go north on Connecticut Avenue and take the right branch at the Washington Hilton, onto Columbia Road, N.W. This is *Adams Morgan,* perhaps the most ethnically diverse neighborhood in the city, which is evident from its restaurants. The Latino Festival is held here every year.

Follow Columbia Road to Sixteenth Street, N.W.; turn left on Sixteenth and drive north about 4 miles past Walter Reed Army Medical Center on the right and bear right on Alaska Avenue. This area is known as *Shepherd Park,* another ethnically diverse neighborhood. In the late 1950s when realtors were trying to incite racial prejudice and fear to coerce homeowners to sell their houses cheaply, the people in Shepherd Park banded together to form Neighbors, Inc., an association dedicated to maintaining the multiracial character of the neighborhood. Continue on Alaska Avenue until it intersects Georgia Avenue, and turn right. On your right you pass the other side of the Walter Reed Army Medical Center. About 6 miles south on the left is *Howard University.* Notice the expansion of the campus, the new dormitories, and the new businesses along Georgia Avenue. Incidentally, several Jamaican restaurants can be found along Georgia Avenue as well as new stores in the old bakery and car barn on Georgia Avenue and Barry Place, N.W. *LeDroit Park* is around the corner from the Howard University Inn. This inn is an integral part of the University's School of Business where the students put their academic skills to practical use. It also houses two restaurants, one with an excellent jazz band.

LeDroit Park

LeDroit Park forms a rough triangle bounded by Second Street, N.W., on the east, Sixth Street, N.W., on the west, W Street, N.W., on the north, and Florida Avenue on the south.

LeDroit Park began as a Washington suburb catering to Victorian taste. In 1873 Amzi L. Barber, one of the white founders of Howard University, bought forty acres of university land. With the help of his father-in-law, real estate broker LeDroit Langdon, Barber hired architect James McGill and an assortment of workmen. In four years they produced forty-one houses of various styles at a total cost of $200,000. By 1887, LeDroit Park consisted of sixty-four houses on streets named for trees and surrounded by a fence that separated it from black residents in neighboring Howard Town. The fence was an indignity, and one day in July 1888, a group removed a wooden section. The barbed wire fence that replaced it lasted two years before it too disappeared.

The first black to move to LeDroit Park was Octavius Williams, a barber at the Capitol who bought the residence at 338 Spruce (now U) Street. By World War I the area was almost completely

The Elks Home, Rhode Island and Florida avenues, LeDroit Park. Photograph by Scurlock Studio.

black. It produced many luminaries, among them poet Paul Laurence Dunbar; Anna Cooper, awarded a doctorate by the Sorbonne; statesman John Mercer Langston; Duke Ellington; Civil War hero and Congressional Medal of Honor winner Major Christian Fleetwood; the U.S. Army's first black general, Benjamin Davis; Nobel Prize winner Ralph Bunche; Senator Edward Brooke; Robert H. Terrell, the city's first black municipal judge; and his wife, civic leader Mary Church Terrell.

By the 1970s newspapers were describing LeDroit Park as an inner-city slum with a glorious past. Nevertheless some old families refused to move, and in 1974 the neighborhood was listed on the National Register of Historic Places. Of the original sixty-four houses, fifty remain. One resident who never sold out was the former mayor of this city, Walter Washington, who still lives in the residence of the late Reverend Bullock in the 400 block of T Street, N.W. Just east of his house on the corner of Fourth and T streets, N.W., is the Washington, D.C., residence of the Reverend Jesse Jackson.

Garnett C. Wilkerson, former assistant superintendent of the Colored Schools in Washington, D.C., lived at 4006 U Street, N.W. The houses in this block are examples of Italian Renaissance townhouses, the only ones in the Washington, D.C., metropolitan area. Around the corner on Fourth Street, N.W., lived the Byrd family. Marguerite Byrd married Harry Belafonte and is now the widow of the late Dr. Edward Maziquie, a local physician and president of the Board of Trustees at Morehouse College in Atlanta, Georgia. One of Marguerite's brothers was an architect, and a sister taught music at McKinley High School. Colonel West Hamilton owned a print shop on U Street, N.W. and served in many capacities in the community, including that of school-board member. He lived to be over 100 in the 300 block of U Street, N.W. The Carters have resided at 4002 U Street, N.W., since 1912. James Martin Carter taught math at Armstrong High School and English at Dunbar High School for a total of forty-four years. Both Armstrong and Dunbar are *Shaw* area public schools. Dr. Marion Carter, the daughter of James M. Carter, now resides in the house. She received a B.S. degree from Wellesley College; master's degrees from Howard, Middlebury, and Georgetown; and doctorates from Catholic University and Georgetown University. Her mother's sister is married to the noted tenor Todd Duncan.

Arthur DePriest lived at 419 U Street, N.W.; a neighborhood in the far northeast section of town is named after him. In the 1930s and 1940s, it was a fashionable neighborhood for "colored" people of means. Dr. Anna J. Cooper lived at 201 T Street, N.W., an impressive residence. She was a principal at the Dunbar High School, earned her Ph.D. from the Sorbonne in Paris, and was president of the Frelinghuysen University, a private university in her home during the 1920s to 1940s. The house is in disrepair today. Judge Terrell and Mrs. Mary Church Terrell, a civil rights

*Dr. Anna J. Cooper on the veranda of her home in LeDroit Park, c. 1940.
Photograph by Scurlock Studio.*

activist, lived at 326 T Street, N.W. He founded the Terrell Law
School which graduated many prominent black lawyers. Ernest E.
Just, the noted biologist and professor at Howard University, lived
at 412 T Street, N.W. Paul Lawrence Dunbar, for whom Dunbar
High School in Shaw is named, lived briefly at 312 U Street, N.W.

The old Foster home has a distinctive character with its slant-
ing ceramic tile roof. Dr. Foster was a dentist whose offices
were near the historic old *Howard Theater* (624 T Streets, N.W.).
(His last wife, Dr. Marguerite Williams Foster, taught geography
at the Miner Teachers' College. She grew up in LeDroit Park and
earned a Ph.D. in geology from the Catholic University of
America [620 Michigan Avenue, N.E.].) The Howard Theater
was the first legitimate theater for blacks in the District and

featured entertainers such as Lena Horne, Louis Armstrong, and Moms Mabley.

Today LeDroit Park, like so many in-town neighborhoods, is experiencing regentrification. Whites are moving back into the neighborhood, as they are to Shaw, because of the convenience to downtown. It is no longer an exclusive neighborhood for blacks or whites, but is merely a nice place to live despite the urban problems that plague it.

The best eating place in the area, Harrison's Restaurant on U Street at New Jersey Avenue, N.W., has closed. At one time is was a residence, like most of the restaurants in Adams Morgan. At a former barbecue pit at Fourth and U streets, N.W., passersby always saw a pig rotating over a fire. Today, except for fast-food places, the only restaurants in LeDroit Park are in the Howard Inn on Georgia Avenue between Adams and Bryant streets, N.W.

Many students at Howard University live in LeDroit Park because of its proximity to the school. However, today the new residence halls on Barry Place, N.W., have attracted many students who would otherwise rent in LeDroit Park and Shaw. Howard maintains two dorms in LeDroit Park, one on Third Street and the other on Oakdale Place, N.W. Many houses in this area have been owned by whites and rented to blacks. It is possible that the white owners are now reclaiming them.

Shaw

Shaw consists of a group of neighborhoods given a common name by the federal government in 1966 to identify them as part of an urban renewal project. The area is found roughly between North Capitol and Fifteenth streets, N.W., and between M Street and Florida Avenue, N.W. The Shaw neighborhood and the public junior high school are named for Colonel Robert Gould Shaw, who led a regiment of freedmen in the Union Army during the Civil War. Born in 1837 in Boston, Massachusetts, he briefly attended Harvard University before the war. He died in action in South Carolina.

Corner of Seventh and T streets, Shaw, late 1940s. The marquee of the Howard Theater is visible at the left in the distance. Photograph by Scurlock Studio.

Shaw consisted of open farmland just before the Civil War. Seventh Street was a bustling commercial district, serving as the route that connected Tidewater Virginia to the south and the Maryland farms to the north with the docks in southwest Washington. By 1900 the area was entirely populated by blacks.

Ironically, Shaw's decline began in the early 1950s with desegregation, when the residents left their traditional neighborhoods and went downtown to shop and find entertainment. The Reverend Walter E. Fauntroy, then a young pastor at New Bethel Baptist Church, believed that urban renewal had always resulted in removing blacks. To counter that trend and keep Shaw a black community, Fauntroy founded the Model Inner City Community

Organization (MICCO), a group committed to nonviolent land reform through the encouragement of development and construction. The 1968 riots following Martin Luther King's assassination, however, proved a great setback to this community. Key to the survival of Shaw as a neighborhood was the replacement of the long-neglected Shaw Junior High School, and the new (1986) D.C. office building at Fourteenth and U streets, which employs 1,000 people, is a sign of the District's commitment to the revitalization of the area.

Shaw is a neighborhood of churches with the most influential black churches, including store-front churches, within its borders. They serve as an active part of Shaw's revitalization, working to bring affordable housing to Shaw's residents. Perhaps the most outstanding religious structure in Shaw is the gold-domed *United House of Prayer for All People* at Sixth and M streets, N.W., which includes a cafeteria with excellent and well-priced food. Bishop McCollough, who led this church for many years, died in 1991. He and his religious organization have shown a commitment to providing affordable housing in the Shaw area. When the last brick was laid on his garden apartments, the last payment was made, and the building project was debt-free. At present (1991) his church is completing another garden apartment complex along Seventh Street between M and N streets, N.W. The *Lincoln Westmoreland apartment building* (1730 Seventh Street, N.W.) was a unique joint-development project undertaken by the black Lincoln Temple United Church of Christ and the white Westmoreland Congregational Church in Bethesda, Maryland. Begun in 1971, the ten-story apartment building initiated Shaw renewal, and other church-sponsored housing complexes followed. *Gibson Plaza* (1301 Seventh Street) for low- to moderate-income families was a joint venture begun in 1973 by the local First Rising Mount Zion Baptist Church and MICCO, the community development organization. The largest such project (263 units) was sponsored by Immaculate Conception Church at 1330 Seventh Street (Seventh and N streets, N.W.). Financed by the Bible Way Church of Our Lord Jesus Christ World Wide and completed in 1975, the *Golden Rule* complex (901 New Jersey Avenue) added eighty-five townhouses and forty garden apartments to the neighborhood. *Foster House* (801 Rhode Island Avenue, N.W.) is also on church-owned property, with the land held by the New Bethel Baptist Church. New Bethel is pastored by the former D.C. representative to Congress, the Reverend Walter Fauntroy.

Take the Metro (Green line) to Seventh and R streets, N.W., and proceed to the Lincoln Westmoreland at 1730 Seventh Street, N.W. Across the street is the *Watha Daniel Library* at Eighth Street and Rhode Island Avenue, N.W., a neighborhood branch of the D.C. public library system. It is named after a local neighborhood activist who lived on Ninth Street in the Shaw area.

At the turn of this century, Seventh Street was an open sewer and fields and cow pastures abounded in the Shaw area. In fact, my former home at 1718 Eighth Street, N.W., was built by a dairyman as his residence. When I renovated the house, I found built into the floor a stone container designed to hold milk; Mrs. Ada G. Piper, a former owner, told me that the sheds in the back were for the cattle, but the milk was stored in the house. In the 1200 block of O Street the only old frame house was owned by a farmer who grazed his cattle across the street on the present site of the Iowa Apartment and townhouses.

Among the several houses in the Shaw area that are musts because of their historically significant residents or their architecture, is *Benson House* at 1502 Vermont Avenue, N.W., one of the most outstanding examples of restoration in the area. James L. Wells, a nationally known local artist who taught art at Howard University, resides at 1333 R Street, N.W. The *Bethune Museum Archives* at 1318 Vermont Avenue, N.W. is the former home of Mary McCloud Bethune (b. 1875; d. 1955), the founder of the Bethune-Cookman College and a national black activist. Today art shows are presented at the museum of the archives. The former home of Blanche Kelso Bruce (b. 1841; d. 1889), the first Afro-American to receive a full term as a U.S. senator from Mississippi, is located at 909 M Street, N.W. Mr. Bruce also served as a trustee for Howard University and a recorder of deeds for the District of Columbia.

The house at 1833 Vermont Avenue, N.W., was formerly the residence of the late Amanda Hilliard, a professor at Howard

University and founder of the Iona Whiteley Home for Unwed Mothers. Ruth E. Clark, who was for many years associated with the Madeira School in Virginia and also worked for Alice Roosevelt, is a longtime resident. Students from Ethiopia, Uganda, and the United States have also lived here. The building at Twelfth and O streets, N.W., currently a home and office, was once an exclusive, high-priced hand laundry.

No field trip of Shaw would be complete without seeing the home of the late Carter G. Woodson (b. 1895; d. 1950), a black historian and founder of the Negro Life and History Association in 1915. That organization has become the *Association for the Study of Afro-American Life and History* at 1401 Fourteenth Street, N.W. Woodson, a prolific researcher, writer, and publisher, taught at Howard University, which is within walking distance of his home. *Shiloh Baptist Church* with its relatively new family center is just down the street at 1500 Ninth Street.

Logan Circle was originally named Iowa Circle, but was renamed in honor of General John A. Logan. General Logan commanded the Army of the Tennessee during the Civil War, and he later became the commander of the Grand Army of the Republic. It was in this capacity that he designated May 30 as Memorial Day. He also served in the Senate and House representing the state of Illinois.

Return to the Metro stop at Ninth and R.

There are two good eating facilities in Shaw: one is in the well-known *Shiloh Baptist Church* at Ninth and P streets, N.W., and the other is the *United House of Prayer* cafeteria at Sixth and M streets, N.W., in the basement of the religious facilities. Both serve soul food; however, I prefer the cafeteria in the United House of Prayer because of the greater variety of food and the more spacious, pleasant atmosphere. Other tasty soul food can be found on the edge of the Shaw neighborhood at the famous *Florida Avenue Grill* at Eleventh Street and Florida Avenue, N.W. *Frenchie's* is another very good ethnic cafeteria in the 1300 block of H Street, N.E. The owners, an elderly couple from Alabama, take great pride in the food preparation, its appearance, and the cleanliness of the facilities. One of the best eating places for ethnic food in Washington, D.C., is *Adelis* at Fourteenth and U streets, N.W., across from the *Reeves Municipal Center.* It provides a buffet lunch, all you can eat for $6.99. The lunch tastes home-cooked, with a good choice of entrees and desserts. I recommend it for lunch, although Adelis serves only lunch whereas the others serve breakfast, lunch, and dinner.

Of course, home to a plethora of ethnic restaurants is the *Adams Morgan* area around Eighteenth Street and Columbia Road, N.W. This neighborhood has the best variety of residents as well as food, with a mix of Hispanic Americans, Caribbean Americans, Africans, Afro-Americans, and Americans of European descent. Many of the restaurants serve tasty native cuisine. Don't forget *Georgetown.* There are many excellent restaurants along M Street, N.W., and along Wisconsin Avenue, N.W., although they tend to be more pricey than those in other areas. To be honest, Georgetown and Adams Morgan are perhaps the safest areas to dine in the evening although all areas are relatively safe for lunch. There are a few places in the far northeast and southeast and on upper Georgia Avenue that serve good food—soul food—but their distance from the central business district discourages a visit since time is limited, and there are so many excellent options near the downtown area.

Epilogue

This tour through two Washington, D.C., neighborhoods hints at the vibrant life of the black community here. Of the city's 800,000 residents, nearly three quarters are black. Because of past decades of rigid segregation, the black neighborhoods in their separateness formed a "secret city." What we see in these communities today results from the dynamic and dramatic changes of the last forty years.

△ Day Three

GEORGE WASHINGTON'S POTOMAC—MOUNT VERNON TO GREAT FALLS

by Ronald E. Grim, *Library of Congress*
and Paul D. McDermott, *Montgomery College*

This tour is based on Herman Friis's popular field trip, *Geographic Reconnaissance of the Potomac River Tidewater Fringe of Virginia from Arlington Memorial Bridge to Mount Vernon* (Washington, D.C.: Association of American Geographers, 1968). It focuses on the historical geography of the area along the Potomac River from Mount Vernon to Great Falls.

Most of our travel is on the George Washington Memorial Parkway, which parallels the Potomac River from Mount Vernon to the western side of the Washington Beltway (I-495). One of the nation's first landscaped parkways, the segment south of Alexandria was completed in 1932 as part of the Washington's Birthday bicentennial celebration.

Although the trip is structured around several sites and activities associated with George Washington (b. 1732; d. 1799; pres. 1789 to 1797), the first President of the United States, our intent is not to overemphasize the historical or geographical significance of one man. Rather, our objective is to use these associations as a framework that concentrates on the late colonial and early national periods of American history. This is an important time in the area's

George Washington's Potomac

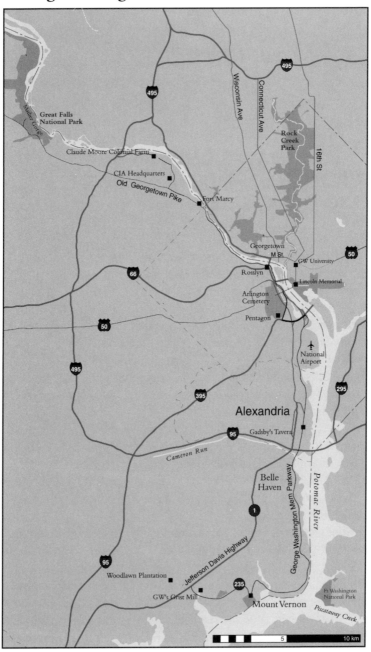

geographical development because it marks the height of the agrarian plantation settlement pattern associated with Tidewater Virginia and the beginning of urbanization in the Washington, D.C., area. By examining the historical remnants, restorations, and reconstructions from this period, we can appreciate the effects of 200 years of urbanization that have transformed a rural agricultural landscape into an integral part of a major urban area.

The Region

PHYSICAL LANDSCAPE

The key to understanding this area is Friis's use of the term, "Tidewater Fringe," in describing its physical location. The field trip begins in the upper reaches of the Chesapeake Tidewater and straddles the Fall Zone, the approximate boundary between the Coastal Plain and the Piedmont. The contrast between these two physiographic zones can be observed in the panoramic views of the river and shoreline at the beginning and end of this field trip. At Mount Vernon, the river is broad and placid and the hills low and rolling, while at Great Falls, the falls, the narrow rocky gorge, and terrain are more rugged.

The Atlantic Coastal Plain is a very broad region, for the most part low-lying and flat. Here most of the rock type is sedimentary and easily eroded. Much of the Coastal Plain is dissected by the movement of streams toward the Chesapeake Bay. In earlier times, rivers flowing into the bay created valleys that have since become flooded. These flooded or drowned river valleys are termed estuaries.

The Piedmont is characterized by gently rolling hills, a mixture of metamorphic and sedimentary rocks, and the sporadic occurrence of higher mountains known as monadnocks. A classic example of a monadnock in this region is *Sugar Loaf Mountain* in western Montgomery County, Maryland. It rises to a height of 1,200 feet.

When plotted on a map, the boundary between these two physiographic regions forms a highly irregular line. However, this boundary is frequently equated with the more generalized Fall

Zone or Fall Line, as it has been traditionally known. It has been so called because many of the rivers and streams flowing toward the Atlantic Ocean form a series of falls or rapids in this area as they cross the boundary between the two provinces. This zone of falls and rapids has been traditionally associated with urban origins during the colonial period, because the falls presented an absolute head of navigation to ocean-going vessels, as well as a potential source of water for industrial development.

CULTURAL GEOGRAPHY

This area was also transitional in terms of its cultural geography. Tidewater Virginia was noted for its tobacco culture, large plantations, slavery, and lack of urban centers, while the Virginia Piedmont and Great Valley were noted for wheat farming, small farms, lesser use of slavery, and an emerging system of central places. Colonial Fairfax County, which encompasses the majority of our itinerary, showed elements of both economic systems. Slave holdings are a rough index of the size of farm operations and their relative position of Fairfax County. According to the first federal census of 1790, 37 percent of the county's total population was slave. This percentage is similar to the values of other Piedmont counties, while the counties with the highest percentages (55 to 65 percent) were mainly in Tidewater and those with the lowest percentages (less than 20 percent) were west of the Blue Ridge. Even more revealing is the size of slaveholdings per household within the county. Approximately 52 percent of the households held no slaves, while 3 percent held more than twenty slaves and only eight households owned seventy each. The combination of tobacco and wheat as agricultural crops is apparent in the location of tobacco warehouses in the southern portion of the county and grist mills in the interior and northern part of the county on small streams tributary to the Potomac.

Although an integrated network of towns had not developed in the area during the colonial period, five town sites had been platted immediately downstream from the Fall Zone before the site of the nation's capital was selected in 1790. Three of these (Alexandria in Virginia and Bladensburg and George Town in Maryland) had their origins in the 1740s and 1750s and were viable, functioning towns. The other two (Carrolsburg and Hamburg, which were incorporated in the present site of Washington, D.C.) were only towns on paper. Alexandria, the largest of these towns, had a population of 2,700 in 1790, making it the fourth largest settlement in Virginia behind Richmond, Norfolk, and Petersburg.

THE POTOMAC RIVER

This field trip follows a segment of the Potomac River. In colonial times the river was referred to as the "Pawtowmack." The river originates about 335 miles to the west of Mount Vernon. In its meandering journey toward the Chesapeake Bay, the Potomac flows through different landscapes—mountains, farmland, urban settlements, and coastal plain. By the time it reaches the bay it has traveled 400 miles and has collected run-off from an area of 14,670 square miles in four states—Maryland, Pennsylvania, Virginia, and West Virginia.

Along most of the course, the river flows gently. At Great Falls, the nature of the river changes. Here, the flow is turbulent and dangerous as the course narrows and descends through the gorge. The change is caused by a vertical descent of some seventy-six feet over a horizontal distance of approximately one quarter of a mile. After passing over the falls, the river continues its descent as it passes through Mather Gorge and Little Falls. Upon reaching Georgetown, the nature of the river again changes. The channel becomes deeper and wider. More significantly, it is now characterized by tidal action—usually one high and one low tide each day. At this point fresh water begins mixing with salt water. Below Georgetown the river is termed an estuary. By the time the river reaches Mount Vernon it has increased its width to about 1 mile with a twenty-five-foot depth. Above Georgetown the river is less than 1,200 feet wide and is generally more shallow—sixteen feet or less.

The Potomac has an uneven flow pattern. A daily average of 83 thousand gallons of water per second move down its channel. During a flow year (October to September), the amounts recorded

Potomac River Drainage Basin

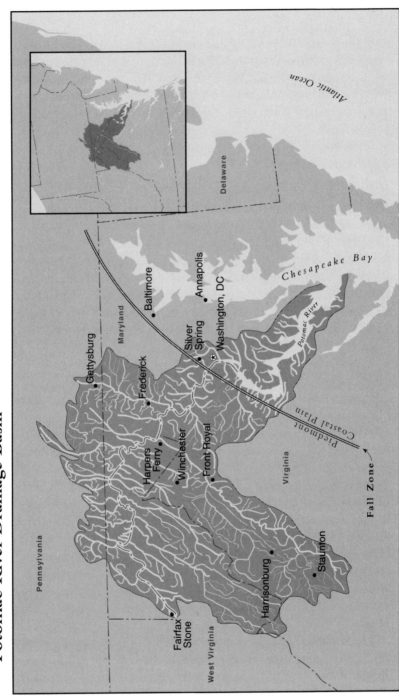

vary dramatically. Late summer months are characterized by low flows—typically 9 thousand gallons a second or about 10 percent of its average flow. Early spring is distinguished by floods or otherwise heavy flow periods when 1 billion or more gallons flow downstream per second. During an average year more than a trillion and a half gallons flow into the Chesapeake Bay.

THE NATION'S NEW CAPITAL

In 1790 the U.S. Congress authorized George Washington to select a site for the nation's new capital within this physical and cultural setting. The Potomac River presented a situation that was essentially in the middle of the north–south extent of the original thirteen colonies, but Washington also selected a site within the area he was most familiar with—one near his beloved Mount Vernon and his hometown of Alexandria. Hoping to capitalize on the potential of a Fall Line location, Washington undoubtedly envisioned that the new city would become the nation's entrepôt. The city has never been known for its port facilities, but by the middle of the twentieth century it developed into a major metropolitan area, based instead on its governmental and service functions, as well as tourism.

Itinerary

From Exit 1 on Interstate 495 take U.S. 1 south. The first 7 miles of the journey follow a portion of U.S. 1, which is known locally as the "Jefferson Davis Highway," in honor of the President of the Confederacy during the Civil War. This road follows the approximate route of an Indian trail named the Potomac Path. Later, it was part of the "Old Colonial Post Road," a road connecting Boston, Massachusetts, to Charleston, South Carolina. While the Fairfax County welcoming sign at the beginning of the route advertises the county as the "gateway to American history heritage," the present-day landscape along this four-lane highway provides meager support for the claim. The extensive commercial and strip development along this major suburban artery includes numerous local and regional shopping centers, as well as at least one of almost every fast-food establishment represented elsewhere in the metropolitan area. As we approach the southern portion of the stretch, there is strong evidence of the historical commercialization of the area with the use of the names "Mount Vernon," "Woodlawn," and "Belvoir" for streets, subdivisions, apartment complexes, and commercial establishments. Note also the colonial "Mount Vernon"–style architecture characterizing various businesses and schools.

WOODLAWN AND WASHINGTON'S GRIST MILL, VIRGINIA

Turn left from U.S. Highway 1 onto the Mount Vernon Highway (Virginia Route 235). On the hill on the southwest corner of this intersection is Woodlawn Plantation, the home of George Washington's nephew Lawrence Lewis and Martha's granddaughter Eleanor Parke Custis. On the occasion of their marriage in 1799, Washington gave the Lewises this 2,000-acre estate. The mansion was designed by William Thornton, the first architect of the U.S. Capitol. It was built on the hill overlooking Dogue Run and provides a view of both Mount Vernon and the Potomac. This property, which is now maintained by the National Trust for Historic Preservation, is a good example of an early nineteenth-century plantation.

George Washington's Grist Mill is a reconstruction of a mill originally built by George Washington in 1770 on this site. Powered by the erratic flow of Dogue Run, this mill is representative of numerous other mills in operation in the upper Coastal Plain and the Piedmont during the late eighteenth and early nineteenth centuries, reflecting the general shift from tobacco to wheat cultivation in this portion of Virginia and Maryland. Adding to the industrial significance of this operation, Washington also maintained a distillery and cooper shop at this site. (A cooper shop constructed barrels and other containers from wood.) Other functioning mills exist in the Washington, D.C., metropolitan area, for example, Pierce Mill on Rock Creek in the District of Columbia, the Colvin Run Mill in suburban Fairfax County, and Adelphi Mill in suburban Prince Georges County. These mills were used by early settlers to grind grains—typically wheat, corn, or rye—into flour and meal. Although grains could be marketed in bulk, flour was preferred, because it commanded higher market prices. Most grist mills in the region were constructed on small streams such as Dogue Run or Rock Creek—both tributaries of the Potomac. These streams were blocked by small dams that diverted some of the flow to flumes. Water passing through the flume turned a water wheel which was connected to gear works and burr stones in the mill. Flour resulted from grain passing between the burrs and the grinding action of the stones.

MOUNT VERNON TO ALEXANDRIA, VIRGINIA, 7.4 MILES

Our second stop is *Mount Vernon,* the home of George Washington (b. 1732; d. 1799). This restoration, which was begun in 1858 by the Mount Vernon Ladies' Association, presents the Mansion House area as it existed at the end of the eighteenth century during the last years of Washington's life. The preserved area consists of approximately 500 acres, only a small remnant of the 8,251 acres Washington acquired between Dogue and Little Hunting creeks. These holdings were divided into five working farms: Mansion House, Union, Dogue Run, Muddy Hole, and River farms. Mount Vernon is often portrayed as a fine example of a southern eighteenth-century plantation. However, it must be noted that what we see here represents the material possessions of one of the county's wealthiest men at the height of his career. Certainly, the plantation is representative of Virginia's larger and wealthier plantations, but not of Tidewater's entire settlement pattern. The *Mansion House* with its magnificent river view, flanked by a variety of outbuildings (kitchen, office, craft buildings, barns, stable, and sheds), and formal and kitchen gardens, is typical of the large self-sufficient plantations associated with Tidewater Virginia. In the same manner as these other large plantations, slaves provided the labor to operate the Mount Vernon complex. Two censuses taken in 1782 and 1790 indicate that Washington was the largest slave owner in Fairfax County.

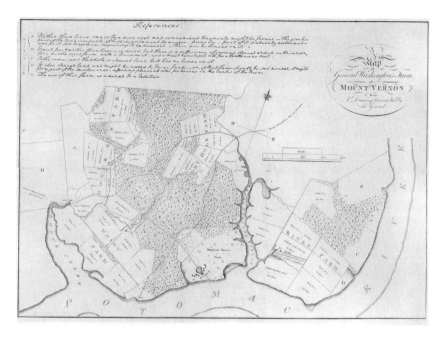

Map of George Washington's lands at Mount Vernon, 1793. Photograph courtesy of the Library of Congress.

In some ways, however, Mount Vernon was not typical of other Tidewater plantations. Although Washington grew to-bacco, he was deeply concerned about its soil-depleting charac-teristics. He experimented with soil-conservation techniques and different agricultural products. Botanical experiments were conducted in the greenhouse and the botanical garden near the mansion. This research eventually resulted in a shift in crop types on his plantation from an emphasis on tobacco to wheat. Upon leaving the Mount Vernon complex proceed north on the George Washington Parkway.

Fort Washington, which sits on the Maryland side of the Poto-mac at the mouth of Piscataway Creek, was one of the first defenses constructed for guarding the seaward approaches to Washington, D.C. The fort, on a site selected by George Washing-ton in 1795, was completed in 1808, bearing the name Fort

Warburton; it was renamed Fort Washington in 1813. The fort fell to the British attack the next year. Consequently, after the war, the fort was rebuilt in its present configuration, representing an outstanding example of an early nineteenth-century coastal fortification.

The marina to the right, and the residential development and golf course to the left preserve the name *Belle Haven,* which Scottish merchants applied to this area before the town of Alexandria was established. *Great Hunting Creek,* a large tidal estuary, known as Cameron Run in its upper extremities, provides the southern boundary of this independent city, which currently has a population over 110,000.

ALEXANDRIA, VIRGINIA

Encompassed by Fairfax County, *Alexandria's* growth has moved through several stages since its founding. The town was established in 1749 at the site of the Hunting Creek tobacco warehouse, which began operation in 1730. The warehouse, located near the junction of Hunting Creek and the Potomac River, was the focus of considerable Scottish merchant activity during the 1730s and 1740s. The actual warehouse site was recorded on a map drawn by Washington when he was seventeen. At this time he was learning the trade under the tutoring of county surveyor John West. Washington also drew a plat of the town based on West's 1749 survey. The town, as originally laid out, consisted of eighty-four half-acre lots. One lot was eventually purchased by Washington, which today is represented by a reconstructed house at 508 Cameron Street.

Despite these associations with Washington, Alexandria is also important in a geographical context as an example of the urban process in Tidewater Virginia where slow urban growth was the norm. During the seventeenth century there were no towns except Jamestown. Various legislative attempts to create towns were passed with little success. The town act of 1690 did encourage some town growth in the lower Chesapeake at sites such as Norfolk and Yorktown, while the Tobacco Inspection Act of 1730 provided the impetus for small river towns (Tappahannock, Urbanna, Port Royal), and Fall Zone towns (Richmond, Fredericksburg, and Alexandria). Paralleling the delayed settlement of the Upper

Map of the Alexandria site drawn by George Washington about 1748. Courtesy of the Library of Congress.

Potomac, Alexandria was the last Virginia Fall Zone situation to experience urban development. The town's early economic growth focused on a tobacco-inspection warehouse, the trading activities of several Scottish merchants, and head-of-navigation port facilities.

Turn right on King Street, proceed east 0.3 mile (four blocks), turn left on Fairfax Street, and disembark at Ramsey House for a walking tour of Alexandria. The tour ends at *Gadsby's Tavern* (138 North Royal Street), opened in 1770. It is an excellent example of taverns and inns in colonial Virginia and Maryland situated along major arteries connecting settlements.

In our walking tour of "Old Town," we will see restorations and re-creations of eighteenth- and early nineteenth-century structures, as well as twentieth-century residences and commercial buildings designed in historically compatible styles. In most cases older homes are still used as residences while older institutional, commercial, and industrial buildings have been adapted for new uses. There are very few remnants from the earliest years except for residences of a few early Scottish merchants (William Ramsay, John Carlyle, and John Dalton). A greater number of preserved buildings date from the last quarter of the eighteenth century and the first half of the nineteenth century. Most of these structures are houses in the Georgian, Federal, and Greek Revival architectural styles, but structures also remind us of the town's early service functions: Market Square, taverns and inns, the Anglican and Presbyterian churches, the apothecary shop, craft shops, merchants' stores, banks, doctors' offices, and warehouses. Our tour focuses on sites associated with early urban functions and services.

The strong emphasis on historical preservation in Alexandria results from the active participation of the city government (City Council, the Historical Resources Division and its Urban Archaeology Program, and the Department of Planning and Community Development) and Historic Alexandria Foundation, a nonprofit organization promoting the preservation and restoration of structures and sites of historical and architectural significance. The focus of the preservation effort is not the creation of a museum capturing one period, but the preservation of the elements of a living, changing city. There has been a positive attempt on the part of the city government to encourage the preservation of structures older than 100 years and the construction of new or "infill" structures with comparable architectural styles. The design of these newer buildings may copy an older style or incorporate selected elements of an older style in a primarily contemporary motif.

Proceed one block north on Fairfax Street, turn left on Cameron Street, and proceed 0.3 mile (four blocks). Turn right (north) on Washington Street, which becomes the George Washington Parkway north of the city limits.

NATIONAL AIRPORT TO KEY BRIDGE, VIRGINIA, 4.4 MILES

Traveling north along the Potomac we see an area dominated by twentieth-century development. *Crystal City* on the west side of the parkway is characterized by modern high-rise offices, hotels, apartments, and shopping centers. Toward the east and the Potomac River, National Airport was constructed on land reclaimed from its shore. The airport was opened in 1940, at which time Hoover Airport adjacent to the Pentagon was abandoned. *National Airport* is now undergoing expansion to handle larger amounts of traffic. Increased air traffic has engendered the anger of citizens in the Potomac River corridor who complain about the increased noise and safety problems. Planes flying into and out of National must follow the circuitous path of the river—especially the northwest approach. The danger presented by flights was documented in the 1982 crash of an Air Florida flight adjacent to and over the Fourteenth Street Bridge. Seventy-eight people were killed including several commuters going home during the snowstorm! Even with such dangers, the airport has continued to expand as a result of its proximity to Washington, D.C., and continued support by Congress.

The *Pentagon* is the largest structure on the south side of the Potomac River. It houses the Department of Defense operations and supports employee services including restaurants and department stores. It is visible to the southwest of the Fourteenth Street Bridge as you proceed westward on the parkway.

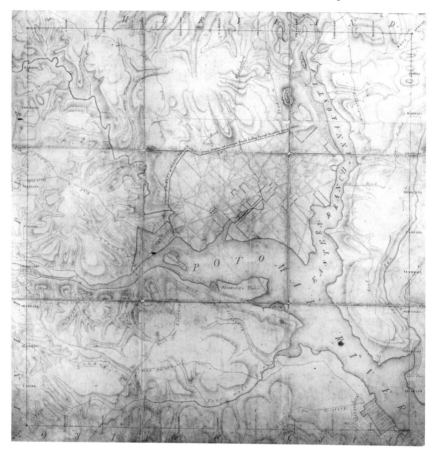

Andrew Ellicott's map of the District of Columbia, based on surveys conducted in 1791 and 1792. Photograph courtesy of the Library of Congress.

This area, as well as Alexandria, was included in that portion of northern Virginia ceded to the federal government as a part of the ten-mile square reserved for the nation's new capital. However, by 1846 this portion, which remained rural, was returned to the state of Virginia because the new city had not experienced the growth anticipated. This retroceded area was designated Arlington County, which today is almost as urbanized as the District of Columbia.

Enter Arlington Circle, following signs for "US 50, Rosslyn and Key Bridge." Follow the exit ramp for "Rosslyn and Key Bridge." Turn right onto Lynn Street and continue for 0.5 mile (approximately six blocks) through Rosslyn and across Key Bridge.

Rosslyn, like Crystal City, is an area of recently constructed high-rises, apartments, hotels, and offices, some of which are rented to the federal government as office space. The growth in this area has been rapidly transforming an area that at the end of World War II was no more than a village at the terminus of a streetcar line.

Key Bridge, named for Francis Scott Key, the composer of the national anthem, "The Star-Spangled Banner," was opened in 1923. It replaced Aqueduct Bridge, which was part of the Alexandria–Georgetown Canal built in the mid-nineteenth century to carry barge traffic across the Potomac. The canal linked the more extensive Chesapeake and Ohio Canal at Georgetown and the port of Alexandria. Abutments of the old aqueduct can still be seen along the banks of the Potomac slightly north of Key Bridge.

GEORGETOWN

After crossing Key Bridge turn right onto M Street, N.W. Proceed 0.4 mile (eight blocks) through Georgetown. *Georgetown,* like Alexandria, was one of the other towns at the head of tidewater. Founded in 1751, it also developed as a tobacco-inspection warehouse site. The town's early growth was related to its fine port and wharf facilities near the mouth of Rock Creek. Here agricultural goods—mainly wheat, flour, and tobacco—were exported to Europe and the West Indies, while manufactured goods—like textiles—were imported. Port operations remained important to the community until silting forced closure of the port in the mid-nineteenth century. Some of the key sites in Georgetown include the *Old Stone House* at 3051 M Street, N.W. This is the oldest remaining structure in the community, having been built in 1765. Today the house is maintained by the National Park Service. Below M Street you can walk along the towpath of the original Chesapeake and Ohio Canal. In Georgetown, the canal is characterized by flow through a series of scenic locks. During the summer, you can take a barge trip for a short tour on the canal above the developed area.

Georgetown was a prosperous community for approximately 100 years. Its growth was spurred by the federal government and the development of trade up and down the Potomac River. Of special significance in this development was the construction of the Patowmack Canal and later the Chesapeake and Ohio Canal. Both canals facilitated the movement of trade along the river corridor. Many industries arose to take advantage of the canals, for example, Washington Mills, whose flour products are still sold in supermarkets in the area, although the mill site now contains a condominium.

After the Civil War, Georgetown's prosperity declined. By 1890, the district had become a low-rent area. Nevertheless, in the 1930s the area again started gaining in popularity, until today it is one of Washington's most fashionable and prestigious districts. Housing and land values are high. Typically a federal rowhouse is priced at about $500,000 (in 1991). Unlike Alexandria, Georgetown is not an independent city. In 1800, it was incorporated into the nation's new capital. It remains today a distinctive section of the District of Columbia.

CHESAPEAKE AND OHIO CANAL

Turn right on Thirtieth Street. Disembark at the *Chesapeake and Ohio Canal* and walk along the towpath to Thirty-first Street. The old canal is a piece of nineteenth-century America. The canal was completed in 1851 and operated until 1924. As a functioning transportation system, the canal connected Cumberland, Maryland, with Georgetown, a distance of 184.5 miles.

Construction on the canal began on 4 July 1828, with the intention of connecting the Chesapeake region with the Ohio River, thus, its name. Ironically, on the same day the Baltimore and Ohio Railroad was started. Digging the canal proved to be a very expensive enterprise. Whereas the profitable Erie Canal in New York State cost $20,000 per mile to construct, the C & O cost upward of $60,000. Much of this increased cost could be attributed to the need to build seventy-five locks, eleven aqueducts, and a 3,117-foot tunnel. Considerable additional expense was encountered in the digging of the canal through bedrock in some places, like the Great Falls area.

During its economic lifetime, barges along the canal carried an assortment of goods to various communities adjoining its path. The primary trade items were agricultural produce such as wheat, building materials (stone and lumber), and coal. Unfortunately, this was not a profitable enterprise. Each year, income generated by the movement of these goods amounted to $100,000, yet operating expenses were usually $1,000,000. This meant that canal operations were heavily subsidized by the states and the federal government.

Today the canal forms the basis of a unique National Park—the Chesapeake and Ohio National Historical Park, created by an act of Congress in 1972. The park is the outcome of the work of Supreme Court Justice William O. Douglas (b. 1898; d. 1980), who actively lobbied for its preservation.

WASHINGTON CIRCLE TO ARLINGTON CIRCLE, 1.9 MILES

Bear right onto Pennsylvania Avenue. Proceed 0.4 mile (approximately three blocks) to *Washington Circle* and turn right on Twenty-third Street. Continue 0.8 mile (approximately nine blocks) to the *Lincoln Memorial*. On this segment of the field trip we travel through the western portion of the original city as it was planned and designed by Pierre Charles L'Enfant (b. 1755; d. 1825), the French engineer whom Washington engaged for this purpose. As we travel along Pennsylvania Avenue and around Washington Circle, observe the "baroque" street pattern that L'Enfant employed. Starting with a basic grid pattern, he superimposed diagonal streets and circles to emphasize the monumental character of the city. Continuing on Twenty-third Street, we pass *George Washington University,* one of the multitude of places named for our first President. At C Street, N.W., pass the U.S. State Department on the left and the Old U.S. Naval Observatory on the right. The planned town of Hamburg occupied this area. As we approach the *Lincoln Memorial,* we can again observe the monumental proportion of L'Enfant's "baroque" plan.

Cross Arlington Memorial Bridge. As we cross the bridge, we have an excellent view of another site from the first half of the nineteenth century—*Arlington House* or the Custis-Lee Mansion. Constructed on a 1,100-acre plantation between 1804 and 1817, this Greek Revival mansion was first the home of George Washington Park Custis (Martha Washington's grandson), and later his son-in-law, Robert E. Lee. The only remnant of this antebellum plantation is the mansion house, several dependencies, and surrounding gardens. The property was acquired by the federal government after the Civil War for use as a national cemetery. In front of the house is the tomb of Pierre Charles L'Enfant.

Turn right at *Arlington Circle,* this time following the signs for George Washington Parkway. As we reenter the George Washington Parkway, we pass *Theodore Roosevelt Island,* which has been maintained in its natural state by the National Park Service since 1931 as a memorial to the twenty-sixth President of the United States (1901 to 1909) in recognition of his role in the conservation movement. Originally known by its Indian name "Analostan" or "Anacostian," it was renamed by its successive owners, "My Lord's Island," "Barbadoes," and "Mason's Island." The latter name was applied during much of the eighteenth century when the Mason family owned the island. George Mason (b. 1725; d. 1792), one of George Washington's neighbors, helped draft the U.S. Constitution and wrote the first ten amendments known as the "Bill of Rights."

GEORGE WASHINGTON PARKWAY TO GREAT FALLS, VIRGINIA, 12 MILES

From *Overlook 2,* look down into the valley of the Potomac and observe the floodplain of the river. Notice how the river's width has decreased from what is was near Mount Vernon. The river now is characterized by numerous rapids and cascades. These features characterize the Potomac throughout the *Great Falls* region. The nature of the river changed as we passed from the Coastal Plain below Georgetown–Rosslyn to the Piedmont. This boundary is visible as we ascend the George Washington Parkway from the river's edge adjacent to Rosslyn to our present position. During

Tobacco hills prepared for planting at Claude Moore Colonial Farm.

major floods much of the plain below is covered by raging water. This flow scours the plain of any vegetation, hence the lack of mature tree development along its surface. The most devastating flood in recent years accompanied Hurricane Agnes in 1972.

Fort Marcy was constructed early in the Civil War to protect Washington, D.C., from attack along the Georgetown Pike from the west. It was one of many forts strategically positioned around the city to resist Confederate attempts to capture the nation's capital.

Exit the parkway and go west on Chain Bridge Road. Immediately after passing the entrance to the Central Intelligence Agency, turn right onto Old Georgetown Pike (Virginia Route 193). Make another right turn, following the sign to the Claude Moore Colonial Farm and proceed 0.7 mile to parking lot.

In terms of settlement features, *Claude Moore Colonial Farm* represents a significant contrast to Mount Vernon, Woodlawn, and the Custis-Lee Mansion. The Claude Moore Colonial Farm at

Turkey Run is a re-creation of a small-scale, low-income home-stead of the late eighteenth century. Originally developed by the National Park Service, this living museum is now managed by a nonprofit, publicly supported corporation. Designed to portray the life and material possessions of a poor tenant or struggling free-holder, the site includes approximately 100 acres, of which twelve are cultivated with tobacco, corn, an orchard, and a kitchen garden. The significance of this size farmstead can be judged from the 1782 enumeration of Fairfax County in which approximately 50 percent of the households owned no slaves, suggesting a large number of small agricultural operations.

After visiting the farm, turn right (west) onto Old Georgetown Pike (Route 193). *Old Georgetown Pike* is an example of the roads and turnpikes constructed in the early nineteenth century to focus trade of the Virginia Piedmont and the Shenandoah Valley into the towns east of the Fall Zone. Several of these roads, such as the Leesburg Pike and Little River Turnpike, connected this Piedmont hinterland with Alexandria. The Old Georgetown Pike, however, was an attempt by the Georgetown merchants to capture a portion of the trade from the Virginia Piedmont.

Turn right on *Old Dominion Road.* This thoroughfare follows the right-of-way once traversed by the Washington and Old Do-minion Railroad. The railroad (trolley line) provided access for visitors from Washington, D.C., to the Great Falls of the Potomac during the first third of the twentieth century. On both sides of the Potomac, facilities were built to provide food, entertainment, and recreation. Most of these have now disappeared. Today, the Great Falls area is administered by the National Park Service.

GREAT FALLS PARK

The chief attraction for the 500,000 people who visit the park is the *Great Falls of the Potomac.* The seventy-six-foot drop of the falls is the greatest single descent of the Potomac within the Fall Zone. Although numerous rapids and rocky areas exist elsewhere along the river, this immediate section is the most rugged. During the colonial period, Great Falls was regarded as an obstacle to inland navigation, particularly for ocean-going vessels. Typically, these

The Great Falls of the Potomac River.

ships made their last port of call at either Georgetown or Alexandria downstream. To tap the commerce of the Piedmont hinterland, the Patowmack Company, with George Washington as its president, was founded in 1784 to construct a series of canals that would bypass the falls and other unnavigable stretches along the river. Adjoining the canal at Great Falls was the colonial settlement named *Matildaville,* founded in 1790 by Henry "Lighthorse Harry" Lee (b. 1756; d. 1818), the father of Robert E. Lee (b. 1807; d. 1870). The town and canal prospered until the 1820s, when they were eclipsed by the activities of the Chesapeake and Ohio Canal, which was built on the Maryland side of the Potomac.

Currently, Great Falls marks the Potomac's passage across the Fall Line. This location is about 15 miles above the land boundary between the Piedmont and Coastal Plain. The falls result from 2 million years of erosion. The river has gradually carved its way into the metamorphic rocks characterizing this portion of the Piedmont. The formation here is identified as the Peter Creek Schist, a particularly hard rock which was not eroded as fast as the rock material downstream.

When the Peter Creek Schist was metamorphosed, a number of faults and joints developed. Some of these joints and fractures are used by the Potomac to ease its path to the ocean. Whereas the Potomac normally follows a gently meandering path toward the coast, at Great Falls it suddenly changes course. Within a distance of 5 miles, the river makes two abrupt shifts in direction. Each change is separated by a long, linear gorge. Known as *Mather Gorge,* this feature illustrates strong structural control. Notice how long and straight the gorge is. In this case, the river is probably following the path of least resistance created by the fault. It assumed this route as the region was uplifted and the river began downcutting into bedrock. After moving through the gorge for several miles, the river again shifts its course eastward. Farther downstream, it moves through a maze of channels and crosses one last fall complex, *Little Falls* near Chain Bridge.

PATOWMACK CANAL

One of the most significant engineering achievements in the early history of our country was the construction of the *Patowmack Canal,* conceived by George Washington to facilitate safe passage of freight around major obstacles in the Potomac River. For years, before its initiation, colonists used canoes or small rafts to float their produce to marketplaces in either Georgetown or Alexandria. Sometimes, lives and goods were lost as they tried to take their goods through the fall complexes along the river. To reduce these losses, the Patowmack Canal Company constructed a series of bypass canals.

Company promoters including Washington argued that the most efficient way to develop the Potomac River system was to use the river itself as the primary channel of movement. Only at locations presenting major obstacles were bypass canals constructed. The company's decisions were motivated by the need to keep construction costs down and to quickly ease shipping problems along the river. In any case, their plan was only partially successful. The Potomac River's erratic flow proved more difficult to tame and use than they had envisioned, and the cost of building bypass canals was high in terms of capital and time.

The Great Falls-skirting canal was begun in 1786. Construction of the canal completed in 1801 and opened to river traffic in 1802. The operation continued until 1830 when it was superseded by the Chesapeake and Ohio Canal on the Maryland side of the Potomac River. When finished the canal was a little over a mile long. For most of its course, the channel width measured twenty-five feet except at the locks where it narrowed to less than fourteen feet. The canal contained five locks, all in its southern portion. These structures were designed to lift or lower river craft from Mather Gorge to the level of the river upstream—a vertical distance of seventy-six feet.

Although not very deep (four to five feet), the canal was deep enough to allow the passage of a wide assortment of boats. Thomas Hahn, a local canal historian, documented five different types—log rafts, gondolas, dugout canoes, sharpers, and keelboats. Log rafts and gondolas were designed for a one-way trip downriver. Upon reaching their destination, the freight was unloaded and the vessel dismantled for lumber. Their owners would either walk or hitch a ride home.

Sharpers were sixty to seventy-five feet long and five to seven feet wide. These vessels were designed to move either upstream or downstream as each end of the craft was pointed. When fully loaded sharpers carried fifteen to twenty tons of goods—usually agricultural produce. The typical products shipped were wheat, flour, corn, whiskey, and "pig iron." The pig iron was manufactured at small furnaces upstream—an example being Antietam Furnace near Shepherdstown, West Virginia.

To move the freight downstream required a voyage of three to five days. The exact length of time depended on the number of miles traveled. Freight originating at Cumberland, Maryland, could cover a distance of 185 miles in five days. A return trip upstream by sharper required nine to thirteen days. Today we can travel by car to Cumberland in about four hours.

Travel on the river was seasonal. Water flow was either too high in the spring or too low in the late summer to permit easy travel. Movement of freight was coordinated to the fluctuating flow of the river. Two periods of heavy traffic occurred—one in late winter and early spring, the other in fall.

Return

From this point we reverse our route and return to Washington, D.C.

As we begin to retrace our route, it is possible to reflect on the significance of George Washington's Potomac. While the total distance of this field trip is less than 50 miles, we traced a route that emphasized transition, both in a geographic and a temporal context. In terms of the former we traversed the zone that marks the boundary of two major physiographic regions, the Coastal Plain and the Piedmont. Besides the changes that are apparent in the physical landscape, the transition is also evident in a temporal and cultural context. We focused on a period that witnessed the beginning of the shift from a rural agrarian settlement pattern, based on the mixed economy of tobacco and wheat, to the establishment of an urban settlement that has become one of the nation's largest metropolitan regions.

A primary participant in this geographic and temporal setting was George Washington, first President of the United States. Although he was not a professional geographer, his vision for the region certainly included a geographical perspective. His decisions for locating the nation's capital were in part influenced by the desire to have equal access to the original thirteen states. Another consideration was his view that the capital could not function solely upon governmental operations; it must also have economic viability. The basis for this visibility would be the development of the Potomac River as a major trade route. With access to trade moving up and down the river corridor, he envisioned the development of a major market site and its associated activities within the city. Unfortunately, these never materialized, as witnessed by the remains of both the Patowmack and Chesapeake and Ohio Canal systems.

The L'Enfant plan, executed under Washington's supervision, continues to dominate the city's planning and circulation. Certainly much of the city's attraction is based upon the original layout for buildings, public spaces, and streets. As the city has grown beyond L'Enfant's plan, Alexandria and Georgetown, which were the dominant urban settlements during Washington's lifetime, now have been engulfed into its modern infrastructure. Ironically, the attractiveness of both sites continues to be based upon the colonial origins and associations. Even though George Washington had a great vision for this city and its surrounding hinterland, it is not likely that he would have foreseen the extent and importance that the city has attained in a few hundred years and which is now being commemorated in the bicentennial of its founding.

△ *Day Four*

COLONIAL VIRGINIA— JAMESTOWN, WILLIAMSBURG, AND YORKTOWN

by **Christine Drake,** *Old Dominion University*

This field trip provides an insight into the geographical environment and main historic sites of colonial Virginia. It highlights some of the major events of the period between 1607, when the first permanent English settlement in North America was established at Jamestown, and 1781, the date of the momentous battle of Yorktown that led to the final defeat of the British and their recognition of American independence. We will focus on the beginnings of permanent English settlement on the North American continent and the environment in which it occurred and consider the site and situation of the two colonial capitals of Virginia— Jamestown (1607 to 1699) and Williamsburg (1699 to 1780). We will examine early human–environment interactions, including the growth and development of a typical plantation (Carter's Grove), and also look at the origins of some of America's fundamental institutions, such as Congress and the Supreme Court. This historic triangle of Jamestown–Williamsburg–Yorktown contains many exhibits, restored and reconstructed eighteenth-century buildings, and the re-created living history of the colonial period interpreted by costumed guides.

Colonial Virginia

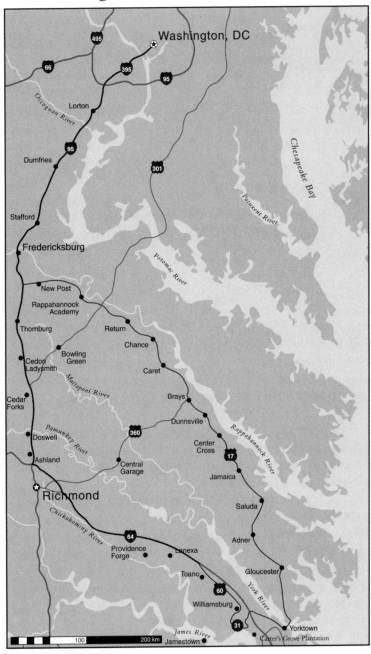

The New World had been discovered more than 100 years before English settlers successfully established their first permanent settlement at Jamestown, Virginia. Indeed, there was considerable British activity, both exploratory and colonizing, before the seventeenth century began. King Henry VII (b. 1457; d. 1509), in 1497, commissioned John (b. 1450; d. 1498) and Sebastian (b. 1476?; d. 1557) Cabot to cross the Atlantic to search for Cathay and claim a portion of North America for England. West Country fishermen followed the Cabots and fished off the coast of North America, putting in from time to time along the cold, forbidding Newfoundland coast to cure their catches. Later in the sixteenth century, English fishermen came to the Chesapeake Bay and stopped off for short periods to rest and reprovision. Navigators knew the winds and currents from frequent crossings of the Atlantic. The French focused their exploratory and colonizing efforts on the land around the St. Lawrence River and Gulf of Mexico. By the middle of the sixteenth century the Spanish had settled in the Caribbean, the Andes, and Florida (St. Augustine was established in 1565) and in 1570 to 1571 founded an abortive Spanish Jesuit mission in the Chesapeake Bay area. Like the French and the Spanish, the English tried for decades to find a passage to India and the alluring riches of the Orient. In the late 1570s Sir Humphrey Gilbert (b. 1539?; d. 1583) and Sir Walter Raleigh (b. 1552?; d. 1618) attempted to find the Northwest Passage to Asia, and even established a short-lived colony at St. John's, Newfoundland. Later expeditions sought a milder, more southerly site for a colony, along the Outer Banks of what is now North Carolina (then part of "Ould Virginia," named after England's Virgin Queen, Elizabeth I [b. 1533; d. 1603]). Here, on Roanoke Island, the first child of English parents, Virginia Dare, was born in 1587. But the outbreak of the Anglo–Spanish War in 1588 prevented the resupplying of the colony and put a stop to further colonizing. By 1590, when John White returned to the shores of the New World, the colony on Roanoke Island had disappeared (the "Lost Colony"), and no trace of the original colonists was ever found.

In his *Discourse of Western Planting,* published in 1584, the Oxford geographer Richard Hakluyt (the Younger) (b. 1552?; d.

1616) discussed all the advantages of establishing settlements in North America, even if they failed to yield gold or a passage to the Orient. His reasons included trade and the creation of secure and profitable sources of raw materials and agricultural commodities, as well as religion, emigration, and defense. Hakluyt envisioned Virginia as a great agricultural settlement that would produce "vines, olives, oranges, lymons, figges, etc.," along with iron, salt, cables, and cordage (E.G.R. Taylor p. 317). His cousin Richard Hakluyt (the Elder) was even more enthusiastic, anticipating the production of sugarcane as well. Both based their knowledge of what they thought would grow from comparable latitudes in Europe (along the Mediterranean), not realizing how different an East Coast climate is from a west coast Mediterranean climate (because of the continental influences of unhindered cold Arctic air blowing in the winter, and the heat and humidity of the summer). Thus only vines and figs would grow in Virginia, while the frosts of winter killed citrus trees or prevented them from fruiting in any part of eastern North America north of central Florida (even though oranges grow at Seville and Valencia in Spain at the same latitude as the Chesapeake Bay) (B. W. Blouet).

Not until 1604, when peace was reestablished between England and Spain, did the merchants of England recognize the wisdom of Hakluyt's insistence that England stood to profit from American settlements. It took a further year of lobbying before King James I (b. 1566; d. 1625) issued a charter of incorporation and a land grant to a group of merchants and other influential public figures. The charter divided North America in half, giving the northern part to the patentees from Bristol and Plymouth, and the remainder of the continent to those from London. Seven Londoners organized themselves as the Virginia Company of London, and set about mounting an expedition to begin permanent settlement in North America.

Three vessels were chartered: the *Susan Constant* and the *Godspeed,* chosen for their cargo capacity, and the *Discovery,* selected for its maneuverability in coastal waters. Commanded by Christopher Newport (d. 1617), the ships eventually left England on 20 December 1606. Traveling via the Canary Islands and Martinique in the West Indies, the fleet, after more than four months at sea, finally entered the Chesapeake Bay. The colonists explored the capes at the entrance to the bay, erecting a cross at the southern one, named for Henry, the Prince of Wales, and landing also at the northern cape, named for the prince's younger brother, Charles.

Colonial Virginia

JAMESTOWN

The Virginia Company had issued detailed instructions to the colonists, even though the drafters of the orders could have had little idea of the lands that were to be occupied. The settlers were told to find a safe port at the entrance to a navigable river that ran inland, preferably in a northwest direction, "for that way you shall soonest find the other sea" (W. M. Billings, p. 19). So for about two weeks they explored the banks of the Powhatan River, which flows from the northwest, and renamed it the James River in honor of their sovereign, James I. They visited several native villages— notably Kecoughtan and Paspahegh—and finally selected a site for their new settlement of *Jamestown* on a peninsula that ran out from the north bank of the James. Here the water was deep enough along the shoreline for the mariners to moor their ships to the trees and unload their cargoes directly ashore. The settlers began their colonization of the New World on 14 May 1607.

This pear-shaped peninsula, approximately 2 miles long and about 1 mile wide, with only a narrow isthmus connecting the western end to the bank of the James, appeared easy to defend against the native Americans (whom the Europeans called "Indians" because they had expected to reach India by going westward). It also seemed safe from possible Spanish assaults, located as it was 60 miles from the open sea. Game and trees abounded and the soil appeared fertile. The disadvantages of the site, however, were not so readily apparent in mid-May—the surrounding marsh which bred enormous swarms of mosquitoes, the lack of drinking water, the proximity of the Paspahegh Indians whose land the colonists had appropriated, the extremes in climate which were greater than

An authentically re-created home inside the palisaded Jamestown Fort at Jamestown Settlement.

the English had ever experienced, and the erodibility of the soil and its continual need for fertilizing. In any case the first settlers thought they needed to be near their ships, partly because they were the connecting link with supplies from England, and partly because the ships with their cannon at first provided their only real security from the Indians.

The English settlers could have learned much from the Indians, who had lived in this part of Virginia for at least 10,000 years. By 1607 the Coastal Plain up to the Fall Line where the rivers stop being tidal, a region known as Tidewater, was home to some three dozen tribes, all of whom were associated in a loosely knit political organization ruled by the great Werowance, a man known to the English at Powhatan (b. 1550?; d. 1618). Each tribe had its own chief, who was occasionally a woman (lines of kinship were also traced through the mother). They knew how to take their living from the land without unduly disturbing the environment's natural balance. They were skilled huntsmen, harvesting fish and game with implements fabricated from stone, wood, or bone. They cultivated beans, corn, melons, squash, and tobacco in large community fields for the chiefs, and in small plots for their families, which men cleared by slashing and burning and women farmed. These they intercropped in rows on mounds, which produced strong stalks and root systems and which also reduced weeds and soil erosion and contributed to the retention of moisture. Intercropping corn and beans helped maintain soil fertility. Indeed, the Indians frequently staggered their corn planting so as to give three harvests, in August, September, and October. They also possessed native remedies to a variety of illnesses, which often had greater curative powers than did European medicine at that time, and had a complex culture with a well-defined division of labor. Further, they knew the wisdom of leaving the low-lying, mosquito-infested, swampy ground during the hot, humid summer months. The Indians both helped and distrusted the English, bringing them food which enabled them to survive their first winters, but also attacking and killing them from time to time.

However, the English harbored prejudices against these native Virginians—indeed, against anyone who was neither English nor Christian. In regarding the Indians as inferior and barbarian and treating them with contempt, the English not only failed to learn their survival skills but provoked them to hostility that led to a number of massacres and wars. These hostilities ultimately decimated the Indian tribes and led to their almost complete destruction as a people. Today, the offspring of the survivors of the Pamunkey and Mattaponi tribes live on reservations in King William County, or have been partially assimilated into American culture.

The early English settlers confronted enormous difficulties, both physical and social. Physically, the extremes of climate, the brackish and contaminated water, inadequate food and nutrition, and outbreaks of disease led to the death of large percentages of their early numbers. By the end of September 1607, only 54 of the original 104 colonists remained alive, and only 38 survived the first winter; two years later (during the winter of 1609 to 1610) increased numbers of settlers and inadequate food supplies led to the "Starving Time" in which 440 of the 500 settlers died. Socially, quarrels over leadership, the inclusion among the settlers of many gentlemen who were unwilling or unskilled at working with their hands, and Indian attacks undermined early chances for success. Indeed, in May of 1610 the surviving settlers packed up and abandoned their colony, only to learn of a new contingent of settlers, supplies, and fresh leadership arriving in the Chesapeake Bay, which persuaded them to return and try again.

The settlers made serious attempts to establish industries, particularly in iron and glass, but the turning point in changing a struggling colony into a thriving business came with John Rolfe's (b. 1585; d. 1622) experimentation with growing tobacco. He succeeded in developing the desirable West Indies species of tobacco, *Nicotiana tabacum,* in place of the Indian variety, *Nicotiana rustica* (which produced a biting taste when smoked). Smoking had become the rage in England ever since some of Sir Walter Raleigh's colonists had introduced the habit in the 1580s and Raleigh had made the practice acceptable at Queen Elizabeth's court. Despite King James I's dislike of smoking, by 1618 more than 50,000 pounds of the leaf had been shipped home from Virginia. A tobacco-based economy had been established in the New World, and Jamestown's survival was assured. Private land-ownership attracted new settlers, who acquired their own land and brought indentured servants and, later, slave laborers. Plantations were developed (such as Carter's Grove) and new government was established. Representatives known as burgesses were elected to Virginia's first General Assembly held at Jamestown in July 1619, a forerunner of the Congress of the United States.

After several years of relatively calm relations, assisted by John Smith's (b. 1580; d. 1631) associations with the Indians and the marriage of Powhatan's daughter, Pocahontas (b. 1595?; d. 1617), to John Rolfe, the Indians struck out against the English. Angered by the contempt with which the English treated them, resentful of their increasing loss of land, and with their existence as a race of free people threatened by the growing numbers of English settlers, the Indians simultaneously attacked the entire line of English settlements. In March 1622 they massacred 347 men, women, and children, eliminating almost one third of the colony's population. Jamestown escaped destruction only because its inhabitants got wind of the impending disaster. The resulting war, together with other problems—including incompetent leadership, inadequate funds, lazy colonists, disagreements about purposes, and unrealistic expectations—led to the dissolution of the London Company in 1625, and the proclamation of Virginia as a royal colony by the new monarch, Charles I (b. 1600; d. 1649). It remained as such until the American Revolution. Jamestown, by virtue of being the first settlement, became Virginia's capital and remained the seat of government for the rest of the century.

During this period, Virginia, known as the Old Dominion, began to flourish as more and more colonists arrived from England and the number of great tobacco-growing plantations on the shores of the Chesapeake increased. In addition, many settlers arrived to farm their own small acreages; most were poor farmers living in simple wooden structures. The need for more labor led to the importation of ever-increasing numbers of Africans. In early days they came, as did many white immigrants, as indentured servants. However, as time passed, more and more of the Africans became indentured for life—slaves, in other words—while the indenture system died out for whites. However, there were always some free blacks, who had either served out their indenture or been freed. They worked, as did many white settlers, as small farmers, tradespeople, and crafters.

The economy of the colony became more diversified with the addition of craft industries and service occupations. However, the development of the large plantations, with their direct trans-Atlantic maritime links, retarded the growth of towns. In addition, mid-seventeenth-century colonists had to confront problems similar to those of the pre-royal-colony days: the Indian War of 1644 to 1646 and subsequent raids, inept leadership, and Bacon's Rebellion in 1676 (which began in response to the government's unwillingness to protect the lives and property of the planters from Indian attacks, and finished as an all-out attack on the weak government of Governor Sir William Berkeley [b. 1606; d. 1677]).

Historic Plantations of Colonial Virginia

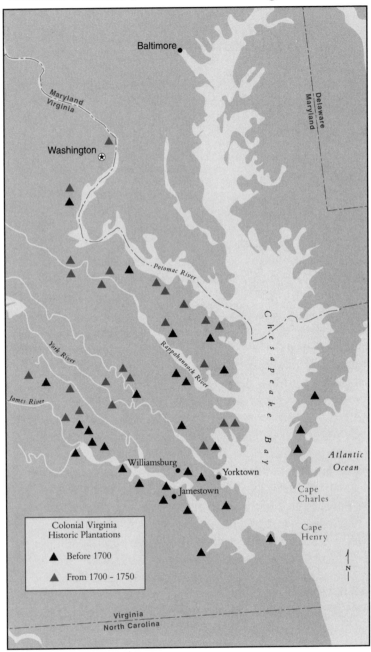

Although John Smith had pronounced Jamestown's site "a verie fitt place for the erecting of a great cittee," a view shared by many company investors, colonists, royal officials, and governors, Jamestown never developed into anything more than a small town with several dozen buildings and a resident population that seldom numbered as many as 200. It housed the state house and capitol complex, the governor's residence, a substantial brick church with three-story tower, a number of houses of varying size and construction, from frame to brick to rude thatched cottages made of plaster and lath ("wattle-and-daub"), and industrial buildings including a warehouse, brick kilns, a bakery, a pottery kiln, and breweries. Its location on a restricted peninsula site, its unhealthy climate, and the decreasing need for a defensive position as the Indians were pushed back into the interior help to explain its limited growth. In addition, at various times in its history (1608, 1655, 1660, 1676, and 1698) fires devastated the town.

Indeed, Jamestown never fully recovered from the 1676 fire, which Nathanial Bacon (b. 1647; d. 1676) deliberately set in his final act of rebellion. It took years for most of the buildings to be reconstructed or repaired, and the governor's residence was never rebuilt. By the late seventeenth century the "scraggly little village" no longer projected an image befitting a wealthy American colony, and indeed Jamestown never lived down its reputation as a disease-ridden, indefensible settlement. Another fire in 1698 reduced Jamestown to ashes. In 1699 the royal governor, Francis Nicholson (b. 1655; d. 1728), persuaded the General Assembly to move the seat of government inland to a site known as *Middle Plantation* 5 miles from Jamestown. It was this place that grew into the city of *Williamsburg*. Jamestown gradually slipped into decay and finally disappeared altogether. Jamestown's legacy consists of just the church tower, which remains as Jamestown's sole surviving seventeenth-century structure, and the foundations of some of the houses and other buildings.

WILLIAMSBURG

Willamsburg, then known as Middle Plantation, was settled originally in 1633 as an outpost to defend against Indian attacks. It even served as a substitute capital during Bacon's Rebellion in 1676 and

1677, when Jamestown was burned to the ground. By 1690 it had developed into a small village with widely scattered houses, a church, several stores, a tavern, and two mills. In 1693, the College of William and Mary was founded there, making it, after Harvard, the oldest college in the colonies.

Middle Plantation was located on high ground between the York and James rivers and was therefore relatively free of mosquitoes and disease. Its inland location was thought to be safe from naval bombardment. As home to the College of William and Mary, one of the colony's principal institutions, it offered cultural and educational attractions. In addition, several of Virginia's leading politicians lived nearby. It was also at a crossroads along the main post road that ran from Charleston and Norfolk to Baltimore, Philadelphia, and New York. Finally, Middle Plantation offered a relatively undeveloped area upon which an appropriately planned capital city could be constructed, unhindered by many previous buildings.

Williamsburg was laid out with a specific town plan which is clearly in evidence today. In the center of the town is a large open area, known as *Market Square,* which served the eighteenth-century need for regularly held markets and fairs. Crossing Market Square is the east–west Main Street (now called *Duke of Gloucester Street*), which extends from the *College of William and Mary* (with its lovely Wren building at the apex) at the western end, "downtown" to the *Capitol* building at the eastern end of the town. Designed to be ninety-nine feet wide and nearly 1 mile long, this street was a broad, open avenue that accentuated the linear aspects of the city plan.

To the west of Market Square, the city was laid out in the shape of a square, centered on *Bruton Parish Church* (first built in 1683 slightly to the north of its present location, and replaced in 1715 on its present site). The *Governor's Palace* was located at the head of a wide green avenue running north from the church. The main Duke of Gloucester Street is flanked by two back streets, Nicholson to the north and Francis on the south. City planners clearly anchored the town on the College, Church, and Capitol, three physical symbols of a traditional city. Governor Nicholson also stipulated that each house lot should be one half acre in size, so that each household should have enough space for a free-standing

The original Williamsburg home of George Wythe, lawyer, burgess, signer of the Declaration of Independence, and teacher of Thomas Jefferson.

Three houses on Duke of Gloucester Street in Williamsburg.

Bruton Parish Church in Williamsburg.

A reconstruction of the first Capitol in Williamsburg, used between 1704 and 1747 as the seat of the General Assembly and the General Court.

A pastoral scene in Colonial Williamsburg.

The reconstructed Governor's Palace in Williamsburg, which housed seven British royal governors and the first two governors of the Commonwealth.

dwelling, garden, and orchard. The plan even specified the design of the houses (not less than a "tenn foot pitch," meaning from the ground floor to the second floor) and their setback from the street (six feet). The contrasts with the cramped quarters of the narrow and medieval row-housing at Jamestown and with its restricted peninsula site are readily apparent. Although three different house plans are common, one type of house came to be characteristic of Williamsburg: a story and a half in height with a steep, shingled roof, a great brick chimney at one or both ends, and windows on each side of the doorway, with dormers in the roof. Wood framing faced with weatherboarding was the most common construction method for small houses in the Virginia colony throughout the eighteenth century, with brick used mostly for larger homes.

Unlike Jamestown, which never became more than a small, underdeveloped administrative center, Williamsburg grew along with the colony through the eighteenth century. The college and the workings of government and court attracted newcomers. Taverns were established to feed and house those in town on government business. Lawyers settled there to be close to the court. More and more stores were opened to provide merchandise to out-of-town shoppers, and the number of available services expanded. Proximity to the Capitol attracted many of the artisans, shopowners, and tavern-keepers, who competed for the business of visitors to the Capitol; while the western end of town provided a more pastoral atmosphere, with larger, more elegant townhouses and ornamental and practical gardens. Much of the heavy and domestic work around town was performed by blacks, most of them slaves. By the eve of the American Revolution nearly 2,000 people, roughly half white, half black, lived in the capital city.

Williamsburg played a considerable role in the struggle for independence. Indeed Virginia's revolution began in Williamsburg on 26 May 1774, when the House of Burgesses, although dissolved by Governor Lord Dunmore, met at the Raleigh Tavern to form a Virginia Association that ruled Virginia in defiance of British authority. The first Virginia Convention encouraged the other colonies to meet at Philadelphia in the First Continental

Congress, where, under the presidency of Peyton Randolph, Virginians (including George Wythe, Thomas Jefferson, Benjamin Harrison, Thomas Nelson, and Richard Henry Lee) took the lead in seeking the redress of America's grievances and a union of all the colonies to accomplish this goal. On 15 May 1776 Virginia's leaders (including Patrick Henry, Edmund Pendleton, Robert Carter Nicholas, George Mason, and James Madison) created a new, free commonwealth in Virginia and called upon the Congress in Philadelphia to declare the independence of the American people from the tyranny of King George III (b. 1738; d. 1820). Acting on the resolution of the Virginia Convention, Richard Henry Lee (b. 1732; d. 1794) presented a motion for independence in the Continental Congress. A committee of five, headed by Thomas Jefferson (b. 1743; d. 1826; pres. 1801 to 1809), prepared the draft declaration, which was adopted without dissent on July 4.

Although Williamsburg had grown into a far more impressive urban community than Jamestown, not all eighteenth-century Virginians approved of the capital's location there. After several earlier attempts to relocate the capital, in 1780 (four years after the Declaration of Independence) proponents of a new capital prevailed, arguing that Richmond offered better military defense, a healthier climate, and a more central location. Indeed, Richmond was considered "more safe and central than any other town on navigable water." However, despite the loss of its status as the capital, Williamsburg did not die as Jamestown did, but continued to be a county seat and to house two important institutions—the College of William and Mary and the Public Hospital for the Insane. Throughout the nineteenth century Williamsburg served as an important market center for nearby farmers and their families. In the 1920s, thanks largely to the inspiration of Reverend W.A.R. Goodwin, rector of Bruton Parish Church, who recognized the value of the many eighteenth-century buildings still standing, and the commitment and resources of John D. Rockefeller, Jr., Williamsburg was restored to its eighteenth-century condition. Today the Historic Area of Williamsburg is both a museum and a living city.

YORKTOWN

The colonial period in Virginia ended with the climactic battle of Yorktown that was pivotal in leading to the end of the Revolutionary War and the recognition by Britain of American independence. By the summer of 1781, the United States had been at war with England for over six years (the first shots of the Revolutionary War, or War of Independence, had been fired in April 1775 on village greens in Lexington and Concord, Massachusetts). After the devastating winters of 1777 to 1778 at Valley Forge, Pennsylvania, and 1779 to 1780 at Morristown, New Jersey, in which many soldiers froze or starved to death or gave up and returned home, American fortunes were at a low ebb. Only the strong leadership of commander-in-chief George Washington (b. 1732; d. 1799; pres. 1789 to 1797) kept the Continental Army together. But in the summer of 1780 American troops received a major boost to their cause when 6,000 French troops arrived at Newport, Rhode Island. France had been sending supplies to the Americans all along, but only after France and Britain declared war against each other in 1778 did French King Louis XVI send troops to the American states and engage the British directly.

When the French arrived, the British were operating on two fronts: General Sir Henry Clinton (b. 1738?; d. 1795) was occupying New York, while General Lord Cornwallis (b. 1738; d. 1805) was leading through the southern colonies an army that had already captured Savannah and Charleston. The main U.S. army under Washington was stationed along the Hudson River north of New York City. On learning that the French fleet, with more than 3,000 French troops, was sailing into the lower Chesapeake Bay in July 1781, Washington moved most of his troops south to fight Cornwallis, while deceiving Clinton into believing he was about to attack him in New York.

Cornwallis, meanwhile, was in Yorktown, having been ordered by Clinton during the summer to provide a deepwater, protected harbor for the British fleet in the lower Chesapeake Bay. However, after a brief skirmish with the French at the Battle of the Virginia Capes in which their ships were damaged, the British fleet returned to New York, leaving the French, commanded by Admiral

F.J.P. de Grasse (b. 1722; d. 1788), in control of the lower Chesapeake. The 8,300 British soldiers occupying Yorktown were heavily outnumbered by the approximately 17,600 American and French soldiers gathered in Williamsburg. Cornwallis constructed a main line of defense around Yorktown, consisting of ten small, enclosed forts (called redoubts), batteries with artillery, and connecting trenches. However, the American and French troops began encroaching on these defenses, capturing redoubts 9 and 10 on 14 October 1781. The British tried first to attack the allied center, and then to evacuate Yorktown by crossing the York River in small boats to the fortified Gloucester Point; but a violent storm scattered the boats and aborted the evacuation plan. Cornwallis saw the futility of further conflict and sued for peace. The surrender took place on October 19—the very day Clinton sailed for Yorktown from New York with thousands of reinforcement troops.

Although the British still had 26,000 troops in North America, British resolve to continue the war weakened as a result of the defeat at Yorktown. The war had been lengthy and costly, and Britain was engaged also in military struggles in India, Gibraltar, the West Indies, and Ireland. Thus, in March 1782 the British Parliament passed a resolution to end the war against the United States. Later that year commissioners from both sides signed provisional articles of peace. In September 1783, the Treaty of Paris was signed, which ended the war and acknowledged American independence.

The Itinerary

JAMESTOWN SETTLEMENT, ONE TO TWO HOURS

This site has a unique museum of outdoor living history and indoor gallery exhibits that show the fascinating story of Jamestown's origin—its English inhabitants and the native Americans who lived in the area. The following options are available:

1. a short introductory film, "Jamestown: the Beginning";
2. three permanent exhibition galleries:

Historic Jamestown/Williamsburg Area

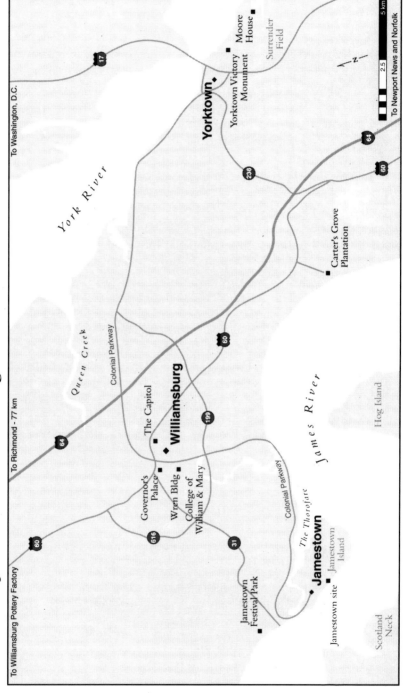

- ☐ the English Gallery deals with the beginning of Jamestown in sixteenth-century England, where merchants, mariners, and colonists joined together to plan their venture to the New World;
- ☐ the Powhatan Indian Gallery explores the land and lifestyle of the Powhatans before the English arrived in 1607;
- ☐ the Jamestown Gallery traces the history of the Virginia colony from its early struggle to survive to its establishment as a successful, permanent colony by the end of the seventeenth century;
3. the outdoor, authentically re-created world of early seventeenth-century Virginia:
   - ☐ a Powhatan Indian village with its bark- and mat-covered dwellings, tool-making, hide-tanning, food preparation, and other living demonstrations;
   - ☐ the palisaded Jamestown Fort, with its homes and small gardens, wood fires, thatching, tool-making, blacksmithing, and weapon-repairing;
   - ☐ full-scale replicas of the three ships, the *Susan Constant, Godspeed,* and *Discovery,* which first brought the colonists to the New World.

At each outdoor stop, costumed interpreters, using seventeenth-century skills and technology, present a view of the daily life of the Jamestown colonists or of their native American neighbors.

JAMESTOWN SITE, ONE HOUR

A short visit is available to the actual site of the original Jamestown settlement, about 1 mile from the Jamestown Settlement Living Museum. More than 700 feet of James River shoreline were lost to erosion between 1607 and 1935 (when the present concrete seawall and riprap retaining-wall were completed), including the original landing site and fort. Nevertheless one can still see some of the remains of the old town, including the old church tower, the only seventeenth-century structure still standing, and the foundations of many homes and other buildings of New Towne, which was developed after 1620 to the east. Other monuments include statues of Pocahontas, daughter of Chief Powhatan, whose marriage to John Rolfe in 1614 helped to improve relations between the native Americans and the English; and of Captain John Smith, explorer, author, soldier, and president of the Virginia Council from 1608 to 1609, whose strong leadership (with his rigid discipline of "he who will not work, will not eat") enabled the young colony to survive and grow. A Memorial Cross marks some 300 shallow graves hastily dug by the colonists during the winter of 1609 to 1610, known as the "Starving Time."

CARTER'S GROVE, ONE HOUR

Carter's Grove was an early seventeenth-century plantation, destroyed by the Indian massacre of 1622 and reestablished as the site of small farmsteads. Then, at the end of the seventeenth century, it became a large, prosperous plantation built on growing first tobacco and later corn, wheat, and apples, using enslaved African labor.

English settlers arrived in 1619, occupying land formerly inhabited by native Americans, and built *Wolstenholme Towne*. This was the administrative center for a plantation financed by a consortium of British "adventurers" who named their company the Society of Martin's Hundred—probably in honor of Richard Martin, recorder of the City of London. The term "hundred" means a tract capable of sustaining a hundred families. By 1622 the new Virginians were firmly established on their 21,500-acre tract, with its ten-mile frontage along the James River. Named for Sir John Wolstenholme, one of the society's most influential shareholders, the "towne" never became more than a village of perhaps thirty to forty inhabitants. It housed officials and probably stored tobacco and lumber for export to England. In the great Indian uprising of 22 March 1622 most of the homes were destroyed and half the settlers killed or carried off. *Martin's Hundred* recovered and continued through the seventeenth century as the site of a number of small farmsteads.

The farmsteads were consolidated at the end of the seventeenth century by one of the wealthiest and most powerful of the gentlemen planters, Robert "King" Carter, who specified in his will that the land "in all times to come be called . . . Carter's Grove." Like

Part of the eighteenth-century slave quarters at Carter's Grove.

many plantations in Colonial Virginia, such as Shirley and Berkeley, Carter's Grove's prosperity was built on the cultivation of tobacco for the English market. "King" Carter's grandson, Carter Burwell, inherited the property and built an elegant brick mansion with detached flanking dependencies and a remarkable series of carved, paneled rooms. After the turmoil of the Civil War, Reconstruction, and agrarian reform, Carter's Grove was restored and expanded in the early twentieth century with architecture and furnishings from the eighteenth century.

The following options are listed in their order of appearance. Options 3 and 6 and a view of the mansion from the river side are especially recommended.

1. A fourteen-minute multi-image slide presentation on Carter's Grove.
2. A small display of documents and interpretations of plantation and Indian life (twenty minutes).

3. The eighteenth-century slave quarters, which has been care-fully reconstructed on its original site and provides important perspectives on eighteenth-century plantation life through its dwellings, corn crib, garden plots, and chicken enclosures; it was used by slaves who provided labor for the agricultural tasks in the fields and woods at Carter's Grove. An interpretive lecture by African-American guides makes the site come alive (twenty to thirty minutes).

4. An explanation of the construction and changes at the mansion followed by a tour of this eighteenth-century mansion (restored in the 1920s), which provides an insight into life as it was lived at Carter's Grove in the 1930s and the eighteenth-century heritage of ideas and styles that so deeply influenced that life (forty-five minutes). If you decide to bypass the tour, go around the house to see its location with sweeping lawn and gardens reaching down to the James River.

5. Archaeological museum (thirty minutes).

6. Wolstenholme Towne. Although as much as half of the town may have been lost to erosion by the James River, archaeologists have discovered and others have partially reconstructed some of the palisades, fences, and buildings, including the "Company Compound" and store. The voice of the archaeologist who directed the excavations can be heard at eleven barrel-housed stations around the site (forty-five minutes).

WILLIAMSBURG

Williamsburg is the restored and reconstructed eighteenth-century capital of Virginia from 1699 to 1780.

In 1699 the capital of the Virginia colony was transferred from Jamestown to Williamsburg, which was named in honor of King William III. For eighty-one years Williamsburg was the thriving capital of Virginia at a time when the American dream of freedom and independence was taking form and the colony was a rich and powerful land stretching westward to the Mississippi River and north to the Great Lakes. Colonial Williamsburg is a restored and

Colonial Williamsburg

rebuilt eighteenth-century colonial town, with eighty-eight original eighteenth-century structures among its more than 500 buildings.

You can have lunch at a reconstructed tavern in the historic area (the King's Arms Tavern or Christiana Campbell's Tavern).

There is an enormous amount to see here. Approximately 1,200 eighteenth-century-costumed interpreters work in the historic area. Walk up and down Duke of Gloucester Street, absorbing the architecture. Recommendations of places to visit include:

1. the Capitol—A reconstruction of the first Capitol building that served between 1704 and 1747 as the seat of the General Assembly and the General Court. (The second Capitol building, built in 1753 after the first was gutted by fire, was also destroyed by fire in 1832.) Built in an H-shape, the buildings housed both the House of Burgesses (the lower house of the legislature, consisting of two members elected by the landowners of each county and one member each from Jamestown, Williamsburg, Norfolk, and the College of William and Mary) in the east wing, and the Council (made up of twelve leading colonists appointed for life by the king, who also assisted the governor by acting as a council of state) in the west wing. Disagreements over bills between the two houses could be worked out on neutral territory in the second-floor chamber located between the two wings over the entrance portico. The General Court, the highest court of the colony and a forerunner of the United States Supreme Court, consisting of the governor and the twelve members of the council, met in the General Courtroom on the first floor of the west wing. (Thirty-minute tours are given every fifteen minutes).

2. a tavern—Wetherburn (restored) or Raleigh (reconstructed). A colonial tavern not only served liquor but offered a lodging for travelers, meals, and a place for socializing and entertaining. A thirty-minute tour shows both the public and private spaces in the tavern, the outbuildings (including the kitchen, slaves' quarters, stables, and dairy), and the vegetable garden and yard.

3. the home of a wealthy local civic leader (depending on which is open on the day of your trip): George Wythe, Brush-Everard, or Peyton Randolph.
4. craft shops with costumed specialists at work: cooper, wigmaker, printer-bookbinder, blacksmith, shoemaker, windmill, silversmith, cabinet maker, wheelwright, harness-maker, milliner, and gunsmith.
5. Bruton Parish Church (organized in 1674)
6. the Public Gaol
7. the Governor's Palace (extra fee charged)
8. the Wren building at the College of William and Mary (founded in 1693)
9. gardens
10. a variety of museums: Abbey Aldrich Rockefeller Folk Art Center, De Witt Wallace Decorative Arts Gallery, and Archaeological Exhibit

YORKTOWN BATTLEFIELD, FORTY MINUTES

Yorktown was the site of the last major battle of the American Revolution, a turning point that led to the independence of the United States and significantly changed the course of world history. As we drive through the battlefield, we will see the British inner defense line, behind which the British endured a three-week siege; the grand French battery (the largest gun emplacement on the first allied American–French siege line); the two small British fortifications, known as redoubts 9 and 10 (redoubt is a French word meaning a small, earthen fort), which were captured by French and American troops on the night of 14 October 1781; the Moore House, where officers from both sides met to negotiate the final terms of the surrender of General Lord Cornwallis's army on October 18; and the Surrender Field, where the British and German mercenary troops under Cornwallis's command laid down their arms.

Tidewater Maryland

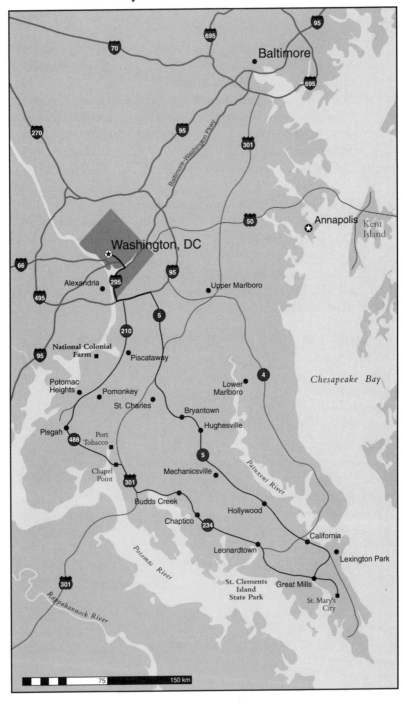

△ Day Five

COLONIAL TIDEWATER—TOBACCO IN SOUTHERN MARYLAND

by Robert D. Mitchell, *University of Maryland, College Park*

Travelers using Maryland Routes 3 and 301 south of Baltimore, to avoid metropolitan Washington en route to Richmond and points south, generally are unaware that they are passing through one of the areas of earliest European settlement in North America. Southern Maryland is positioned near the northern end of the Coastal Plain that extends westward from the Atlantic Ocean beyond tidal range to the Fall Zone of the rivers tumbling off the Piedmont. Traditionally the five counties of Anne Arundel, Prince George's, Charles, Calvert, and St. Marys, all between the Chesapeake Bay and the Potomac River, comprise the region.

A trip southward on Routes 3 and 301 reveals a place whose 1,400,000 residents still reflect the rural, provincial, small-town world that has long characterized this relatively out-of-the-way region. Only along its northern margins in Prince George's and Anne Arundel counties has there been a marked change to residential and commercial subdivisions with the spread of the suburbs of Washington, D.C., and Annapolis, Maryland. This settlement expansion has accounted for more than 80 percent of Southern Maryland's population increase since 1950. Black migrants from Washington, D.C., and states to the south comprise a substantial component of the increase, making Prince George's County the most populous, black, suburbanized county in the United States (730,000 residents, 51 percent black). Farther south, the low-lying to gently rolling countryside is covered with fields, farms, forests, and small towns, none of which contains more than 20,000 people. Observers view a seemingly unvarying agrarian landscape of corn, soybeans, wheat, hay, and tobacco, with a scattering of livestock. The region offers few major tourist sites save for St. Mary's City, Maryland's first capital, 75 miles southeast of Washington. Otherwise, the local road system terminates at numerous isolated sites along the bay and its rivers, the Patuxent and the Potomac.

The colonial era has left few vestiges on the landscape of Southern Maryland. Images of a sophisticated Williamsburg or an imposing James River plantation notwithstanding, most Europeans who occupied the Tidewater lands around Chesapeake Bay after 1600 built their settlements of wood. This was not log-cabin country but rather a land of frame structures based on simple English cottages or more substantial hall-and-parlor plans. Fewer than a dozen such colonial structures have survived, even in preserved form, in Southern Maryland. Most of the colonial sites on this field trip, except for parts of Port Tobacco and Chapel Point, contain structures that have been reconstructed in our own time and thus represent interpretations of colonial settlement landscapes which themselves deserve close scrutiny. The most enduring relics of the colonial era are to be found more in the fields than in the settlements. Of the region's five principal crops, tobacco and corn (maize) were cultivated by the native Indians, wheat and hay were introduced by Europeans, and soybeans emerged commercially only forty years ago. Today's tall, high-yielding, hybrid corns, used—like winter wheat and soybeans—for livestock feed, are far removed from the small flint and dent corns of the precolonial period. Tobacco is more representative of colonial times, both in its slightly modified form as *Nicotiana tabacum,* and in its locational persistence as a commercial crop for more than 350 years. In no other region of North America has tobacco been cultivated so continuously.

The Changing Status of Tobacco

Tobacco was *the* cash crop of the colonial Chesapeake Tidewater. Although corn was the most widely raised crop during the colonial period, it was tobacco cultivation (begun in Tidewater Virginia) that molded Chesapeake society and economy. Tobacco was primarily responsible both for the presence of slavery and dispersed plantations, and for the general absence of towns. While it is no longer grown in the Virginia Tidewater or on Maryland's Eastern Shore across the bay, tobacco has persisted commercially in Southern Maryland since the late 1630s.

No other crop, however, has been affected so adversely by the changing social habits of Americans during the second half of the twentieth century. For almost four centuries, Maryland's tobacco farmers defied the adage of Sir William Sandys, first secretary of the Virginia Company, that "you cannot build an empire on smoke." But since the early 1960s, cigarette consumption in the United States has declined by 25 percent and tobacco producers have found it increasingly difficult to stay in business. Southern Maryland's tobacco industry reflects this trend. Since acreage peaked at almost 40,000 acres during the early 1950s, harvested tobacco has declined steadily to only 7,000 acres in 1991, with a commensurate decline in tobacco farms from more than 5,000 to fewer than 2,000 (many of which are now part-time operations). By comparison, Southern Maryland farmers devote 35,000 acres to soybeans, 30,000 acres to corn, 17,000 acres to hay, and 11,000 acres to winter wheat.

Prince George's County was Maryland's leading tobacco county and one of the most productive agricultural areas in the South during the late colonial period. By this time tobacco had become entrenched in North Carolina and was about to diffuse to Kentucky, the two leading tobacco-producing states today. Increasing suburbanization since the 1950s has also eliminated tobacco production from the northern parts of both Prince George's and Anne Arundel counties, leaving the more southerly St. Marys (2,300 acres) and Charles (1,700 acres) counties currently as Maryland's principal tobacco areas. Relic tobacco barns remain

A modern tobacco landscape in early August. Photograph by Robert D. Mitchell.

amidst suburbia, and along the Patuxent River, which runs through the historic heart of tobacco country. One can still find ruins of tobacco landings or jetties where the crop was transferred to vessels for transport to London, Bristol, or Glasgow.

The contemporary tobacco landscape contrasts considerably with the colonial landscape not only in terms of acreage and relative significance but also in terms of farming and marketing practices. Maryland farmers continue to produce a special kind of air-cured tobacco, known as Type 32, which is highly prized for cigarette manufacture in Western Europe. It is grown in Coastal Plain areas where light sandy-loam soils, very low relief, and a growing season of 185 to 190 days provide excellent conditions for its production. Seedbeds are plowed and prepared outdoors in October and left over the winter. The following March the seedbeds are sown and packed. Muslin covers are generally draped over the young plants for six to eight weeks after which the plants are sown

Harvested tobacco for curing. Photograph by Robert D. Mitchell.

by machine in rows three feet apart in well-drained fields. About 6,000 plants are sown per acre. The fields are sprayed periodically with chemical pesticides and herbicides to keep down weeds and to destroy insect pests. As they mature, hired laborers remove sprouts on the sides of the plants by hand. This practice (termed "suckering") enhances the growth of large leaves, and the tops of the plants are broken off below the seedhead to permit the lower leaves to develop (called "topping"). The plants, now containing sixteen to twenty large leaves, grow for another few weeks before being harvested beginning in mid-August. This is accomplished by cutting the stalks close to the ground by hand and leaving them to wilt in the field until they can be pierced and strung on a tobacco stick and hung in a curing barn. These tall, generally unpainted barns dispersed throughout the landscape measure about forty feet long and sixteen feet wide, and have hinged side-boards to facilitate air flow.

Tobacco cures slowly on the racks until the end of the winter or very early spring under natural air conditions. The dry, brittle, reddish brown leaves soften in the rising spring humidity and are then removed from the barn. The leaves are graded into bunches of twelve to fifteen (termed a "hand") and placed in large piles (called "burdens"). Maryland tobacco is not subject to government price supports or quotas, unlike most American tobaccos, which provides for a flexible marketing situation. The burdens are no longer packed into huge wooden barrels (known as "hogsheads") but trucked to loose-leaf auctions held during April in Hughesville, La Plata, and Waldorf in Charles County and in Upper Marlboro in Prince George's County. During a hectic, two- or three-week period the entire Maryland crop of some 25,000,000 pounds (at 3,600 pounds per acre) is sold to American and European tobacco companies at $1.60 to $1.80 per pound.

Itinerary

What are the origins of such practices and how did they create the tobacco world of the seventeenth and eighteenth centuries? To answer these questions we begin our journey from Washington, D.C., in reverse chronological order. Our first visit is to the National Colonial Farm at Accokeek, which represents plantation life during the late colonial period (1740s to 1775); at Port Tobacco and Chapel Point we will examine the social and environmental contexts of Maryland's tobacco world; and our final destination is St. Marys City, Maryland's first foundation in 1634, where we will explore the origins of colonial society and economy.

THE PISCATAWAY

Our journey out of Washington on South Capitol Street takes us across the Anacostia River appropriately on the Frederick Douglass Memorial Bridge. Douglass (b. 1817?; d. 1895), the great nineteenth-century abolitionist, was born a slave on a tobacco plantation on Maryland's Eastern Shore. We continue on South Capitol past reclaimed land on which Bolling Air Force Base is

Accokeek Creek, a typical tidal marsh. Photograph by Robert D. Mitchell.

located and cross the District of Columbia boundary line where the route becomes Maryland Route 210, aptly named Indian Head Highway. Amidst this former tobacco-growing area, now converted to suburban development, lie the diverse remains of Indian life at contact time. We are reminded of this as we cross Piscataway Creek 8.5 miles south of the D.C. line. Named after the dominant native group in the area, the Piscataway, the tidal creek was deep enough in the seventeenth century for smaller tobacco ships. In the vicinity are the remains of an Indian village where Governor Leonard Calvert (b. 1606; d. 1647) negotiated an agreement with the "Emperor" of the Piscataways, which led to relatively peaceful relations for the early European settlers. Excavations have revealed the remains of Indian skeletons and artifacts including many trade beads. Ebenezer Cook (b. 1708?), the self-styled "poet laureate" of Colonial Maryland, caricatured the Piscataway Creek world in these terms:

I crost unto the other side,
A River whose impetuous Tide,
The Savage Borders does divide;
In such a shining odd invention,
I scarce can give its due Dimention.
The Indians call this watry Waggon
Canoo, a Vessel none can brag on;
Cut from a Popular-Tree, or Pine,
And fashion'd like a Trough for Swine.

As we turn right off 210 to Bryan Point Road, however, we pass through land still sacred to the Piscataways. The present *tayac,* or leader of Piscataway descendants, still conducts a quiet ceremony each spring at the site of Moyaone on the Potomac floodplain. Mayaone was located on John Smith's (b. 1580; d. 1631) 1612 map of "Virginia," at a site destroyed by Virginians after the Indian uprising of 1622. We approach this site by turning right off Bryan Point Road to the trail across Accokeek Creek. From the board-walk you can get an excellent view of the tidal wetlands so characteristic of much of the shoreline of Chesapeake Bay and the banks of the Potomac River.

NATIONAL COLONIAL FARM

Bryan Point Road terminates at *National Colonial Farm,* a reconstructed 160-acre tobacco plantation of the mid-eighteenth century, which is a cooperative venture of the Accokeek Foundation, Inc., and the National Park Service. Established in 1958, the farm is on the Potomac River opposite George Washington's somewhat grander tobacco plantation at Mount Vernon on the Virginia shore.

The main settlement site contains a small, frame farmhouse constructed with a board-and-batten exterior and a steeply pitched, wood-shingled roof (with some acknowledgment of twentieth-century residential needs), a separate out-kitchen for food preparation and cooking, a smokehouse for preparing beef and pork, and an outhouse. Adjacent to the residence ensemble is a kitchen garden, an herb garden, and a grape arbor for wine production.

The barnyard complex consists of a livestock barn, pig pens, and chicken houses, although most livestock roamed relatively freely, and free-standing "zig-zag" or "snake" fences were constructed to protect crops. The farm maintains a breeding program to produce animals that closely resemble those of colonial times, including red devon cattle, dorset horn sheep, turkeys, and guinea fowl. The crop area remains the heart of the plantation, however. A typical late colonial farm for a household of five persons would have had between 10 and 15 percent of its total area (some fifteen to twenty-two acres) cleared for crops. Within this area corn would occupy eight to ten acres, tobacco three to four acres, wheat three to four acres, vegetables and berries the remainder. The most important vegetables, beans and squashes, were often sown in the cornfields, a triple-cropping practice learned from the Indians.

The success or failure of the farm enterprise depended ultimately upon the production of tobacco. Colonial planters dubbed tobacco "the fifteen-month crop" because it took not only an entire year to prepare, cultivate, and process the plant but another three months to transport and market the crop in Britain. This meant that next year's planting had been accomplished before the previous year's crop had been sold. Hence Ebenezer Cook's lament about the uncertainties of tobacco production in his poem, "Sotweed Redivivus":

> *Too long, alas! Tobacco has engross'd*
> *Our Cares, and now we mourn our Markets lost;*
> *The plenteous Crops that over-spread our Plains,*
> *Reward with Poverty the toiling Swains;*
> *Their sinking Staple chills the Planters Hearts,*
> *Nor dare they venture on unpractis'd Arts;*
> *Despondent, they impending Ruin view,*
> *Yet starving, must their old Employ persue.*

TOBACCO IN COLONIAL MARYLAND

Most of the tobacco grown in Southern Maryland was of the Orinoco variety (*Nicotiana tabacum*), a versatile product but not

Indian tobacco, Nicotiana rustica. *Photograph by Robert D. Mitchell.*

Colonial tobacco, Nicotiana tabacum. *Photograph by Robert D. Mitchell.*

as highly regarded as the Sweet-Scented variety cultivated in parts of the Virginia Tidewater. Orinoco tobacco was diffused from the Caribbean and had been imported by Virginians to replace the tobacco variety cultivated by local Indians (*Nicotiana rustica*). Rustica grows less than two feet tall and had a high ratio of seedheads to leaves. Orinoco is a more vigorous variety, which was transformed during the 1640s into a commercial plant seven to eight feet tall, when planters learned to top off the seedheads so that plant energy could be diverted to the leaves and stalks.

In January and February tobacco seedbeds were prepared from freshly cleared land, and wood ash was added. Land clearance usually involved adopting the Indian practice of slash-and-burn agriculture which meant girdling trees, allowing them to die, and leaving the stumps in the ground. By the mid-eighteenth century, however, such practices were less common as the greater availability of labor and draft animals made more thorough clearance possible.

Transplanting the young plants from seedbeds to fields was a process that usually lasted a month, from late April to late May. Field preparation contrasted just as markedly from current practice. Plows were not common in the Chesapeake Tidewater until very late in the colonial period. Planters were more likely to employ the traditional Indian method of hoe-hill cultivation rather than plow cultivation. This involved the use of several types of wooden-shafted iron hoes to loosen the soil and create small mounds nine to twelve inches high. Each mound received one tobacco plant. Spaced three to four feet apart, one acre could accommodate about 2,700 to 3,200 plants (less than half of a modern planting). A typical planter, cultivating three or four acres of tobacco, would require the help of two or three workers. By the early eighteenth century such labor requirements were met with the purchase of African male slaves, together with the likely use of a female domestic slave for household tasks. The initial high costs of such purchases prevented as easy access to the planter ranks as had been the case during the seventeenth century. Slaves and their offspring remained in bonded slavery for life. "Surplus" slaves were taught other skills, rented out, or sold to other planters, thus making the creation of black family life extremely tenuous.

Although not as labor-intensive as rice, sugarcane, or cotton, tobacco production required year-round attention. As soon as the ground had thawed in early to mid-April the tobacco fields were prepared. In some years this would simply involve hoeing the fields used the previous year and building the individual tobacco hills. Planters seldom fertilized the fields, fearing that the application of animal manures would produce bad-tasting tobacco. Consequently, tobacco could be grown in the same field for only three or four years before the soil became "exhausted" and yields declined significantly. Because systematic crop rotation was not yet practiced in the Tidewater, planters employed a kind of field-rotation system whereby new acreage was cleared periodically for tobacco cultivation. This was labor-intensive work—chopping trees, clearing underbrush and burning it, breaking the soil with hoes, and scattering ash on the new field before making hills. Transplanting the young plants from the seedbeds could consume four to five weeks because the process could only be done after wet weather.

Planters turned their attention to their cornfields even before all the tobacco was in the ground. Cornfields were also prepared in hoe-hill fashion, with the hills arranged six to seven feet apart to accommodate mature gourd-seed stalks eight to ten feet tall. To conserve time and labor, former tobacco fields were often used as part of the corn acreage. Corn acquired its water and nutrients from the soil at a deeper level than the more shallow-rooted tobacco. The corn hills, moreover, were often sown with nitrogen-fixing beans, which used the cornstalks as vine support (unlike the ground-hugging soybeans of today), and with pumpkins and other squashes that spread over the ground and helped to choke out weeds.

Tobacco, on the other hand, had no such "helpers." Hence slaves had to pay constant attention to the field. By late May, when the plants had grown to a height of about three feet, and displayed many thin leaves, skilled slaves "topped" the plants. Topping was followed by "priming" (removal of bottom leaves), by periodic "suckering" (which required strong thumbnails), and by occasional weeding and regular worming (especially for hornworms

A late colonial tobacco landscape. Photograph by Robert D. Mitchell.

and grubs which fed on the leaves). The plants reached full height by mid-July. Weeding and worming continued until, by early August, closer attention was paid to signs of spotting and discoloration which heralded harvest time. By the third or fourth week in August cutting began. The plants were cut at the base with a tobacco knife and stacked in the fields to wilt throughout September and early October.

After the tobacco was cut, planters again turned their attention to the cornfields. Early in September winter wheat was sown either in former tobacco fields or between the corn hills to conserve space. It would be harvested in June of the next year at a time when labor could be drawn from tobacco weeding and worming. Corn harvesting was a more prolonged activity which lasted from late September through October, by which time tobacco "sticking" was in full swing. Slaves carried the sticks to the barn where they arranged them in racks to allow free air flow to cure the leaves during November and early December.

A late colonial tobacco barn. Photograph by Robert D. Mitchell.

By late November or early December, depending on the availability of damp weather, "sweating" took place. The brittle leaves were taken down carefully, arranged in bundles on the barn floor, covered with sacking, and allowed to build up humidity so that the leaves would be pliable for "prizing." This involved binding the leaves in small bundles ("hands") and stacking them in larger piles to maintain moistness before packing into hogsheads. Packing was begun in January under damp weather conditions. Slaves would stand in the casks and build up the tobacco leaves in smooth layers until the casks were full. The pressure was applied by levers, weights, and screws to pack the leaves tightly, after which more tobacco was added and pressed until the hogsheads were tightly packed. The head was secured, hoops tightened around the cask, and the hogshead weighed and marked with the planter's initials or mark. Filled hogsheads varied in weight between 750 and 1,100 pounds. A middling planter with five acres in tobacco, with a yield of between 700 and 800 pounds per acre, would require four or five hogsheads for his or her annual crop.

After 1747, when the Maryland legislature reluctantly passed a Tobacco Inspection Act as a quality-control measure (seventeen years after Virginia), hogsheads had to be transported by wagon, boat, or by rolling to the nearest inspection warehouse along the Potomac or Paxtuxent rivers. The casks were opened and inspected for trashy tobacco which could reduce prices in Britain; negligent planters could be asked to repack their hogsheads. Once inspected, planters received tobacco notes indicating the weight of each cask. These notes operated legally as money which could be used to pay taxes or personal debts. The first casks would be available for shipping by late November and loading would continue throughout the winter. By March the last of the hogsheads stored in public warehouses were ready for shipping to British markets. As Ebenezer Cook described the process in *The Sot-weed Factor:*

> *With this sly [planter] soon I struck*
> *A Bargain for my English Truck,*
> *Agreeing for ten thousand weight,*
> *Of Sot-weed good and fit for freight,*
> *Broad Oronooko bright and sound,*
> *The growth and product of his ground;*
> *In Cask that should contain compleat,*
> *Five hundred of Tobacco neat.*

Even after the tobacco was on board ship, it remained the planter's responsibility until it arrived safely in the care of British merchants. Risks and uncertainties were high because damage or spoilage could occur during the two-month journey to market. Prices received for the tobacco were also beyond the planter's control, and part of the profit invariably went to pay off the previous year's consumer debt. The appearance of Scottish factors and their stores in Southern Maryland after 1740 facilitated the planter's purchases of imported manufactured and luxury goods. Only occasionally did planters require the services of stores in small towns such as Upper Marlboro on the Patuxent, Bladensburg on the Anacostia, and Georgetown on the Potomac. Thus it is not surprising that the largest colonial settlement in this overwhelmingly rural region, Annapolis, never contained more than 2,200 inhabitants, a quarter of whom were slaves.

PORT TOBACCO

The relative absence of towns, however, did not mean the absence of orderly society. Our visit to *Port Tobacco,* once a small tobacco center and county seat of Charles County, will emphasize this point. It will also allow us to explore the controversial relationship between tobacco cultivation and the siltation of the Chesapeake Bay and its tributary streams.

We return to Route 210 and continue south for 8 miles, until the junction with Route 225 at Potomac Heights. Turn left and continue on Route 225 for 6 miles, passing through Ripley, to the traffic light at Marshalls Corner. The landscape now manifests more rolling land, covered extensively with scrub and pine woodlands on poorer, sandy soils. We turn right at the light onto Rose Hill Road and follow this road for 2.5 miles. We are in fact passing through a late seventeenth-century land grant known as *Betty's Delight* which contains a small, frame, colonial house and the unusually fine, two-story, brick-nogged, frame house of *Rose Hill* (private) overlooking the Port Tobacco Valley. At the junction with Chapel Point Road, turn left and travel 200 yards to Port Tobacco Road on the right and arrive at Port Tobacco within 0.5 mile.

The Potopaco Indians who had a village here during the early seventeenth century. The English settlement, founded in the 1640s, was known officially as Charlestown but referred to locally as Port Tobacco. Tobacco did indeed become the small settlement's life line. It had become an active port on the Potomac by the early eighteenth century (as witness Warehouse Landing Road) and became the seat of Charles County in 1727 (and remained so until fire destroyed the courthouse in the 1890s and officials moved the county seat to La Plata). By 1775, the town contained about fifty houses, supporting a population of about 250. But the head of the creek had silted up to form a tidal marsh and only small craft could now reach the town, which went into prolonged decline and substantial abandonment during the nineteenth century. Only three eighteenth-century houses and a reconstruction of a fourth house, as well as a reconstructed brick courthouse (of the 1820 period), represent something of the colonial world arranged around Courthouse Square.

Chimney House (1765) is a two-and-one-half story frame dwelling with an unusually large double chimney. Adjacent Stagg Hall (1732) has a brick chimney freestanding above the second floor. Quenzel House and Store across the square is a reconstruction of a "saltbox" frame house and store that occupied this site. The recently opened Catslide House represents a middling family home built about 1700. Archaeological excavations have revealed the sites of several other eighteenth-century structures, including an Episcopal church.

The reconstructed, second county courthouse dominates the square and reminds us of the importance of the county as the principal unit of local government throughout the Chesapeake Tidewater. For many colonial settlers the courthouse functions of government and justice, under the framework of English civil law, represented one of the few occasions for monthly social gatherings in this region of dispersed plantations. The county justices, usually selected from among prominent planters, oversaw the public life of the community ranging from registering land grants and adjudicating debt suits to appointing tithe takers and road overseers. A thirty-minute film in the courthouse provides a historical view of the influence of tobacco on the region, as well as of later events that affected the town. These events include its association with the Confederate underground during the Civil War and with the search for John Wilkes Booth (b. 1838; d. 1865) after he assassinated President Abraham Lincoln (b. 1809; d. 1865; pres. 1861 to 1865) in 1865.

For our purposes, however, the film raises questions about the processes of erosion and siltation that had overtaken the Tidewater region by the end of the colonial period. Settlers clearly were aware of the soil and marsh accumulating at the head of many tributaries of the Potomac as well as the middle and upper sections of the Patuxent. As our indomitable Ebenezer Cook described it:

> . . . *unthinking Swains*
> *At Ax and Hoe, like Negro Asses tug,*
> *To glut the Market with a poisonous Drug:*
> *Destroy sound Timber and lay waste their Lands.*

Land clearance and preparation for tobacco long have been regarded as the principal contributors to soil erosion and soil depletion, leading to the gradual siltation of formerly navigable streams. Recent research, however, suggests that most stream sediment is trapped in marshes within 0.5 mile of stream mouths and thus cannot account for the siltation of entire estuaries. Rather, coastal erosion in the Chesapeake Bay and along tidal rivers, which is capable of producing sediment loads several times larger than tributary-stream erosion, appears to have been a major reason for the accumulation of sediments along many tributary mouths during the late colonial period. The environmental effects of tobacco cultivation, therefore, may have been no worse than forms of European farming practices that involved large-scale land clearance for plow agriculture.

CHAPEL POINT

A short drive (2 miles) south on Chapel Point Road and a steep climb out of the Port Tobacco Valley brings us to *Chapel Point* with its commanding view of the Potomac Valley. Named after a chapel built during the 1660s, this site was the focus of one of colonial Maryland's most distinctive and contentious groups, the Jesuits. Today the site is occupied by St. Ignatius Roman Catholic church (1790), St. Thomas Manor House, (enlarged several times since its construction in the late seventeenth century), and the cemetery, which includes a memorial to the pioneer priests who came to convert the local Indians.

The site complex is a reminder of Maryland's unusual origin as a Catholic foundation within an overwhelmingly Protestant colonial system. Yet the Jesuits here and at St. Mary's City proved to be a mixed blessing to the Lords Baltimore. Anxious to avoid creating the appearance of a Catholic colony, the proprietors were sympathetic to the Christianizing mission of the Jesuits but attempted to control them by preventing them from owning land. The Jesuits, for their part, tried to avoid this restriction by registering an 8,500-acre estate around Chapel Point in the name of a settler who was actually a priest. It was in this manner that the Jesuits not only created chapels to serve both Indian and settler communities but also established working plantations where they cultivated corn, wheat, and grapes, and raised cattle and sheep. But their members seldom exceeded a dozen at one time. They were suppressed during the religious upheavals at the turn of the eighteenth century. Finally all authority for them to be in the colony was rescinded in 1773, leaving few converted Indians and fewer relics of their "errand into the wilderness."

ST. MARY'S CITY

From Chapel Point we follow Route 427 for 2 miles to Route 301 which we take south for 5 miles before turning left onto Route 234. This route is Maryland's "Tobacco Road" which is bordered for several miles with active tobacco farms. Continuing south we pass through the village of Chaptico, named after the Chaptico Indians, cross Clements Manor which was under Jesuit control, and reach the Route 5 junction 7 miles south of Chaptico. A short trip brings us to Leonardtown, the second and present county seat of St. Marys County. Originally named Shepherd's Old Fields, suggesting previous Indian clearings, residents built a courthouse here in 1710 facing Breton Bay. Eight miles to the south we pass through Callaway and, a mile farther on, Great Mills, a reminder of a short-lived experiment in wool production during the late nineteenth century long after Southern Maryland had gone into rapid decline when planters emigrated and agricultural marketing concentrated in Baltimore. Less than 6 miles later we enter the manor lands associated with Maryland's establishment at St. Mary's City. Our principal theme now becomes one of origins and intents.

Commensurate with his status, Cecil Calvert (b. 1605; d. 1675), the second Lord Baltimore, planned a most traditional colonial foundation that made few concessions to the New World environment. He intended the new colony to be under complete proprietary control, with feudal land tenure, a manorial system, and a Catholic landed aristocracy, resting on strong family tradition, religious toleration, and a diversified, mixed-farming economy. But the difficulties that beset the early colonists at St. Mary's City after 1634 in creating a profitable enterprise encouraged them to emulate Virginia's example and participate in a tobacco-oriented world that was already contributing to the North Atlantic economy.

The landscapes around St. Mary's City yield few clues either to the founder's intent or to the physical structure of the original settlement. One clue, off to the right on Route 5, is the Father Andrew White Memorial, erected to commemorate the most active of the early Jesuits. Father Andrew was so active among the Indians at Piscataway and Port Tobacco that he was banished to England after a revolt against proprietary leadership in 1644. As we edge south and have our first sight of the St. Mary's estuary, which flows into the Potomac, we can appreciate Father White's description of the latter body of water:

> This is the sweetest and greatest river I have seen, so that the Thames is but a little finger to it. There are noe marshes or swampes about it, but solid firme ground, with great variety of wood, not choaked up with undershrubs, but commonly so farre distant from each other as a coach and fower horses may travale without molestation.

We pass through Pope's Freehold, a 100-acre tract patented in 1641 and later leased to tenants. Archaeological excavations have unearthed the site of a substantial frame house thought to have been built in the late seventeenth century. The tract borders on Fisherman Creek, a boundary of the original 1,200-acre tract of the St. Mary's Town Lands, which we cross and continue on for one third of a mile before veering right on Route 584 into *St. Mary's College of Maryland* in the current heart of the Town Lands. We continue past the college, a small liberal arts institution now part of the University of Maryland system, to the Visitor's Center 1 mile beyond on the right. The center and its displays reflect the most extensive archaeological and historical research ever conducted on colonial Maryland. The St. Mary's Town Lands offered a unique opportunity to excavate an entire seventeenth-century settlement with its surrounding lands because the site was virtually abandoned when the colonial capital was moved north to Annapolis in 1695, and no subsequent urban development obliterated the colonial foundations. The Maryland legislature founded the St. Mary's City Commission in 1966 to preserve, research, and develop the original Town Lands.

Leave the Visitor's Center for *Godiah Spray Plantation,* a reconstructed working farm of the late seventeenth century. Neither the plantation nor Godiah Spray actually existed. What we see is a careful reconstruction of a typical farm and its residents pieced together from contemporary records and accounts, from archaeological investigations, and from existing structures and artifacts. We are presented, therefore, with a current interpretation of early life in the Maryland colony literally "from scratch." In spite of Father White's comment about open woodland, it is likely that the pioneer colonists encountered a relatively dense hardwood forest dominated by oaks and hickories. Without suitable tools, the colonists reverted to Indian practices of slashing and burning the forest, girdling the larger trees with an ax, letting them die, and using wood supplies for housing, fencing, and fires.

The principal structures on the plantation (originally a generic term referring to any farm unit in the Tidewater) are the large twenty-foot by thirty-foot, two-and-one-half-story dwelling house and two tobacco barns. All represent an amalgamation of old traditions and new adaptations to the colonial environment. Thus the farm house has a foundation of cedar posts-in-ground instead of one of stone. The timber-frame style is of English origin, but it is covered with clapboard including the roof (instead of thatch). The pantry has a dirt floor, although pine flooring is found elsewhere. The fireplace is mostly brick, as in England, but with a wattle-and-daub (white oak and clay mud) chimney. The "hall" or general-purpose room and the chamber above have plaster walls

The reconstructed Godiah Spray farmhouse at St. Mary's City. Photograph by Robert D. Mitchell.

and leaded-glass casement windows (sufficiently novel to be a status symbol in seventeenth-century Maryland).

The tobacco barns represent a distinct innovation because tobacco cultivation was banned in Britain. The nearest "tobacco house" is a traditional British-style storage barn, but with posts in the ground, a clapboard roof, and interior runners to support tobacco poles. The second barn represents a transition to a colonial style, with a frame structure, clapboard exterior, and side entrances. Innovations made during the early eighteenth century, such as a larger four-pen interior, wider gable-end entrances, and side slats, created a colonial barn (as at Accokeek) which was the prototype for the tobacco barns of the nineteenth and twentieth centuries.

Livestock and crops had to be accommodated in new ways. Because land was obtainable on an individual rather than a communal basis, each farmer had to make his or her own decisions not only about settlement arrangements but also the arrangement of the fields. With no common land for animals, concern over wild predators, and the tendency for cattle to become mired in the mud flats of tidal creeks, livestock eventually had to be fenced in. The construction and maintenance of the fences, however, was a heavy task. A hog pen, hen house, and cow pen were derived from traditional British farm patterns, but new modes of fencing took advantage of the abundant wood. Two fence types are evident at the Spray Plantation. A zig-zag rail fence surrounds the larger fields, while smaller gardens and yards are surrounded by sharpened pickets lashed to or nailed on post-and-rail fences (although nails were a scarce and imported item in seventeenth-century Maryland). The early acceptance of maize, instead of wheat, for food, and tobacco for commerce meant the need to learn Indian hoe-hill cultivation practices, which were still common a century later at Accokeek.

Across the fields in the woods is the *Tenant's House,* a simple one-room-with-loft cottage which represented a typical "starter" home for new immigrant or freed servant families. The building reflects a transition to colonial traditions, with clapboard over a frame structure, steep clapboard roof, a large wattle-and-daub chimney, shuttered (and glassless) windows, and a dirt floor. Many of Maryland's early settlers came as male indentured servants from the British Isles. To pay off their indebtedness for their ocean voyage and subsequent upkeep they served an established planter family as farm hands until their four- or five-year indenture period was completed. This was how early tobacco planters acquired the labor needed for tobacco production. The memorial to Mathias de Sousa, which we will pass later on the riverbank, indicates that selection by race initially was not a factor in acquiring suitable labor. Once free, former servants were likely to lease land and "sharecrop" a planter's output until they could afford to purchase land themselves, acquire a wife, and begin a new family.

During the third quarter of the seventeenth century, however, attitudes toward labor supply began to change. The supply of servants began to decline. Their short-term service within a growing tobacco economy came under evaluation; simultaneously the appearance of African slaves in the Virginia Tidewater became more frequent as slave prices gradually fell. Slaves were purchased for life, cost less than servants to maintain, and their offspring were also born into lifetime slavery. By the 1680s, planters in Southern Maryland had begun to follow suit, and they were further encouraged by the fall in slave prices following the Royal Africa Company's loss of monopoly in trading slaves in 1695. By the first decade of the eighteenth century, slaves outnumbered servants on Maryland plantations by almost four to one, thus setting the course for a new social geography that had no precedent in Western Europe. This social geography had two novel dimensions: a white European farm population stratified socially in terms of its ability to acquire wealth in land and slaves, and a slave caste faced with legal bondage and no opportunity for upward social mobility.

The drive back to the Town Lands takes us into two other dimensions of Maryland's first colonial settlement: the reconstructed brick State House of 1676, and the "living history" reconstructions of other town buildings. Begin at the beginning with a walk down to the river. Here we find a full-scale replica of the fifty-ton pinnace, the *Dove,* the supply ship that accompanied the larger *Ark* of London carrying the 140 original settlers to Maryland. This "numerous crew," as Ebenezer Cook described them,

> *In Shirts and Drawers of Scotch-cloth Blue*
> *With neither Stockings, Hat, nor Shooe . . .*
> *Figures so strange, no God design'd,*
> *To be a part of Humane Kind:*
> *But wanton Nature, void of Rest,*
> *Moulded the brittle Clay in Jest,*

who were soon to find themselves

> *. . . in a Hut supinely dwelt,*
> *The first in Furs and Sot-weed dealt.*

St. Mary's City with known sites, circa 1676

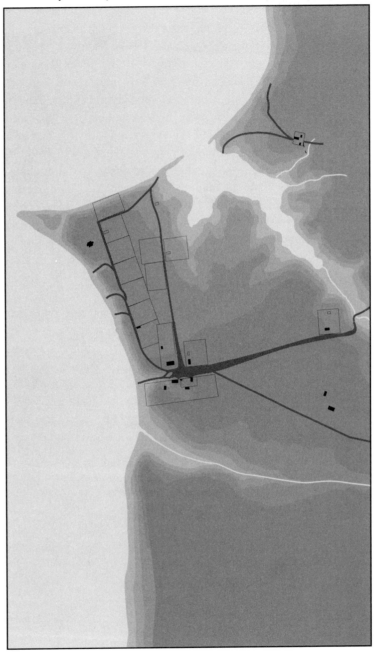

Retracing our steps from the *Dove,* we pass the *Mathias de Sousa Memorial,* dedicated to the first black Marylander who arrived on the *Ark* in 1634 as an indentured servant. After completing his servitude in 1638 he became a trader and participated in the legislative assembly of 1642. The origins of tobacco cultivation in Maryland, as in Virginia, did not involve slavery. Seventeenth-century Maryland remained a land of opportunity for young farmer's sons and indentured servants from England.

The other dimension of early Maryland that is evoked by our traverse of the Town Lands is the novelty of Chesapeake settlement. The apparent open, haphazard arrangement of the existing structures, from the statehouse to van Sweringen's Council Chamber Inn, belies Cecil Calvert's seeming intent to create a designed settlement. Archaeological research has deciphered a layout that is not evident at ground level—a baroque axial plan. To appreciate this surprising discovery we should realize that the landing north of the State House and the State House itself form the short side (North Street) of a triangle counterbalanced by the mill dam and the chapel which form the short side of a similarly shaped triangle two thirds of a mile to the east. Both triangles meet as two connected "wings" at a town center currently occupied by the reconstructed Country's House, Cordea's Hope, and Smith's Town Land. The adjacent reconstructed Farthing's Ordinary and van Sweringen's Inn face the street of the first triangle parallel to the river, and help to form the active "center" of the late seventeenth-century town.

The baroque arrangement seems to have been laid out between 1665 and 1670. Only the State House triangle was fully occupied by 1690. Neither the mill dam nor the chapel exists today, thus making it difficult to visualize the second triangle on the ground. Current excavations at the chapel site, the highest area within the original Town Lands, may reveal more about the eastern end of the town. The chapel itself is significant because it was the location of the first Catholic church in English America, built during the late 1630s. The first wooden structure was burned to the ground in 1645. A much larger, cross-shaped, brick structure was built by 1667 and survived for about forty years. The ground beneath and

Comparison of the Triangular Design with the Presumed Locations of Roads

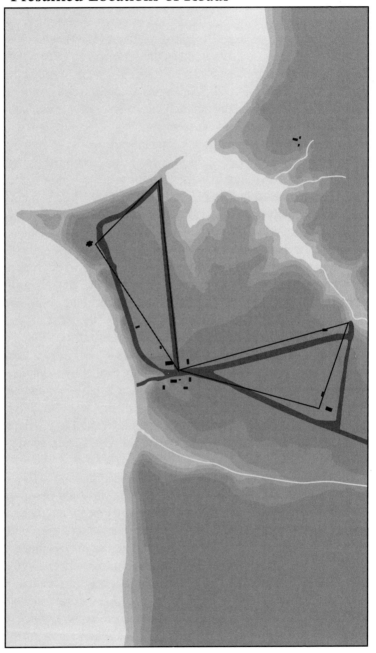

around the chapel site is Maryland's oldest cemetery and contains as many as 400 graves, including that of the first governor, Leonard Calvert (b. 1606; d. 1647).

The Colonial Legacy

The ultimate failure of St. Mary's City, the best known, freely abandoned site in early America, and the modest growth of its northern successor, Annapolis, reveals one of the major paradoxes of British colonial policy. It was in the Chesapeake Tidewater that European rhetoric, which associated cities and urbanism with civilization, broke down. The most successful colonial enterprise on the North American mainland, the tobacco world of the Chesapeake, functioned largely in a dispersed, decentralized fashion in the absence of towns. This focus on tobacco created a new type of British farmer, the colonial planter who saw little need for towns and indeed had become suspicious of one of the fundamental precepts of Western civilization.

Such views were to become symbolized in the words of Thomas Jefferson (b. 1743; d. 1826; pres. 1801 to 1809), himself a Chesapeake planter, during the debate over the direction to be taken by the new American nation. Jefferson wrote in 1785:

> As long as we remain virtuous, and I think we shall be so, as long as agriculture is our principal object, which will be the case while there remain vacant lands in any part of America. When we get piled upon one another in large cities, as in Europe, we shall become as corrupt as in Europe, and go to eating one another as they do there. . . . The mobs of great cities add just so much to the support of pure government, as sores do to the strength of the human body.

This anti-urban sentiment, too, is as much a legacy of the colonial Tidewater as is the declining presence of the "stinking sotweed plant."

The Eastern Theater of the American Civil War

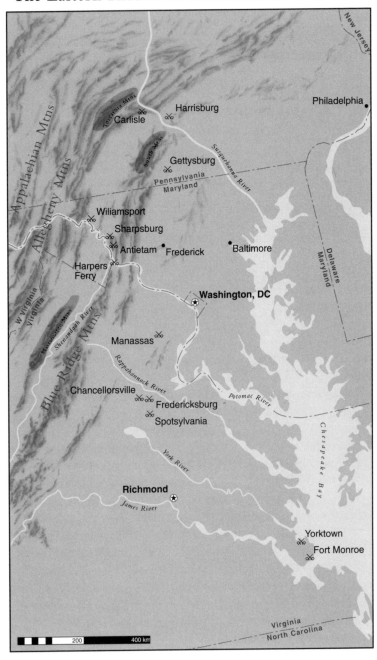

△ Day Six

GEOGRAPHY AND THE CIVIL WAR—THE EASTERN THEATER AND GETTYSBURG

by Harold A. Winters, *Michigan State University*

The American Civil War (1861 to 1865), also known as the War Between the States, was this nation's greatest tragedy. As an ominous precursor to "total war," the casualties for the two sides were roughly equal, and combined, eventually exceeded 1 million. The 1 million includes 600,000 deaths, of which about 200,000 were killed in battle while, with the exception of approximately 60,000 fatalities in prisoner of war camps, the remainder died of disease and illness. With a total population of about 28 million (18.5 million in the North; 9 million in the South, about one third of whom were slaves), one of every twenty-eight people were victims and nearly all of these were males between the ages of fifteen and thirty. Thus, by the war's end about one of every six young men involved was either wounded or dead. And for the South, with its much smaller population, the chances of a soldier's being harmed were as high as one in three. With those kinds of odds just about every citizen, whether in the North or South, was at one time or another acquainted with someone who became a casualty, a situation that happened only once in the history of the United States.

The coalition of southern states, known as the Confederacy, fought for the right to secede from the United States and in so doing sought to preserve a way of life involving an agrarian aristocracy and the right to own slaves. For the North the initial objective was preservation of the Union, but by late 1862 the abolition of slavery became an equally important political issue. Although the main conflict lasted four years and produced widespread grief, suffering, destruction, and death, there is no doubt that, even with the lasting imperfections in the social system, the outcome of this terrible war eventually led to both the enhancement of human dignity and a higher level of individual freedom.

It should be noted that almost all of the military leaders for both sides had been trained at the same place, the U.S. Military Academy at West Point, New York, on the Hudson River. As a result, most tended to believe in the teachings of that institution, which stressed Napoleonic maneuver and the military concepts of Baron Henri Jomini (b. 1779; d. 1869). Furthermore, within the context of existing technology, communications, and logistics, the size and geographic diversity of the land, with its compartments, obstructions, barriers, boundaries, and shields, added a complexity to the application of this military doctrine. Such geographic diversity also offered a distinct advantage to the more astute and aggressive commander who understood the implications and importance of regional and localized geography.

Geographically and militarily the war may be divided into eastern and western theaters that were very different in both the nature of the campaigns and the quality of leadership in the field. Fighting in the west—which occurred mainly in Alabama, Georgia, Louisiana, Mississippi, and Tennessee—involved long, sweeping maneuvers designed to control lines of communication and transportation. The setting was almost wholly rural; at most places the local population was sparse, and activity in this theater never directly threatened respective centers of government. Here, from the outset, the North had the initiative much of the time while, for a variety of reasons, the South was plagued with leadership problems.

For the first two years of the war things were exactly the opposite in the east. Here most of the combat took place within a relatively small part of northeast Virginia, often threatening one capital or the other—Washington or Richmond—and Southern forces had a number of major successes under the skilled leadership of General Robert E. Lee (b. 1807; d. 1870), commander of the Confederate Army of Northern Virginia.

About midway through the war, in July 1863, two widely separated events permanently changed the complexion of the conflict. In the west, it was the Union occupation of Vicksburg, Mississippi, the last Confederate stronghold on the Mississippi River. In the east, it was America's most famous battle, which consisted of three days of fighting at Gettysburg, Pennsylvania, and ended with the defeat and retreat of Robert E. Lee's troops. Although there would be much more fighting, and the war would grind on for another twenty months, these two developments shifted the tide of battle in favor of the North.

Surely geography of the Eastern Theater presented both sides with numerous military opportunities and problems. Yet little is written on the nature of the irregular Virginia coastline, or the character of the rugged Blue Ridge Mountains with their high and low passes, or the importance of the numerous northeast–southwest-trending inland agricultural valleys separated by rocky ridges, or the impact of southeast-flowing rivers.

Thus, the purposes of this field guide are first to account for the major terrain features of the Eastern Theater and relate these to overall military operations; and second, as a case study, to show how details of the geomorphology in and around Gettysburg affected the momentous and pivotal battle that occurred there on 1 to 3 July 1863.

The Terrain

The terrain of the Eastern Theater can be separated into four physiographic provinces, each trending in a northeast–southwest direction. Easternmost is a low, poorly drained Atlantic Coastal Plain interrupted by the Chesapeake Bay, the largest and most deeply penetrating embayment on the eastern shore of the United

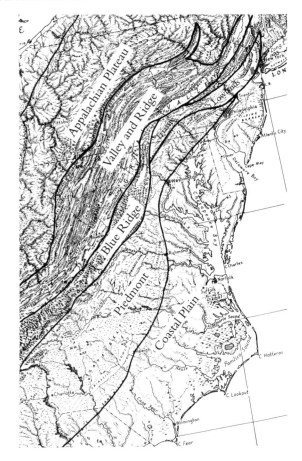

Physiographic provinces of the area. Courtesy of Raisz Landforms Maps.

Diagrammatic structure section through the state of Virginia with the associated relief features. Courtesy of Raisz Landforms Maps.

States. Adjacently situated is the Piedmont, a slightly higher area consisting of low, rolling, stream-dissected hills. Farther west lie the relatively narrow, but much higher and more rugged, northeast-trending Blue Ridge Mountains which, in turn, are bordered by the linear lowlands and mountains of the Valley and Ridge Province. The westernmost boundary of the Eastern Theater was essentially the high, imposing east-facing edge of the Appalachian Plateau. These provinces had topographic characteristics so distinctive that each one profoundly influenced military strategy and tactics in different ways. Thus, to assess the effect of terrain in the Eastern Theater fully and accurately one must understand the nature of these four physiographic divisions.

The origin of this diverse yet scientifically orderly landscape may, in large part, be traced to rock structures that formed hundreds of millions of years ago when, according to plate tectonic theory, an ancestral North America, with a geography quite different in configuration and character than today's, was moving directly toward its equally ancient counterpart of Africa. Eventually these and other continents converged to form the largest land mass known in the Earth's history. Called Pangaea, for a time it combined all of the Earth's continents into one enormous world island.

As movement toward the formation of Pangaea progressed, the central, old, thick, strong, and more stable rocks that form the foundation of North America were altered the least. But rocks along what was then the continent's leading edge, where the crust was somewhat thinner and weaker, were severely deformed at the boundary between converging plates. The massive compression resulted in the formation of numerous northeast–southwest-trending linear structures, all associated with a mountainous zone that can be traced from Alabama and Georgia to New England and eastern Canada. It is likely that at some places the Earth's crust was uplifted to form summits that then may have been as high as the Himalaya of today. All of this ancient mountain building created great thrust faults and giant folds as a 250- to 400-mile-wide (400- to 600-kilometer-wide) section of the Earth's crust was pressed into an area only one third its original width.

By 250 million years ago this collision of ancestral continents came to an end, but the effects were permanently embedded in the remaining rock. Weathering, degradation, and deposition then became the prime forces in creating the evolving topography of what is now the eastern United States. Erosion in the Piedmont, the area central to mountain building and uplift, has been so great that igneous and metamorphic rocks that originally formed deep in the crust are now at the Earth's surface. After more than 200 million years of exposure to the elements, this area has gradually evolved into low, rolling hills such as those immediately west of both Richmond and Washington, D.C.

Farther west, a linear tract of some especially resistant and ancient igneous and metamorphic rocks supports the higher and more rugged Blue Ridge Mountains. Only one low-level water route, the opening formed by the Potomac River and containing the town of Harpers Ferry, West Virginia, extends through the northern extent of these mountains. There are, however, numerous other passes of varying altitude, width, and ruggedness. Known locally as "gaps," some of these were important lines of march during the war. Even so, the Blue Ridge Mountains presented a significant obstacle to east–west movements; they also limited westward visibility from the Piedmont.

Immediately west of the Blue Ridge are the folded and faulted, weak and strong, Paleozoic sedimentary strata, so old that they, too, have been deeply eroded. The result is an abundance of distinctly linear, rocky, and forested ridges supported by more resistant formations, such as sandstone, separated by long, generally narrow, fertile, agricultural valleys developed on more easily weathered limestone and shale. The widest and best known of these lowlands is the Great Valley, so extensive that different areas within it have local names, one derived from the famous Shenandoah River (Shenandoah Valley), another from the town of Hagerstown (Hagerstown Valley).

Farthest west and forming the western margin of the Eastern Theater is the Appalachian Plateau with its high, east-facing boundary escarpment capped by strong, but less deformed, sedimentary formations. Largely because of its physical isolation, this remote, generally infertile, dissected, and rugged upland was of little military importance except that its presence separated the two theaters of war. Here, combat was limited for the most part to skirmishes and scattered cavalry raids, and these generally occurred near the valleys to the east.

A fifth physiographic realm, not mentioned previously, is especially important to this study, although it is smaller and initially not as apparent as the others. Its origin goes back about 180 million years to when the previously formed world island of Pangaea began to break apart, leading to the present arrangement of continents. At many places in eastern North America, tensional forces permitted wedges of the Earth's crust to be down-faulted as the land separated. These sites were then marked by great linear lowlands at the surface, much like the present-day rift valleys of Africa and the depressions occupied by the Dead Sea and Red Sea. As sediments accumulated in these lowlands, magma from deep in the Earth's crust also intruded upward along the weaker zones in the faulted rock; most solidified before reaching the Earth's surface to form the igneous rock called diabase, but some poured out as lava flows that quickly hardened to become especially resistant basalt. This down-faulting, sedimentation, and volcanic activity continued for millions of years, tilting the rock strata as crustal movement progressed.

The accumulation of sediment and the faulting of these rocks occurred during the Triassic Period and represent the earliest events in the gradual separation of Africa and North America and the widening of the Atlantic Ocean; today's width is but a partial measure of the amount of movement that has taken place in the last 180 million years. Since the separation began, both Triassic rock and nearby older formations have been carried northwestward with the drift of the North American continent. Above sea level during much if not all of this time, these down-faulted areas have experienced much weathering and erosion. Where exposed at the surface, the diabase and basalt, which are considerably stronger, support residual hills or ridges. In contrast, the weaker sediments, some with footprints of giant creatures of the reptilian era, were easily eroded to a lower level. The result today is the presence of several "Triassic Lowlands" in and near the Piedmont. Three major Civil War battles—Bull Run I (First Manassas), Bull Run II (Second Manassas), and Gettysburg—were fought on the distinctive terrain associated with two of these areas.

The last and easternmost of the physiographic provinces, the Coastal Plain, formed to a considerable extent from the deposition of material eroded from older rocks in the Appalachians. The accumulation started when North America separated from Africa and Eurasia to create the east coast of an ancestral North America. For over 100 million years rivers have carried weathered material from the Appalachians to the coast to be deposited and distributed along the shore. This resulted in a vast coastal apron of relatively young sediment with much of its surface only slightly above or below sea level. Thus, the low and generally poorly drained Coastal Plain with its highly irregular coastline is quite unlike the other physiographic provinces to the west.

Important River Characteristics

Several aspects of the evolving drainage lines formed especially important elements in the physical setting for the war's Eastern Theater. Curiously, although major topographic and structural trends here extend northeast–southwest, all of the larger rivers drain southeastward to the Atlantic Ocean. This cross-cutting relationship, which is related to the geomorphic history of the area, was of considerable tactical importance because it affected much north–south troop movement and some defensive positions in the Piedmont. For example, the relatively large Rappahannock River, located midway between Washington and Richmond, often served to separate the opposing forces and require crossing in numerous military campaigns.

Accounting for southeast-flowing rivers such as the Potomac, Rappahannock, and James requires understanding of two geological facts: First, the rocks and major structures of the Appalachians, including the Piedmont, are ancient and have been above sea level and subject to erosion for more than 200 million years, ten times more time than is needed to level the highest mountain range; second, most of the topography in the Eastern Theater has evolved in only the last

5 million years, and it is largely the result of weathering and stream erosion of the much, much older underlying crust.

Apparently sometime late in the geological history of the Piedmont, terrain leveling by degradational forces and slight uplift and tectonic tilting of the land toward the southeast combined to permit streams to establish courses consequent to the regional slope, regardless of underlying structural trends. The higher Blue Ridge Mountains to the west now provide the source for most of the larger streams crossing the Piedmont, thus accounting for its widespread dissection. But what becomes of the precipitation and runoff west of these mountains?

In northern and northwestern Virginia, the eastern panhandle of West Virginia, western Maryland, and south-central Pennsylvania, this drainage goes into the Potomac River by way of numerous tributaries, the largest of which is the Shenandoah River. In draining toward Washington, the Potomac River does a curious thing. Instead of completely avoiding the higher Blue Ridge by turning northeastward at Hagerstown, Maryland, to follow the Great Valley and drain toward Harrisburg, Pennsylvania, it extends southeast through ranges of the Blue Ridge, thus eroding two watergaps, the larger at Harpers Ferry, the other at Point of Rocks.

The Potomac's present-day course, like the origin of the Atlantic Ocean to which it eventually drains, was surely established long after the ancient continental collision that formed the underlying crustal structures of the area and resulted in Pangaea. It is also apparent that the river could not have flowed southeastward if the higher Blue Ridge Mountains had existed in the past as they do today. In view of these two conditions, the only reasonable explanation for the river's present position is that at some time during its long history the Potomac River must have flowed southeast on an ancestral surface that lacked any important expression of the present-day Blue Ridge Mountains.

Numerous tributaries must also have flowed southeastward on this same surface. Apparently, however, gradual and widespread uplift of the land resulted in downcutting by all of these streams. Many then eroded nearby weaker strata while incising their channels into the ancient, more resistant rocks of the Blue Ridge. Thus, it is late-geologic, broad-based uplift with accompanying stream degradation (rather than intense mountain building) that accounts for the topographic development of the Blue Ridge Mountains. The largest stream of the area, the Potomac River, had the greatest available energy and thus eroded more rapidly even on the most resistant bedrock. As the Potomac River cut its water gap downward into the emerging Blue Ridge, one of its tributaries, the Shenandoah River, flowing only over much weaker limestone and shale to the west, easily adjusted by lowering its valley floor and expanding its drainage area southwestward.

Meanwhile, other smaller and less energetic tributaries, with courses cutting across the trend of the much more resistant rocks of the Blue Ridge Mountains, were not nearly as successful in eroding downward. In fact, one by one—the smallest first and progressing according to size and remoteness—the headwaters of each stream were, with time, pirated away by the ever-enlarging drainage basin of the more westward and lower Shenandoah River. As the upper headwater drainage for each stream was captured, further erosion of their valleys through the Blue Ridge Mountains ceased. Stream erosion, however, continued to lower nearby areas underlain by weaker rocks. In this fashion notches originally cut by streams now remain as passes, or high openings, across the mountain range. These features, called wind gaps, are known by familiar names such as (from south to north) Rockfish, Swift Run, Chester, Manassas, Ashby's, and Snicker's gap south of the Potomac River. Successively north of Harpers Ferry are Crampton's, Turner's, and Cashtown gaps. All were important as lines of march at one time or another during the Civil War.

Another characteristic of the major southeast-flowing rivers deserves attention because it helps to account for the location of both capitals and their largest intervening city, Fredericksburg, Virginia. River courses on the resistant crystalline rocks of the Piedmont tend to be narrower than those associated with the weaker sedimentary formations of the Coastal Plain. Greater amounts of lateral erosion on the Coastal Plain have formed relatively wide valleys as they approach sea level. Furthermore, the accelerated downcutting at the inner edge of the Coastal Plain combined with the much more resistant rocks of the Piedmont to form a series of rapids and low falls which mark the boundary between the two physiographic provinces. Referred to as the Fall Zone, such places marked the most inland point for uninterrupted navigation from the sea. To go farther required bypass canals or off-loading. Such sites were, in addition, advantageous for water-powered mills or factories. These characteristics, in combination with other factors, favored the establishment of settlements such as Fredericksburg, Richmond, and Washington (along with many others), at the Fall Zone of major rivers.

Finally, one additional characteristic of all large rivers on the Middle Atlantic coast deserves attention. To the south much of the Coastal Plain has been uplifted well above sea level, making it fairly wide and high in the interior. Northward, however, the amount of uplift diminishes and is eventually replaced by subsidence. As a result this plain gradually narrows and then disappears completely beneath the sea off the coast of New England. Between these two extremes is the highly irregular coast of Virginia, Maryland, and Delaware. This type of shoreline formed from partial marine submergence that inundated only the lowermost floodplains of rivers that were formerly barely above sea level.

Thus, in the past, the Susquehanna River flowed within a lowland that is now the Chesapeake Bay to meet the sea east of Norfolk, Virginia. In doing so, it received several large tributaries from the west including the James, Potomac, and Rappahannock rivers. Later, coastal submergence drowned the downstream sections of all these streams, eventually dismembering the lower part of the Susquehanna drainage system to create the great Chesapeake embayment with its numerous large and small estuaries, each proportional to the size of its related river. This geological history not only accounts for the highly irregular coast but also provides for an extensive north–south-trending inland waterway that is protected from the full force of storms at sea. These conditions were of great importance to Union maneuvers early in the war.

Military Corridors and Boundaries

From this comprehensive picture of the Eastern Theater's terrain, two main northeast–southwest-trending military corridors become apparent. To the east is the wider Piedmont with its low, rolling, stream-dissected hills interrupted by several "Triassic Lowlands." To the west are number of northeast–southwest-trending agricultural valleys (the most important being the Great Valley) that provided lines of march as well as food for sustenance. These two corridors are separated by the formidable Blue Ridge Mountains, which are creased by a number of passes and breached in the north at Harpers Ferry by the water gap of the Potomac River. Finally, the theater is bounded on the west by the prominent Allegheny Front of the Appalachian Plateau while the eastern border is the low, poorly drained Coastal Plain with its highly irregular shoreline making overland north-south movement especially difficult. It is in this setting that the war began.

WAR IN THE EASTERN THEATER: JULY 1861 TO JULY 1863

In 1861, although separated by about 160 kilometers (100 miles), the geographic view from both Richmond and Washington was quite diverse yet almost identical. On nearly the same meridian, the opposing Civil War capitals were each Fall Line cities with the same physiographic panorama, both east and west. Midway between them was a major southeast-flowing river, the Rappahannock.

Unlike the geographic scene, however, as the war began the military opportunities presented to each side were markedly different. For example, the North had a superior naval force and occupied Fort Monroe in Confederate territory on the coast of Virginia; thus Chesapeake Bay provided the potential for a large-scale, flanking amphibious operation that could place Union troops a short distance east of the South's capital. On the other hand, the Confederates were well aware that the Piedmont narrows northward, bringing the Blue Ridge and its adjacent Shenandoah Valley much closer to Washington than to Richmond. Thus, by moving troops westward through gaps in the Blue Ridge and using these mountains as a shield, any northeast maneuver in the Shenandoah Valley would threaten the western and northern flanks of the Union capital, a matter of utmost concern to President Abraham Lincoln and the War Department.

Though many battles of the east were fought in a relatively small area within the Piedmont between Richmond and Washington, it is clear that lines of movement for the initial military maneuvers by either side were guided by major geographic characteristics. For the Union, it was the nature of the Coastal Plain and its shore to the east; for the Confederates, it was the form and trend of the Appalachian Mountains.

As the war began both sides had the same two basic concerns. The first was to defeat the enemy's army using the then accepted military doctrine. The second was to protect their center of government, which was generally no farther than 80 kilometers (50 miles) from enemy troops. By the summer of 1861 large numbers of Confederate and Union soldiers faced each other both east and west of the Blue Ridge Mountains. Union demands for action led General Irvin McDowell (b. 1818; d. 1885) to initiate the first large-scale action on the Piedmont. It consisted of an advance toward a railroad junction in Virginia, only a short distance west of Washington, D.C. When the Confederates learned of the Union invasion, they moved reinforcements eastward from the Shenandoah Valley first through the Blue Ridge at Ashby's Gap (west of Paris, Virginia) and then through Thoroughfare Gap in the outlying Bull Run Mountains. The ensuing battle took place near Manassas Junction by a stream named Bull Run and resulted in the defeat and rout of Northern forces.

This first major battle in the east occurred in July 1861 only 40 kilometers (25 miles) west of Washington. The victory by the Confederates not only threatened the Union capital, but in hindsight also demonstrated that (1) neither side was prepared for large-scale war and (2) the war would not be settled by a few simple battles.

Shocked and bewildered by the defeat near Manassas (Bull Run), the Union badly needed an effective offensive if there was to be any hope for an early end to the war. The task was given to General George B. McClellan (b. 1826; d. 1885) who, by the following winter, had devised his plan for victory. Instead of confronting a mobile Confederate army in strong defensive positions on the Piedmont, he would attack and capture Richmond with a flanking maneuver that took full advantage of unique coastal characteristics. The operation would come to be known as the Peninsular Campaign.

The plan was to use the Chesapeake Bay and conduct a southward-moving amphibious operation to land troops at Fort Monroe, a long-established coastal fort near Hampton, Virginia, that remained in the hands of Union forces. With this beach-head occupied, such a movement would avoid both the enemy's army and potentially difficult river crossings on the Piedmont. More importantly, it could enable Northern troops to attack westward on land between the James and York river embayments, threatening Richmond, a mere 110 kilometers (70 miles) away.

In early March the first of McClellan's soldiers landed at Fort Monroe. Although delayed from early April to early May by Confederate defenses near Yorktown (where years earlier the British surrendered to Colonial troops, thus ending the Revolutionary War), they approached Richmond in late May. Fatefully, on May 31 General Joseph E. Johnston (b. 1807; d. 1891), the Confederate commander who had moved his forces so effectively from the Shenandoah Valley to Manassas Junction and Bull Run ten months earlier, was wounded while defending the city; his replacement was General Robert E. Lee (b. 1807; d. 1870).

Earlier in the year, to counter this Union offensive and relieve its threat on Richmond, Lee, using geographic characteristics of the Valley and Ridge Province to splendid advantage, devised an ingenious plan to be executed by General Thomas "Stonewall" Jackson (b. 1824; d. 1863). Now known as the Valley Campaign, it was to become one of the most effective military diversions of this or any other war. In long marches and swift encounters Jackson moved north and south in the Shenandoah Valley, using its intervening Massanutten Mountain and the mountain gaps both to occupy large numbers of Union troops and to threaten their capital. Not only did Jackson win many of his battles, but for three months his Valley Campaign harassed and confused Union leaders to the point that it prevented the major transfer of reinforcements to assist McClellan in his Peninsular Campaign.

For this and many other reasons the Northern invasion across the Coastal Plain gradually lost momentum and eventually ground to a halt just short of Richmond. Lee then ordered Jackson to join him and the combined forces drove McClellan's troops from the outskirts of the capital. Although fighting on the peninsula continued for weeks, this Union offensive proved to be a failure, resulting in the gradual removal of Northern forces.

LEE'S FIRST INVASION OF THE NORTH

With the larger Union army in the east separated into two major units, one leaving the peninsula slowly and the other protecting Washington, Lee decisively and effectively prepared for his first invasion of the North. Before all of the Union troops were withdrawn to end the Peninsular Campaign, Lee moved north across the Piedmont to threaten Washington and once again engage Union forces on the same nearby battlefield known as Manassas, or Bull Run. The result was another Southern victory that in late August forced Union troops to retreat, for the second time, to the defenses of their capital. This sequence of events and the related terrain presented an open path for the Confederate invasion of central Maryland.

Taking full advantage of his second success at Bull Run, Lee divided his forces to capture Harpers Ferry (then a part of Virginia) and invade north-central Maryland, thus cutting important Union lines of communication. This partial flanking maneuver culminated in a great battle along Antietam Creek near Sharpsburg, Maryland, on 17 September 1862. In what turned out to be the single bloodiest day in American history, neither side was victorious, and Lee ordered his troops southward to defensive positions in Virginia. There was, however, one especially important political outcome of the battle; it was Lincoln's presentation of the Emancipation Proclamation which, by Union law, freed the slaves of the South, an act that permanently changed the complexion of the war.

FREDERICKSBURG TO CHANCELLORSVILLE

The Union again went on the offense in late 1862. Advancing southward to Falmouth, Virginia, just across the Rappahannock River from Confederate forces in and near Fredericksburg and about halfway between Washington and Richmond, a new Union commander, General Ambrose E. Burnside (b. 1824; d. 1881), directed a campaign that resulted in a fierce battle on 13 December 1862. To attack westward at Fredericksburg, Union forces first had to cross the Rappahannock. This was followed by fighting through the town. And the day ended with a costly attack on Confederate troops who were in excellent defensive positions at the top of a long bluff bordering the river valley. The result was another major Union defeat, made even worse the following January by Burnside's infamous "Mud March," an abortive offensive effort that brought Northern morale to its lowest point thus far in the war.

The following spring Northern forces with a new commander, General Joseph Hooker (b. 1814; d. 1879), attempted another campaign. It focused on Chancellorsville, less than 15 kilometers (9 miles) west of the previous battleground at Fredericksburg. Here, during the first six days of May, Lee twice separated his forces to outmaneuver and again defeat the Union army. But in doing so the South lost one of its greatest generals, Stonewall Jackson, who was mistakenly shot by one of his own soldiers.

LEE'S SECOND INVASION OF THE NORTH

In June 1863, General Lee began his roundabout march toward the most famous battle in American history: Gettysburg. In a series of carefully planned and deceptive maneuvers, he moved most of his Army of Northern Virginia westward across the Piedmont, through several Blue Ridge wind gaps, and north in the Shenandoah Valley to cross at two Potomac River fords—one by Williamsport, Maryland, and the other on familiar ground near Sharpsburg.

Once across the river, Lee's troops continued north and east within the Great Valley to enter Pennsylvania, shielded from the east by the northern extent of the Blue Ridge Mountains. From there the Confederate forces separated into groups that reached York, the outskirts of Harrisburg, Carlisle, and Chambersburg, thus threatening both Baltimore and Philadelphia as well as all overland lines of communication with Washington, D.C. With Confederate troops only 110 kilometers (70 miles) north of the Union capital, an increasingly frustrated Lincoln appointed a new commander; he replaced General Hooker with General George Meade (b. 1815; d. 1872).

The pursuing Union army marched northward on the Piedmont without precise information about the location or deployment of Southern forces. Lee, too, was largely ignorant of Union movements, knowing only that they were a growing threat. As a result he ordered his separated units to follow roads south and east that converged in south-central Pennsylvania; this just happened to be Gettysburg. Unknown to Lee, small elements of the Union army had already reached the town. Thus, a great battle began, not through careful and astute military planning, but rather as a chance meeting between two moving armies in search of one another. Ironically, the South moved toward the battle from the north and west while the North advanced from the south.

GETTYSBURG

Gettysburg is situated midway between the east and west borders of the huge wedge of the Earth's crust that subsided because of tensional faulting that accompanied the separation of North America from Africa and the break-up of Pangaea about 180 million years ago. The Triassic rocks consist of weaker sedimentary layers intruded at some places by molten material that quickly solidified into resistant diabase and basalt. As an ancestral North America drifted toward its present location there was ample time for the weathering and erosion of less resistant rocks in this area. This resulted in the formation of a major northeast–southwest-trending Triassic lowland that extends from northern New Jersey southward through Pennsylvania into north-central Maryland.

At most places this landscape is only slightly lower than the rolling hills of the Piedmont to the east, but the area is well below the higher and much more rugged terrain associated with resistant rocks to the west. Within this Triassic lowland there are also limited tracts where resistant diabase or basalt is exposed to support ridges of varying size, each somewhat proportional to the extent and thickness of this stronger rock.

Two types of diabase intrusions are especially important to the Battle of Gettysburg. The first and smaller of these supports Warfield Ridge and Seminary Ridge along with its northern continuation, the slightly higher Oak Ridge. Together these form a north–south-trending belt of low hills just west and northwest of the town. On the first day of the battle, July 1, the Confederates captured Oak Ridge. On July 2 and 3 their major position was on the connected Seminary and Warfield ridges, facing Union troops to the east.

The second area of strong diabase extends from Culp's Hill and Cemetery Hill, at the outskirts of the town, southward to Little Round Top and Round Top, a distance of about 4 to 5 kilometers (3 miles). The extent of this diabase is much wider than the first, giving the ridge more height and supporting the especially prominent hills and round tops mentioned previously. One small appendage of the diabase extends a short distance west from the ridge-line to form the rocky Devil's Den. All of the areas underlain directly by diabase presented problems for entrenchment because soils were generally thin or nonexistent and the rock was impossible to excavate with hand tools. But because of greater altitude, locally rugged terrain, and numerous trees, the ridge line offered good visibility and some concealment for many Federal soldiers.

On July 1 Confederate forces, advancing toward the east and south, encountered a smaller number of Union troops on the northwest outskirts of Gettysburg. This engagement rapidly grew in intensity, and during a day of hard fighting, the outnumbered Northern soldiers retreated southeastward through the town and eventually established defensive positions on Cemetery Hill and Culp's Hill. That night additional troops arrived for both sides: The Union deployed forces on these two hills and southward along Cemetery Ridge while the Confederates reinforced the units assigned to Seminary and Warfield ridges as well as in the town. For the North this established their famous fishhook position that coincided with exposures of diabase.

During the next two days of battle at Gettysburg the Confederates attacked three different sections of the Union line without decisive success. Early on July 2 the greatest pressure was on the Union's far right at Culp's Hill. Later that day the heaviest fighting developed at the Union's left, focusing on the Peach Orchard, the Wheat Field, Devil's Den, and Little Round Top. During the third day the main thrust was a brave but futile frontal attack in the afternoon by about 12,000 soldiers, including General George Pickett's (b. 1825; d. 1875) Division, toward the higher Union center marking the last major military operation at Gettysburg.

After their fishhook defensive position was established, the terrain strongly favored the Union forces in just about every encounter. To reach its major objective, each attacking Confederate force eventually had to move forward over slopes that tended in increase gradually in steepness toward an enemy on higher ground and in well-established defensive positions. The Southerners experienced a situation somewhat similar to that faced by Union soldiers at Fredericksburg only seven months before.

Though the attack on the Union center during the final afternoon of battle reached well up on the west side of Cemetery Ridge, this High Tide of the Confederacy never inundated the enemy troops on the Triassic diabase. As Pickett's remaining troops fell back, Lee's retreat from his second and last major invasion of the North began.

There was no Union counterattack late on the afternoon of July 3 at Gettysburg, much to Lincoln's regret. Instead, as had happened many times previously, both armies seemed satisfied to rest in place. The next day Lee ordered his forces to retreat westward through two of the openings in the Blue Ridge Mountains of Pennsylvania—Fairfield and Cashtown gaps. From there the Confederates followed the Great Valley southward.

The retreat, however, was accompanied by a summer rain. By the time Lee's forces reached the Potomac River at Williamsport it was too high to ford because of the low flood, and his bridge had been destroyed by a Union cavalry force. The Confederates were especially vulnerable. But once again the Union force followed slowly and failed to mount a major attack. Gradually the level of the river receded, and late on July 13 Lee was able to cross the Potomac to the comparative safety of Virginia.

AFTER GETTYSBURG

The Southern army again took up positions south of the Rappahannock River and engaged the North in several battles in the fall of 1863. During the spring of 1864 Lee again tried to use regional aspects of the terrain for wide-ranging maneuvers by sending General Jubal Early's (b. 1816; d. 1894) five divisions northward in the Shenandoah Valley and then eastward through South Mountain to the very outskirts of Washington, D.C., but this action had little effect on the overall course of the war. By 1864 it was the Union army, now under the command of General Ulysses S. Grant (b. 1822; d. 1885), that had assumed the initiative in the east.

To gain momentum Grant had developed a set of coordinated plans for all of his armies. One force moved southward into the Shenandoah Valley to sweep Confederate forces out of the area and destroy resources essential for a renewed Southern offensive there, thus eliminating a threat from that direction. Grant also moved troops inland along the south side of the James River toward Richmond to threaten the enemy's capital and right flank. Most importantly, he used his largest central force, commanded by George Meade, to battle Lee in the wilderness west of Fredericksburg near Chancellorsville. When the Battle of the Wilderness was over, Grant refused to rest his troops as other commanders had done previously. Instead he pursued Lee tenaciously, planned the battles of Spotsylvania, North Anna, and Cold Harbor, and kept constant pressure on Lee's right flank by extending his position southward toward, and eventually past, Richmond. This tactic made it impossible for Lee to disengage without exposing the Confederate capital to attack. It also removed the opportunity to use the compartments leading to the north that had served Lee so well in the past.

Until Gettysburg Lee used tactics and the terrain so skillfully that much of the time leaders of the larger and better equipped Union army in the east were confused, frustrated, threatened, or about to be out of a job. After the defeat at Gettysburg all that changed. There are, of course, many reasons for the gradual demise of Southern forces in the Eastern Theater, but one is especially clear. When Lee lost the ability to use geography to his best advantage, hopes for defeating the Union through maneuver and attrition disappeared. His sometimes stunning Napoleonic movements were replaced by Grant's grinding war of annihilation, and the tide of battle in the east shifted irreversibly against the South.

The Approaches to Gettysburg

FROM WASHINGTON, D.C.

Take I-270 north to Frederick, Maryland. At Frederick continue north on U.S. 15 through Thurmont and Emmitsburg. Cross the Maryland-Pennsylvania state line, continue on U.S. 15 to Fairplay, and follow Business 15 to the Gettysburg National Military Park Visitor Center.

Sites of interest along this route related to military and physical geography include:

1. *The Great Falls of the Potomac River.* The rapids and falls of the Potomac River result from an abruptly increased stream gradient near the boundary between the Piedmont and the Coastal Plain. Excellent and easily accessible overlooks are within several hundred meters of the Great Falls Visitor Center (Virginia) off Route 738 about 18 kilometers (11 miles) northwest of downtown Washington. For details see Reed et al., *The River and the Rocks,* U. S. Geological Survey Bulletin 1471 (1980) and "Scenic Geomorphology of Maryland's Piedmont and Blue Ridge," p. 245 in this volume.

2. *Sugarloaf Mountain,* which is 3 miles west of I-270 Exit 32, consists of resistant quartzite (metamorphosed sandstone) and is the largest erosional remnant on this part of the Piedmont. Although this is privately owned property, it is open to the public. A narrow, winding blacktop road leads to three scenic overlooks with the near-summit parking lot offering an excellent view of land to the west. A rough and rocky trail with a number of steep steps leads to a summit view point, also facing west. For details see "Scenic Geomorphology of Maryland's Piedmont and Blue Ridge," p. 249 in this volume.

3. *Scenic Overlook* just past mile marker 28 on northbound I-270. This site, very near the Monocacy Battlefield (9 July 1864), offers an excellent view of the Frederick Valley and the more distant Catoctin Mountain, which is a segment of

the Blue Ridge. For details see "Scenic Geomorphology of Maryland's Piedmont and Blue Ridge," p. 251 in this volume.

4. *Gambrill State Park.* Follow U.S. 40 a few kilometers west from Frederick to Catoctin Mountain. Turn right (north) at the park sign and follow the winding and steep blacktop road to the summit and turn left (south). Proceed a few hundred meters to the parking/turn-around area. The best view is westward from the opening southwest of the parking lot. From here you will see the Middletown Valley in the foreground and South Mountain with its various gaps in the distance. George McClellan's Union forces marched westward across this valley in their pursuit of Lee's army in September 1862, a maneuver that eventually led to the Battle of Antietam (also known as Sharpsburg). For geomorphic details see "Scenic Geomorphology of Maryland's Piedmont and Blue Ridge," p. 255 in this volume.

5. *Catoctin Furnace.* Catoctin, about 25 kilometers (16 miles) north of Frederick on U.S. 15, marks the place where cannon balls used in the American Revolutionary War were cast. Armor plate for the iron-clad *Monitor,* the famous Civil War Union naval vessel, was also produced here.

FROM BALTIMORE, MARYLAND

Follow I-795 to Reistertown, take Route 140 northwest toward Westminster, then exit northbound on Route 97 and proceed to the Gettysburg National Battlefield Park Visitor Center.

Sites of interest related to military and physical geography include:

1. *Parrs Ridge at Westminster.* Parrs Ridge forms a northeast–southwest-trending drainage divide within the Piedmont that can be traced for many miles. High points on the ridge offer excellent views of the Piedmont landscape to the east and west.

It is in this area that Union General George Meade wished to establish his Pipe Creek Line, sometimes referred to as the Westminster Line. By either name it is associated with

Parrs Ridge, a linear prominence on the Piedmont that can be traced from near Gaithersburg, to Mt. Airy, to Westminster, and beyond. In planning the pursuit of Lee's forces in June 1863, Meade originally favored a defensive line here that extended along the bluffs and ridges south and east of Pipe Creek, which is crossed by Route 97 just south of Union Mills. Although his troops met the enemy 25 kilometers (16 miles) to the northwest, Meade favored this position in the event of a Union retreat from Gettysburg.

2. *East Cavalry Battlefield Site,* about 5 kilometers (3 miles) east of Gettysburg. Access is via either Route 116 or U.S. 30. Here, on the afternoon of July 3, Confederate and Union cavalry fought a fierce three-hour battle that ended with the withdrawal of Southern forces, thus ending their attempt to attack the rear of Northern troops on Cemetery Ridge.

FROM PITTSBURGH, PENNSYLVANIA

Follow I-76 (the Pennsylvania Turnpike) east to exit at McKinney (Exit 15). Follow Route 997 south to U.S. 30. Turn left (east) and follow U.S. 30 to downtown Gettysburg where you turn right (south) on Business 15 and proceed to the Gettysburg National Battlefield Park Visitor Center.

Sites of interest related to physical or military geography include:

1. *Chestnut Ridge* (between Exits 8 and 9) and *Laurel Hill* (between Exits 9 and 10) with its major tunnel. Both are related to large upward flexures in the bedrock (anticlines), and each can be traced many miles both to the northeast and southwest.

2. The *Allegheny Front* (with its tunnel of the same name about midway between Exits 10 and 11) is historically the most formidable and lengthy topographic barrier to westward movement in this part of the Appalachians. It is supported by a great thickness of Paleozoic sedimentary rocks, the youngest exposed at the crest of the ridge being Pennsylvanian in age (about 300 million years old).

3. *Tuscarora Mountain* (with its tunnel of the same name between Exits 13 and 14) is a lengthy ridge formed from steeply inclined and highly resistant Silurian sandstone (about 420 million years old).

4. *Kittatinny and Blue Mountain* (both clearly marked by adjacent tunnels) between Exits 14 and 15 are also supported by highly folded and strong Paleozoic bedrock. Mountains such as these and the intervening lowlands make the terrain of the Valley and Ridge Physiographic Province of the Appalachians so distinctive.

5. Between Black Gap and Hilltown, U.S. 30 passes through *Cashtown Gap,* a low but rugged 13-kilometer (8-mile) pass through South Mountain which is the northernmost extension of the Blue Ridge. Many Confederate troops advanced and withdrew along this route before and after the battle at Gettysburg. By reconstructing this as a rough, rocky trail typical of the 1860s, one gets a clearer picture of how difficult it must have been to move an army with artillery, munitions, supplies, and ambulances so necessary to the Confederates at Gettysburg.

FROM HARRISBURG, PENNSYLVANIA

Follow U.S. 15 south and exit at U.S. 30 westbound. In downtown Gettysburg, turn left (south) on Business 15 and proceed to the Gettysburg National Military Park Visitor Center.

Sites of interest related to physical or military geography include:

1. The Harrisburg area is an excellent place to observe multiple *water gaps* through ridges formed from steeply inclined, resistant rock strata. By driving north on combined Routes 22/322 from Harrisburg to cross the Susquehanna River at Benvenue and returning south via Duncannon and Marysville, one may observe three major water gaps from two different views. The nature of the rock strata may be observed in both the high cliffs and the rapids if the river is not overly high. Such great distortion of the strata are related to ancient plate tectonics while the water gaps are the result of much more recent deep erosion by running water.

2. Other good view locations exist at 1) the *Peters Mountain Overlook* (northeast of Benevenue at the intersection of PA Route 225 and the Appalachian Trail and 2) the *Reservoir Park Overlook* (in northeast Harrisburg).
3. At *Dillsburg,* about 16 kilometers (10 miles) south of Harrisburg, U.S. 30 shirts the northern end of South Mountain. This represents the northeastern end of the Blue Ridge Mountains which can be traced southwestward all the way to Georgia.
4. About 16 kilometers (10 miles) west of Dillsburg via Route 74, a straight drive across half of the Great Valley, is the picturesque town of *Carlisle,* with its Carlisle Barracks, Army War College, and Dickinson College. Some Confederate troops were on the west bank of the Susquehanna River near Harrisburg and in Carlisle immediately before they were ordered to Gettysburg.

FROM WINCHESTER, VIRGINIA, AND THE SHENANDOAH VALLEY

Follow U.S. 7 east to Berryville to turn north on U.S. 340, through Charles Town, to Harpers Ferry. Here you have two choices. The first and shortest is to continue on U.S. 340 through the *Potomac River water gap* to *Frederick* where you may utilize the Washington, D.C.–Gettysburg itinerary described previously. The second and longer route includes access to two additional sites of interest: *Antietam National Battlefield Site* and *Washington Monument State Park* (not to be confused with the structure in Washington, D.C.). Take Route 230 north from near Harpers Ferry to Shepherdstown, then follow Route 480 east. After crossing the Potomac River this road changes to Route 34 (Maryland). Continue on Route 34 through Sharpsburg and on to Boonsboro. From Boonsboro follow U.S. Alternate 40 east to Frederick where you may use the Washington, D.C.-Gettysburg itinerary described previously.

Sites of interest relating to physical or military geography include:

1. *Harpers Ferry* is one of the most interesting geologic, geomorphic, historic, and scenic sites in the northern part of the Blue Ridge Mountains. It is also congested and crowded during the tourist season and on pleasant weekends. Parking

Harpers Ferry in July 1865. Photograph by Gardner, courtesy of the Library of Congress.

in the lower part of the town is restricted, and most gain access to the area via National Park Service buses that operate from a Visitor Center south of U.S. 340, west of Harpers Ferry. Here you may obtain maps and information on the area.

Park Service facilities are also located in the town along with numerous shops and cafes. Be prepared for walking on rough sidewalks that in some places are quite narrow and steep. There are several good overlooks in Harpers Ferry, including Jefferson Rock, which may be reached by a set of steep stairs cut into Harpers Phyllite. The best view of the area, however, is from the top of Maryland Heights on the opposite side of the Potomac River. To get to the trailhead, cross the river via the railroad bridge walkway. Only those with rigorous hiking experience should make this trek, and all who do should be sure to obtain a trail map from a park ranger before leaving on a journey that will take several hours.

The National Park Service Visitor Center both west of Harpers Ferry and in town provide much information on the town's history and its role in the Civil War. For information on the bedrock, terrain, and rivers (Potomac and Shenandoah rivers) see p. 258 within "Scenic Geomorphology of Maryland's Piedmont and Blue Ridge" in this volume.

The town, first settled in 1747, is located within the only water gap through the northern part of the Blue Ridge Mountains. The gap first offered a river-level trail to the Great Valley. A canal was constructed later, followed by the telegraph and railroad. A U.S. arsenal was established here in 1796, and this was the site for slave abolitionist John Brown's (b. 1800; d. 1859) 1859 raid, which proved an important precursor to the American Civil War. All of this made the site of growing importance during the 1800s.

As the Civil War developed, Harpers Ferry quickly became of great tactical importance to both sides. Military control here had a major influence on operations in the Shenandoah Valley. For the Union it was especially important for the security of Washington D.C. and the maintenance of westward communication lines.

A major battle took place here on 14 to 15 September 1862. In conjunction with his first invasion of the North, a portion of General Robert E. Lee's troops occupied the surrounding highlands and captured the town with its garrison plus about 12,000 Union soldiers, the largest military surrender in U.S. history. Once this area was secured by the Confederates most of their troops marched 24 kilometers (15 miles) north to take part of the Battle of Antietam (or Sharpsburg) which is briefly described below.

2. *Antietam National Battlefield,* west of the Blue Ridge Mountains and remote from twentieth-century suburban sprawl, remains one of the best preserved and most authentic Civil War battlefields in the Eastern Theater. Start at the Visitor Center which provides much information, including an excellent narrated slide show, relating to the engagement. A driving tour of the battlefield passes, from north to south, a

series of sites especially important to the battle. Factoring in time at the Visitor Center, plan a three- to four-hour visit for a comprehensive understanding of the battle.

The fighting that occurred here on 17 September 1862, was the culmination of General Robert E. Lee's first invasion of the North. Confederate troops, in positions that extended both north and south from Sharpsburg, faced Union forces aligned along or near south-flowing Antietam Creek. Fighting commenced early that morning at the north flank as a series of piecemeal Union attacks that progressed southward throughout the day. In the end, after a combined total of about 22,000 casualties, including approximately 5,000 dead, neither side gained a decisive advantage. Hindsight, however, suggests that it was a tactical victory for the South (using interior lines and effective maneuver, they turned back all Union attacks) but a strategic success for the North (it stopped the invasion).

Lincoln used this opportunity to announce his Emancipation Proclamation which freed the slaves of the South, an act that markedly and permanently changed the character of the war.

3. *Washington Monument State Park* offers a superb view westward of the Hagerstown Valley (the local name for the Great Valley) and the mountains beyond. The access road (Washington Monument Road) extends north from U.S. Alternate 40 about 3 kilometers (2 miles) east of Boonsboro, Maryland. Once in the parking lot, follow the winding trail upward to the observation tower.

For geomorphic details, including discussion of the block field near the base of the observation tower, see p. 256 in "Scenic Geomorphology of Maryland's Piedmont and Blue Ridge" in this volume.

Ten Key Sites on the Gettysburg Battlefield of Special Importance

The itinerary suggested below begins with observations at the National Military Park Visitor Center. Next, observations of a geologic exposure northwest of Gettysburg provides a basis for understanding variations in the area's terrain. This is followed by observations at seven sequentially ordered battlefield sites of special importance. The tour concludes with an optional stop where Lincoln delivered his famed Gettysburg Address. This routing differs markedly from that suggested on the National Park Service map but provides a better geographic and chronologic appreciation of the battle. Even so, the Park Service's map should also be used because it augments the following information.

THE VISITOR CENTER

Start the tour of the battlefield at the Visitor Center. Here you may obtain information on both the park and ranger-conducted programs, visit a fine military museum without charge, hire a guide or rent an audio-cassette for an auto tour, and make purchases in the bookstore. It is also highly recommended that you see the Electric Map presentation in the Visitor Center before you travel over the battlefield. Nearby is the Cyclorama Center where, in addition to exhibits and a short film, one can attend a program focusing on the huge circular painting of Pickett's charge by Paul Philippoteaux (for chronological reasons some might prefer to visit this at the end of the trip, rather than at the beginning). An admission is charged for both the Electronic Map and the Cyclorama Center.

THE RAILROAD CUT

The railroad cut in the northwest outskirts of Gettysburg is the best place to obtain a basic understanding of relationships between bedrock geology and the overall terrain of the battlefield. From the Visitor Center proceed northwest through Gettysburg to Reynolds Avenue railroad overpass and park on a pull-off just north of the bridge. To reach the cut, walk east along the railroad for several hundred meters until you enter the shallow excavation through a part of Oak Ridge. Be observant while doing this because trains are commonplace.

As you approach the cut notice the poorly consolidated red siltstone and shale, known as the Gettysburg Formation, in exposures bordering the tracks. These red beds are the most abundant

Geography of the Gettysburg Battlefield

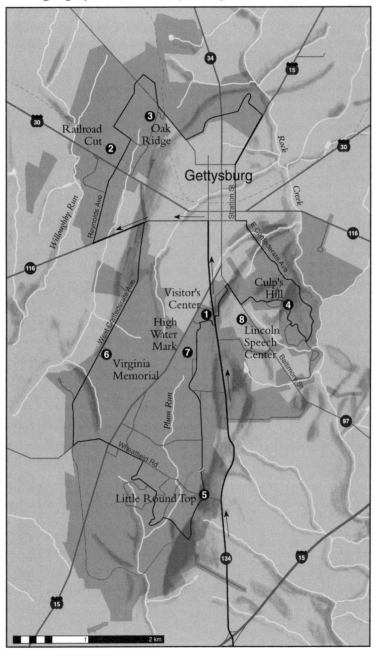

type of rock in the Triassic lowlands of the eastern United States. Close examination will show that the strata are dipping (inclined) northwestward at about twenty degrees from the horizontal, evidence of modest deformation since deposition about 225 million years ago.

By tracing the sediments eastward into the cut, several changes are apparent. First, the beds become more massive, less discernible, and highly fractured. Next, the red shale grades into a harder, grayish-red argillite. Farther on, in a zone about 10 meters (30 feet) wide, the formation has been altered to a fine-grained, black hornfels.

The reason for these changes becomes apparent at the deepest (i.e. middle) part of the cut. Here the bedrock is igneous. Relationships show that this rock originated at a great depth as a superheated liquid that, through upward movement, intruded the red beds and solidified into a very resistant diabase. In doing so, the heat and pressure of the intrusion converted the immediately adjacent Triassic shale into hornfels and the nearby rocks into argillite, a process known as contact metamorphism.

The nature and relationships of these weak and strong bedrock formations account for much of the battlefield terrain. The lowest areas around Gettysburg are associated with tracts of the soft red beds that have been eroded to a reduced level because of their relative weakness. The highest terrain is underlain by diabase intrusions that are referred to either as sills or dikes, depending upon whether or not they extend between or truncate the sedimentary strata. Finally, it is important to note that the dimensions of the lowlands and ridges are directly proportional to the extent of the underlying weak or strong rock formations.

At the railroad cut a relatively thin cross-cutting dike dips from about fifty to seventy degrees toward the east. As a result, the outcrop area of the resistant diabase dike, with the adjacent metamorphic rocks, is relatively narrow but has considerable linear extent; this combination accounts for the width, height, and length of Oak Ridge. On the basis of field evidence it may be inferred that Seminary Ridge is the southern continuation of the same dike. It is also apparent that Warfield Ridge, even farther to the south, is supported by another intersecting dike of similar proportions to those revealed at the railroad cut. The topographic continuity of Oak, Seminary, and Warfield ridges was especially important to Confederate positions during the fighting at Gettysburg. Upon approaching the railroad cut from the west, its form looks much as it did to the advancing Confederates in July 1863, except that the rails were not in place at that time. Recently, however, construction of a new section of track has greatly modified the east section of the cut, making this view markedly different than that at the time of the Civil War. Although this construction is a major modification of this important historic site, the resulting excavations may prove especially interesting to some geologists because the exposure of highly fractured diabase has been greatly expanded.

Another much thicker and more extensive diabase formation of great importance is in the area. Known as the Gettysburg Sill, this material intruded between, rather than through, Triassic strata. Conformable with the beds, this much larger intrusion inclines about twenty degrees to the northwest and supports a 4–5-kilometer (3-mile)–long, hook-shaped upland with a north–south-trending shank (Cemetery Ridge). Little Round Top forms the eye of the hook while Culp's Hill is part of the northeast curvature. By the second day of the battle this land marked the center of the Union position which faced the Confederates on the lower and roughly parallel Seminary and Warfield ridges, about 1 kilometer (0.6 mile) to the west.

Between the ridges lies a linear lowland bordered by sloping ground that gradually increases in steepness upslope toward Cemetery Ridge, supported by the Gettysburg Sill. This terrain characteristic was a formidable factor in Confederate attacks on all three days of the battle, most vividly illustrated by the course of Pickett's Charge on 3 July 1863.

Thus, understanding the geology and geomorphology at the railroad cut accounts not only for the presence of Oak Ridge, but also for the nature of overall terrain characteristics around Gettysburg. Major positions of both armies were most often associated with the areas of diabase while attacks were generally across areas underlain by Triassic sediments. It should now be obvious that the relationships among geology, terrain, and battle are not simply coincidental.

OAK RIDGE OBSERVATION TOWER

Proceed north in a roundabout fashion via Buford Road and the Eternal Light Peace Memorial to the Oak Ridge Observation Tower. From this height it is possible to observe the terrain most important on the first day of the battle. By the evening of 30 June 1863, more than 40,000 Southern troops were converging on Gettysburg from the north and west with some already in place on Herr Ridge about 2 kilometers (1.2 miles) to the west. Fighting began around 8:00 a.m. (0800) the next morning when, near McPherson Ridge, Union cavalry encountered Confederate infantry advancing along the Chambersburg Pike (U.S. 30) toward Gettysburg. Northern infantry soon replaced their cavalry, and through the morning the battle grew in size and ferocity.

Large numbers of Confederate troops continued to arrive on the battlefield and soon the Union soldiers were far outnumbered. Shortly after noon, some of the Southern reinforcements massed at the site of the Peace Memorial and attacked Northern troops on Oak Ridge with its railroad cut. By about 3:30 p.m. (1530), with their defensive positions along Oak and McPherson ridges overrun, Union units were in a general retreat, withdrawing toward and through the town, eventually to take up new positions centered on Cemetery Hill (between Culp's Hill and Cemetery Ridge).

Thus, by sunset on July 1 a chance-meeting engagement between relatively small skirmishing forces had rapidly escalated into an enormous confrontation between two scattered but converging armies. Within twenty-four hours about 70,000 Confederate and 90,000 Northern soldiers would be in the area.

CULP'S HILL OBSERVATION TOWER

Using the National Park Service map as a guide, proceed from the Oak Ridge Observation Tower to Culp's Hill via Mummasburg Road, Howard Avenue, Harrisburg Road, Stratton Street, East Middle Street, East Confederate Avenue, and Slocum Avenue to

Gettysburg after the battle in July 1863. Photograph by Gardner, courtesy of the Library of Congress.

Culp's Hill. Barlow Knoll and Spangler's Spring are two interesting sites to visit along the way.

During the night large numbers of troops continued to arrive on both sides. By early morning on July 2, the armies faced one another in the form of two parallel fishhooks. The Southern line extended along Seminary Ridge, through Gettysburg, and north of Cemetery and Culp's Hill. Union troops were deployed on these same two hills and along Cemetery Ridge north of Little Round Top. It is important to note that, in addition to the high ground, this arrangement favored the Union because of interior lines; that is, its front was half the length of the Confederate's.

The observation tower at Culp's Hill provides a fine view of low-lying land and the town to the north that was captured by the

Confederates on July 1. Equally important, it also displays the formidable defensive position of Union forces on the higher, wooded hills with numerous diabase outcrops and boulders associated with the Gettysburg Sill. The last fighting on July 1, which ended at darkness, occurred at the base of these hills. Confederate attacks also took place here on the afternoon of July 2 to support a major Confederate advance along Emmitsburg Road (U.S. Business 15) on the Union's far left (south) flank, and on the morning of July 3.

LITTLE ROUND TOP

Upon leaving Culp's Hill, proceed west along Slocum Avenue past Cemetery Hill, then southeast on the Baltimore Pike (Route 97) to turn west (right) on Hunt Avenue and then south (left) on Taneytown Road (pronounced Tawneytown). Passing Leister House, the headquarters of the Union Commanding General George G. Meade, continue to Wheatfield Road and access Little Round Top via Sedgwick Avenue.

Most of the combat on July 2 took place on the southern part of the battlefield, and it was especially fierce in the afternoon. Here Union forces suffered about 65 percent of their total casualties for the three days of fighting. The high intensity of the battle is at least partially explained by the fact that commanders from both sides ordered offensive action in this same area on the same day. During the previous night Lee ordered Southern forces on his right (south), directed by General James Longstreet (b. 1821; d. 1904), to prepare for an attack on July 2 northeast along Emmitsburg Road (U.S. Business 15) and directed toward Cemetery Ridge. For the North, General Daniel E. Sickles (b. 1825; d. 1914), in command of Union troops near Little Round Top, also ordered his forces to advance toward Emmitsburg Road on July 2. Sickles moved first. By its nature this maneuver greatly weakened the Northern left flank and eventually placed Sickles's soldiers in an exposed salient that could receive Confederate fire from three directions. It also left Little Round Top largely unprotected. By mid-afternoon Sickles's poorly positioned forces were along Emmitsburg Pike in direct line with Longstreet's planned attack which commenced about 4:00 p.m. (1600).

Leister House on Cemetery Ridge, General Meade's headquarters, at the time of the battle. Photograph by Matthew Brady, courtesy of the Library of Congress.

These actions resulted in intense combat in the Wheat Field, the Peach Orchard, and Devil's Den. Meanwhile Confederate soldiers were occupying Devil's Den and approaching the undefended Little Round Top. Fortunately for the Union, in reconnoitering the area, Brigadier General Gouverneur K. Warren (b. 1830; d. 1882), Meade's chief engineer, recognized that Southern occupation of the hill would seriously threaten Northern positions all along Cemetery Ridge. He quickly ordered nearby Union troops onto Little Round Top. Although fought over bitterly, it was Warren's last-minute action that prevented Confederate troops from capturing this vital site.

Little Round Top is one of the best places in the area to observe characteristics of the Gettysburg Sill. Here the formation dips gently (twenty to twenty-five degrees) toward the northwest and is about 550 meters (1,800 feet) thick; thus the outcrop area is about 1.5 kilometers (1 mile) in width and is easily traced northward along Cemetery Ridge to Cemetery Hill and Culp's Hill and beyond. The resistant nature of the diabase easily supports steep slopes and low cliffs; it also limits soil development and use for farming. As a result, the ridge was well-timbered in 1863, and the trees, along with numerous boulders and hollows, provided good defensive positions that were greatly enhanced by the high ground facing the enemy on the lowlands.

Although the composition and age of the diabase here is essentially the same as that at the railroad cut, a comparison of these two places shows how a change in rock structure and thickness can produce marked differences in terrain characteristics. The outcrop area for a thin and steeply dipping resistant formation (such as at the railroad cut) is much less than that related to a thick and gently inclined unit (as here on the Gettysburg Sill). As a result the terrain associated with the former is narrow and linear while that of the latter is both lengthy and wide.

DEVIL'S DEN

This jumble of rocks, cliffs, and boulders is associated with a mass of diabase that extends westward from the Gettysburg Sill. Although much lower than Little Round Top, once occupied it offered much cover for Confederate troops facing Northern forces on the ridge to the east. The Den was especially useful for Confederate sharpshooters because of its proximity to Union lines.

The rounded boulders, residual rock masses, openings, and crevices here are largely the result of chemical decomposition of the diabase. Slight variations in the rock along with water seepage in and along the joints (cracks) have facilitated differential chemical weathering, leaving the stronger sections of the formation little affected while more susceptible parts are eroded away. The result of this is a natural, low-lying, yet formidable fortress central to the Southern part of the battlefield.

WARFIELD RIDGE OBSERVATION TOWER

Proceed north to Wheatfield Road, follow it west and turn left (south) on West Confederate Avenue, and proceed the short distance to the observation tower.

This tower is built on the slightly higher ground of Warfield Ridge, which is associated with a north–south-trending diabase dike. About 0.75 kilometer (0.5 mile) to the north this ridge intersects Seminary Ridge which is supported by a different dike, the one exposed at the railroad cut.

The top level of this tower, about 200 meters above sea level (660 feet), has the same altitude as the summit of Little Round Top. A sweeping view to the east reveals the Peach Orchard, the Wheat Field, Devil's Den, and a panorama of the west side of Cemetery Ridge. Immediately to the west is Dwight D. Eisenhower's (b. 1890; d. 1969; pres., 1952 to 1960) farm, now a National Historic Site, and in the far distance is South Mountain, the northernmost extension of the Blue Ridge Mountains. In general, the woods of the nearby landscape mark areas of diabase while the tracts cleared for agriculture are underlain by the weaker Triassic red beds.

This site is an ideal place to review Confederate maneuvers within the Southern part of the battlefield on July 2.

THE VIRGINIA MEMORIAL

In many ways this is the most poignant site on the battlefield. Here, on the afternoon of July 3, an estimated 12,000 Confederate troops stepped out of the woods along Seminary Ridge to advance upslope across open fields in a massive frontal attack against the center of Union forces that were in strong defensive positions on Cemetery Ridge. Known as Pickett's Charge, this, the last major maneuver on the battlefield, was a tactical disaster that sealed the defeat of Confederate forces at Gettysburg. More importantly, it marked a turning point in Northern strategy that finally led to the official end of the war in April 1865, when Lee surrendered to Grant in Appomattox, Virginia. Early on the morning of July 3 the Confederates again attacked at Culp's Hill without success, followed by a two- to three-hour lull in the fighting. The bulk of Lee's troops were concentrated along the wooded Seminary Ridge, and many of them had not yet been in combat.

Having assaulted both flanks of the Union position without decisive success on July 1 and 2, Lee ordered the main attack on the 3rd on the Union center. Here Seminary and Cemetery ridges are about 1,200 to 1,400 meters (0.8 mile) apart, well within the range of most artillery on the battlefield. At around 1:00 p.m. (1300) about 140 Confederate cannon commenced firing in a barrage that was to last almost two hours. The Northern artillery returned the fire, and soon visibility was much reduced by the smoke of battle. Because it was difficult for artillerymen to fix targets and view their accuracy, many of the rounds were overshot. Thus the Southern artillery had limited effect on front-line Union troops. Furthermore, in anticipation of an attack, the Union artillery gradually lessened their long-range fire and prepared their cannon for an advance by infantry. This change in tactics led Southern leaders to think erroneously that the enemy was weakened by their barrage, and set the stage for the most famous charge in American military history.

Around 3:00 p.m. (1500) the Southern infantry assigned to the attack moved out of the woods, were aligned in a formation that extended 1.5 kilometers (1 mile) from flank to flank, and began their advance. As they moved forward to come under fire, their pace increased, and as their casualties mounted, there was a tendency to converge toward the center of the Union line marked by the small group of trees directly to the east.

The large Northern force, however, remained deployed along the crest of Cemetery Ridge. By this arrangement, as the Confederates came closer to the Union line they were more concentrated, making them easier targets and increasingly vulnerable to flanking fire from Northern infantry and artillery along the ridge that were not under direct attack.

The maximum advance of the Southern forces on Cemetery Ridge came to be known as The High Water Mark or The High Tide of the Confederacy. It brought a few Southern soldiers to the copse of trees and stone wall, but they soon became casualties or prisoners. Under heavy fire, all who could fell back toward the cover of Seminary Ridge. Half of the soldiers who set out on this famous but futile charge became casualties, and the battle at Gettysburg was over.

CEMETERY RIDGE, THE COPSE OF TREES, AND THE ANGLE

Using the National Park Service's map, proceed north on West Confederate Avenue and return to the Visitor Center. From here follow Hancock Road and its continuation, Sedgwick Avenue, to the parking lot at Wheatfield Road. This drive gives a good opportunity to view Cemetery Ridge and its many memorials. Return by the same route to the parking area near the Copse of Trees and the Angle.

The challenge facing the troops in Pickett's Charge is made most vivid by combining the scene here with that viewed previously at the Virginia Memorial. About 7,000 Union soldiers were concentrated in this small area which was the point of the Confederate attack. And these Union soldiers were supported by many more men and much artillery on both flanks. It has been suggested that here on Cemetery Ridge the Southerners faced a situation similar to the one that led to the defeat of the Northerners at Fredericksburg.

Thus, this is an excellent site to review General Robert E. Lee's strategy in his second and last major invasion of the North and analyze tactics employed by both sides at Gettysburg. More than 150,000 soldiers were in some way involved in the battle, and at the end of three days of fighting 50,000 of them would be killed, wounded, or missing: 27,000 Confederates and 23,000 Northerners.

THE SOLDIER'S NATIONAL MONUMENT AND THE GETTYSBURG ADDRESS

The Gettysburg National Cemetery was dedicated on 19 November 1863. At that dedication President Abraham Lincoln delivered in two minutes his 272-word Gettysburg Address, which is today considered one of the supreme masterpieces of eloquence in the English language. The site of that address is less than 100 meters (300 feet) east of the Visitor Center.

Entrance to the National Cemetery at Gettysburg as it appeared in July 1863. Photograph by Matthew Brady, courtesy of the Library of Congress.

Although it took several years because many were moved from battlefield graves, the bodies of more the 3,500 Union soldiers killed in battle were interred here. Since then, honorably discharged United States veterans and their dependents have been buried here as well.

Lancaster County, Pennsylvania

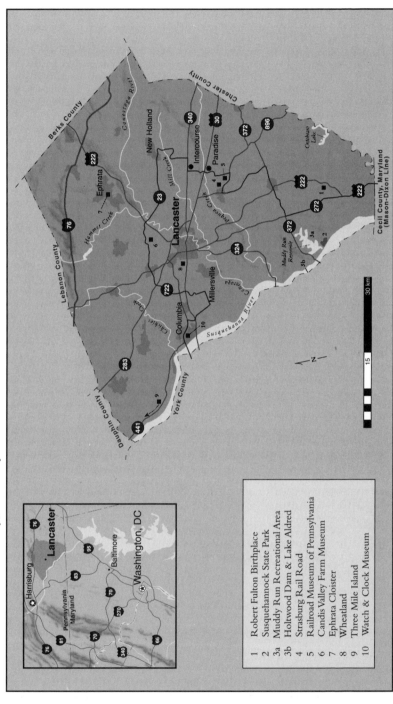

1　Robert Fulton Birthplace
2　Susquehannock State Park
3a　Muddy Run Recreational Area
3b　Holwood Dam & Lake Aldred
4　Strasburg Rail Road
5　Railroad Museum of Pennsylvania
6　Candis Valley Farm Museum
7　Ephrata Cloister
8　Wheatland
9　Three Mile Island
10　Watch & Clock Museum

△ Day Seven

LANCASTER COUNTY, PENNSYLVANIA, AND AMISH COUNTRY

by **Joseph W. Glass,** *Millersville University*

Lancaster County is a land of contrasts. Claiming to be Pennsylvania Dutch, it bears an English name. Renowned for its farming, less than 10 percent of its people live on farms and many of those work at non-farm jobs. Famous for the Amish farming community residing there, less than 5 percent of its population is Amish and not all of them are farmers. Called the Garden Spot of America, but located in the heart of Megalopolis, it is a mix of old and new, tradition and change.

This southeastern Pennsylvania border county lies in the Piedmont with the Susquehanna River flowing along its entire western boundary. Lancaster, its major central place, is approximately 70 miles west of Philadelphia's seaport at roughly 40° north latitude and 76° 15′ west longitude. In the total complex that makes this 945-square-mile space what it is and distinguishes it from all others, this absolute location is virtually the only constant.

Since the early days of European settlement along the Delaware River, Lancaster County has been on a mainstream routeway to the continental interior. The development of passable roads between the Delaware and the Susquehanna in the eighteenth century and its involvement in the nineteenth-century canal era each modified its relative location. Additional modifications followed the building of the Pennsylvania Railroad's Main Line, the Lincoln Highway, and the Pennsylvania Turnpike across the county. More recently, its elapsed time connections with distant places have been drastically reduced by air transport. Parts of the county lie nearly equidistant between the major international airports at Philadelphia and Baltimore. It is even closer to the smaller one at Harrisburg and its own domestic airport is the busiest in the state after those at Philadelphia and Pittsburgh.

Although no survey has ever been made, Lancaster may well be Pennsylvania's most widely recognized county name. Perhaps best known for the farm production from which its farmers received more than 800 million dollars in 1989, the value of its farm receipts leads all other non-irrigated counties in the nation and thirteen entire states. It is surpassed by only eleven large irrigated counties in western states. The agricultural activities responsible for this productivity have resulted in many idyllic farm scenes and pleasing rural landscapes that partially explain why this is one of Pennsylvania's leading tourist attractions. Millions of tourists arrive each year seeking respite from their increasingly urbanized world. Most probably they come with some hopes of satisfying their curiosity about the well-publicized Old Order Amish, among whom are some of the county's hardest-working farmers and whose wives and daughters are its best-known quilt makers. Amish quilts, antiques, and country handicrafts are widely available in the county. Together with seasonal fairs, heritage demonstrations, farm tours, and other farm-related activities, they attract a steady stream of visitors seeking some connection with the rural past.

Selling nostalgia for things rural has turned out to be bigger business than farming itself: Sales revenues generated by tourism in the county exceed its farm receipts. But tourists also come to visit the county's historic sites, museums, parks, and other attractions, including those developed by aggressive entrepreneurs. Of course, being so near other popular tourist destinations—such as Baltimore, Philadelphia, Gettysburg, Hershey, and the state capital at Harrisburg—doesn't hurt tourism in Lancaster County, nor does its megalopolitan location.

But farming and tourism are only a small portion of the whole picture. Lancaster's work force of over 220,000 in January 1991 contained almost 190,000 non-agricultural jobs. Nearly two thirds were in a broad spectrum of service-producing industries, including those related to tourism. The goods-producing industries, making up another third, included eighteen different Standard Industrial Classifications whose employees ranged from unskilled laborers to highly skilled professionals. The three leading classifications accounted for only about a third of these secondary industries and did not include the county's largest single employer. Not only is the county's overall economy diversified, but so are its manufacturing activities.

There is no single cause for this healthy economy. Lancaster's nearly central location in Megalopolis plus effective road, rail, and air linkages play no small role. The work ethic of its people is partly responsible, but it has also been built on its own reputation. Traditionally boasting one of the lowest unemployment rates in the state, the county has been a mecca for job seekers. Existing companies have expanded, new businesses have been started, and branches of national and international firms have been established to capitalize on its advantageous location and the attributes of its labor force.

More jobs induced still more jobs and brought even more residents. The 1990 census counted 420,921 residents—nearly double the 1940 count. Population growth has averaged over 4,600 annually since 1950 and even more in the 1980s. Initially the housing required by these additional residents was relatively unobtrusive. More recently, however, as the population has continued to swell, the conversion of farmland to housing and commercial developments has raised many voices in protest, and various farmland-preservation strategies are being devised. Even they have generated controversy.

Competition among residential builders, commercial developers, farmers, and preservationists for farmland that comes on the market has driven prices of many farms well beyond a level compatible with continued farming. Builders and developers can obtain higher and faster returns on their investments than can

A portion of the field carefully engineered for a pipe-outlet terrace system. Photograph by Joseph W. Glass.

farmers. Nevertheless more than two thirds of the county remains in farms. Most farmland is actually cropland, although poorly drained areas serve as permanent pasture and some steeper slopes are also used as pastures or for woodlots.

Lancaster County's shape resembles a kite. Most of the farmland's maximum local relief and steepest farmed slopes lie in the narrow southern quarter, underlain principally by metamorphic schist. The resultant soils are productive, but require special management practices because of the surface configuration. Contour plowing and strip cropping are common, but farmers are increasingly terracing their fields, building waterways, installing pipe-outlet terrace systems, and using no-till planting.

Stretching across the widest expanse of the county is the well-known Lancaster Plain, a broadly undulating surface underlain by various sedimentary limestones and dolomites. Its gentle swales and lesser local relief minimize erosion in what are the county's most productive soils. Most farmland is cleared and used for crops.

Harder rocks—quartzite, sandstone, and gneiss—underlie sizable portions of the county. The Furnace Hills extend along most of its northern border. Two other separate hilly segments—the Welsh Mountains and Mine Ridge—extend partially into the county on the east, and Chickies Ridge projects from the west. All of these physiographic features possess steep slopes and thin soils that have not been particularly attractive to farmers. As a result, they contain the county's largest expanses of wooded land.

Five months—from the beginning of May to the end of September—is a good approximation of the reliable growing season. It is usually a bit longer and local variations do exist. Normally about forty inches of precipitation is rather evenly distributed through the year with substantial portions coming as soaking rains or winter snowfall. Thunderstorms occur frequently during the summer months bringing heavy rains that magnify erosional tendencies and are often accompanied by damaging lightning, high winds, and hail. Hot summers, and especially the summer nights, offer particularly favorable conditions for corn and other crop growth.

This combination of favorable terrain, productive soils, and propitious climate provides advantageous natural conditions for agriculture. Yet these natural conditions alone were not sufficient to develop either the county's agricultural emphasis or its productivity. After all, Indians had lived in this area for centuries before Europeans arrived without placing a major emphasis on farming. Most of their food was obtained by other means.

Recognition of these natural endowments and the process of capitalizing on them began with the first European settlers. Most of these peasant folk and many who followed them had been farmers in their homelands who had enjoyed residential permanence. With their lives disrupted by war, political oppression, and religious persecution, they were seeking religious freedom and the opportunity to reestablish farming activities and residential permanence for themselves and their children under the benefits of William Penn's Holy Experiment. Lancaster County didn't yet exist when the first of them arrived in 1710, but enough of them did come that the county was established before two decades had passed. The surviving structures that they built—stone churches, houses, and barns—are mute testimony to their intent to stay, but permanent farming required more than permanent buildings. It required proper stewardship of the soil, which they expected to provide sustenance for themselves and their families and for generations to follow. Present-day persistence of their surnames, their religions, a multi-generational farming tradition in some families—including an unbroken succession of family ownership of 115 Century Farms and more than a quarter of all the Bicentennial Farms in the entire state—and the continued high productivity of Lancaster County farmland after 250 years of sustaining its farmers, are clear evidence that they succeeded.

The European peoples were primarily English and Germanic, but they also included many Scots-Irish and smaller contingents of Swiss and Welsh, and a few from other nations. No national group was homogeneous. There was no single kind of English immigrant and the same was true of the others. National, ethnic, and regional differences were compounded by the varieties of their languages, crafts, and farming techniques, as well as by a wide array of religious beliefs and practices which ranged from "plain" to mainstream.

On the eve of the Revolutionary War, Lancaster County contained the most diverse rural population in colonial America. These people lived among one another and learned from one another as they groped for ways to farm successfully in the New World. They observed, adopted, adapted, and became Americans in the process. As an early "melting pot," they contributed to the winning of independence, served as pragmatic models of the value of the First Amendment, and produced a number of what became basic "Americanisms."

The primary objective of early farmers was self-sufficiency through the production of all the family food for the entire year; cash crops were little more than fortunate surpluses. The Pennsylvania barn, with its cantilevered forebay extending outward above the stable doors, eventually became the standard barn used by farmers in this county and far beyond.

In contrast, the primary modern farm objective is maximum production of the most profitable commodities for cash sale and now much of the family food is bought at the grocery store.

Chesapeake Bay-sponsored stream-bank rehabilitation and protection project in the pasture of a Lancaster County dairy farm. Photograph by Joseph W. Glass.

Nowadays, profitable commodities are livestock, primarily cattle and chickens. This county consistently leads the state with the number and value of dairy cattle and their milk products; beef cattle and calves; broilers, layers, and eggs; and turkeys and hogs. Black-and-white Holstein cows and single or multiple silos are prominent ingredients of the rural landscape. Long and low-slung poultry houses are numerous but less conspicuous.

The county's livestock population of nearly 400,000 cattle, almost as many hogs, more than 63,000,000 chickens, and thousands of horses and mules produce a lot of manure. Farmers have always spread it on their fields, but with today's commercial farms containing more livestock, larger quantities of manure are being spread over the fields than ever before. This has contaminated both ground and surface waters by seepage and runoff. Because all of Lancaster County's waters drain into the Susquehanna River, which drains into the Chesapeake Bay, the soil nutrients have become unintentional pollutants of the bay. ("Save the Bay" proponents and the U.S. Department of Agriculture are among the concerned groups attempting to solve this problem.)

Field crops, the intended beneficiaries of the recycled manure, are dominated by corn and hay—livestock feed. Over half of the county's cropland is planted in corn. More than another third is used to grow hay, chiefly alfalfa, but soybean acreage has increased dramatically in the last few years. The remaining tenth of the cropland is divided among winter wheat and other small grains, vegetables, and tobacco. Although tobacco acreage decreased dramatically from about 30,000 in the 1950s to less than 9,000 in 1989—slightly less than 3 percent of the cropland—they have gradually increased since then and the county remains the state's leader in its production. Besides being profitable, tobacco provides distinctiveness to the rural landscape, whether growing in the field or air drying in specially constructed buildings.

Tobacco is also a very demanding crop, requiring much labor to grow, cut, and hang it to dry during the heat of late summer as well as through much of the winter to prepare it for market. Among those who continue to raise it are many Amish farmers whose large families provide the necessary labor. Although many of the county's farmers specialize in large dairy or poultry operations, in cash grain production, or in some combination of these specialities, the Amish farms still tend to resemble more closely the farms of the past. That resemblance is most evident in their use of horses and mules for plowing and other fieldwork.

The Amish

The Amish are just one of more than three dozen religious denominations and four dozen other religious groups—claiming to be non-denominational—to which Lancaster County residents belong. Although several of these are "plain," the most conservative are the Old Order Amish. In contrast to the often conspicuous churches and meeting houses of the county's other religious groups, which are so numerous that they average more than one for every two square miles, the Old Order Amish have no church buildings at all. Instead the members regard themselves as the church and have divided the area they occupy into 100 church districts. Those who reside within a certain district rotate the location of their biweekly worship service among the homes within their district that are large enough to accommodate all district members and their children. Farmhouse capacity limits the size of church district populations. Geographical dimensions, however, vary considerably depending upon the population density of a district's members. Districts are divided and boundaries re-drawn when the population exceeds the worship capacity of the farmhouses.

Amish children do not become church members until they de-cide for themselves to join the church body, usually in their late teens or early twenties. In this respect—the practice of believer baptism rather than infant baptism—and in other ways, the Old Order Amish differ from many other denominations.

Hair and dress styles for both sexes, and the beard without a mustache for married men are among church prescriptions, as is the acceptable type of carriage. Other church rules—the *Ordnung*—include prohibitions against the use of electricity from power companies on their properties, telephones in their homes, owner-ship of automobiles, tractors for motive power, and marriage to anyone who is not Amish.

Less obvious are the high values they place on humility and modesty and the importance of the roles of the family and commu-nity in daily life. Few people know that the Amish are trilingual. The Bible is read in German during their worship services, they converse in the Pennsylvania Dutch dialect at home and with fellow Amish, and speak English with the non-Amish world around them whose members they actually refer to as "English." In fact, many Amish children only begin to learn English at school, as a foreign language.

The horse is crucial to the Amish way of life and tangibly represents their desire to remain separate from worldly ways. Amish mobility is thereby more limited than that of automobile

Amish farmers plowing with horses when weather permits during the winter. Photograph by Joseph W. Glass.

owners and field tasks require more time to perform than they do for farmers who use tractors. On average, therefore, Amish farms are smaller than those owned by the non-Amish whose capital-intensive farming methods include larger and faster fossil-fueled implements. With families that average more than six children, Amish labor-intensive farming successfully compensates despite their smaller farms. Their closely knit families instill responsibility and develop good work habits in their children by involving them in the family activities of the home and farm at an early age.

Children are the lifeblood of Amish society. Because they make no effort to seek converts, their children constitute the sole source of future church members. Fewer than 20 percent of their children decline to become church members or leave the church after having joined. Brought up and socialized in Amish ways within the intimacy of their own Amish home, educated for eight years in their one-room neighborhood Amish schools, and the products of lifetime Amish community associations, these young people become Amish long before they make the conscious decision to be baptized into church membership.

The Amish beliefs have persisted since the early years of the Reformation, and they have existed as Amish since 1693. Fewer than 800 Old Order Amish in the Lancaster settlement were divided into six church districts a century ago. Now almost 17,000 of them have divided themselves into 100 church districts, and more than half the Amish population has not yet reached its eighteenth birthday. Their age structure more nearly resembles that of a developing country than it does that of the United States.

The traditional goal of Amish farm families is to give each son a farm when he marries. The interaction of a farm family collectively supporting itself has been perceived as the ideal manner in which to perpetuate Amish ways and beliefs while promoting the greatest possible separation from worldly influences—this in accordance with biblical instruction to "Come out from among them, and be ye separate, saith the Lord, and touch not the unclean thing; and I will receive you" (II Corinthians 6:17). However, not enough farms are coming on the market to satisfy the needs of their rapidly growing population nor can they afford all those that are put up for sale. Given the competition for land among the Amish themselves as well as from other land-hungry segments of the Lancaster County community, prices are often beyond their means. Many Amish sons cannot follow this tradition that has contributed to their community's ability to endure and thrive.

Some outsiders believe that Amish ways never change. That isn't true. Changed conditions, such as declining opportunities to buy farms, have generated alternative strategies. Numerous Amish-owned stores, metal and wood shops, repair businesses, construction firms, and other commercial enterprises have been established in recent years. They employ family and other church members, often on the same farm property where the business owner grew up. Although their opportunities are limited by only eight years of one-room schooling, other Amish have obtained full-time work off the farm in both "English-" and Amish-owned businesses. Some Amish parents have divided their farms and still others have decided to buy and move to affordable farms elsewhere in Pennsylvania or in other states. The Amish are not only making adjustments within Lancaster County, where they have established a well-honed rapport with land, markets, and neighbors during more than two centuries of residence, but they are also in the testy process of establishing and developing new niches for themselves elsewhere.

Increased contacts with the non-Amish world will likely erode the separation from it the group prefers. More defections from the Amish fold are likely, but as a group the Old Order Amish are survivors. They have a successful record of withstanding religious persecution, political oppression, social change, technological advancement, and an increasingly materialist world for three centuries by devising appropriate strategies. The Amish—and all other residents of Lancaster County—face many dilemmas, chief of which is growth. The area has a fixed quantity of land, and more of almost everything else, including people. Challenges abound in Lancaster County, but in the past its residents have met challenges successfully as they converted a forest-covered frontier into one of Pennsylvania's most desirable places to live, work, and visit. The major challenge now is to sustain that desirability.

Itinerary

This ramble through Lancaster County focuses on rural landscapes that have been shaped by generations of farmers. It avoids the city of Lancaster and all but one concentration of tourist-oriented businesses in order to provide the greatest opportunity for observing the fields and structures essential to various farming activities and for passing through the heart of the county's Old Order Amish settlement. To do this, the route twists and turns along many less traveled roads. Along the way, however, it passes through several small towns (one of which is the county's prime tourist focus), older rural non-farm housing, and ever-expanding portions of modern suburbia.

THE MASON-DIXON LINE

After William Penn received his land grant in 1681, Maryland and Pennsylvania each claimed the full degree of latitude between thirty-nine and forty degrees. Their dispute continued more than eighty years before an agreement was reached to place the boundary at 39° 43′ 18″. Between 1763 and 1768 Charles Mason and Jeremiah Dixon inscribed their names in history by surveying this best known of all U.S. state boundaries. Special stones mark it at 1-mile intervals.

Drive along Route 222, the Robert Fulton Highway in Fulton Township. Both are named for the inventor of the steamboat, who was born nearby.

The average size of a Lancaster County farm is eighty-five acres, but it is much larger here in the county's southern end. Average land values per acre here are near the low end of the county range. Large areas with steeper slopes remain wooded, and poorly drained areas are permanently pastured. Also, since most of this area's farmers have no religious objections to owning and using large fossil-fuel-powered equipment, their capital-intensive farming is more efficient on larger acreages. Until we reach Buck, the smallest farms we will pass will be 90 or more acres, but most will be well over 100 acres and several will exceed 200 and even 300 acres. Many farmers also rent acreage from other landowners. In one neighboring township, for example, a dairyman who owns 196 acres rents five other properties and grows 900 acres of feed crops. Even so, over the years some farmers have sold roadside parcels of land so that now numerous residences and a few businesses, churches, and schools are strung out along several stretches of roadway, but farmland remains behind them.

ROCK SPRING TO BUCK, 12 MILES

Rock Spring Baptist Church on the left (at mile 0.5) was built in 1808 of serpentine, a greenish rock that underlies portions of this area. *Rock Spring School* (mile 1.7) on the left is a former one-roomer. According to the datestone it was established in 1837 and this building was erected in 1890.

Conowingo Creek (mile 3.2), with some permanent wetland pasture beside it, is another small area underlain by serpentine, some of which was used to construct the house on the slope just ahead on the left.

When an Amish family purchased this house from its previous non-Amish owners, they had the electricity disconnected. Photograph by Joseph W. Glass.

Past the creek and Goat Hill Road on the right is a large dairy farm with both upright and trench silos. The county's dairy farms primarily milk Holsteins. Each farm has so many more cows now than was typical of earlier general farming that sizable additions have been added to older barns to accommodate the larger herds.

Route 272 merges with our road from the right at mile 4.3.

Penn Hill Friends Meeting House and cemetery are on the right at mile 4.8. The datestone states that this building was erected in 1823, but Quakers established the meeting itself in 1758.

Bear left at the "Y" and continue on Route 272 (Lancaster Pike). Route 222, the Robert Fulton Highway, winds off to the right, past the inventor's birthplace to Quarryville, Lancaster, and farther north.

Black Bear Structures (mile 6.4), an Amish business, sells a variety of wooden products for outdoor use.

Back along Goshen Road (mile 6.7) is the first of many long, one-story poultry houses we'll see. The 30,000 layers that can be

Hensel Road (mile 7.4) on the right leads to the Robert Fulton Birthplace, operated by the Pennsylvania Museum and Historical Commission. The route is well marked.

housed in it are central to a contract operation involving the farmer, a feed company, and a wholesaler. The feed company owns the chickens and delivers their properly mixed feed to the farm. The farmer houses, feeds, waters, and otherwise cares for the birds. He also collects and prepares their 25,000 or more daily egg production for pick-up by the wholesaler, who markets them as fresh "Lancaster County eggs" in Maryland. The wholesaler pays the feed company for the feed and pays the farmer a contracted price per dozen.

The farm on the left (mile 7.5) belongs to an Old Order Amish family, who has had the power company disconnect electrical service to the property and remove the electric meter that had been used by the previous non-Amish owners. In addition to farming, this family operates a farm greenhouse. They cater to the growing suburbanite market for vegetable and decorative plants. This small-scale farm enterprise is part of a growing trend of cottage industries the Amish have been establishing to provide additional income, to prevent day-long work-place involvement in non-Amish settings, and to maintain their traditional interactive family togetherness.

From mile 8.5, less than a mile to the left along River Road is the *Chestnut Level Presbyterian Church* and both its present and older cemeteries. Many Scots–Irish immigrants arrived and settled in the land disputed by Maryland and Pennsylvania before their agreement was reached. Among the cultural baggage they brought was their Presbyterianism. Numerous congregations were formed because of the limited transportation of those times. Established in 1711, this is the oldest of those congregations in this county.

Telephone booth on an Amish farm. Photograph by Joseph W. Glass.

The fields on the right (mile 8.7) are no-till planted in contoured strip cropping. They also contain carefully engineered artificial terraces and grass-covered waterways specifically designed to minimize erosion.

At *Breezelane Farm* (mile 10.5) small hutches shelter calves that will eventually become part of the dairy herd.

At mile 10.8 is an Amish farm on the right, and just inside the wire fence along the road is a *telephone booth*. Its lead-in wire is stapled down the far side of the telephone pole next to the booth. This booth contains an ordinary household phone, not a coin-operated pay phone. Telephone arrangements such as this are becom-

At mile 10.6, turn left onto Silver Spring Road and follow the signs for 6 miles to visit *Susquehannock State Park* for a picnic, hiking, and a spectacular view of the Susquehanna River. No admission fee.

ing more common among the Amish as they become more involved in non-farm business activities or as their farming and farm marketing become more complex.

The rather public location minimizes the likelihood that it would be used for idle chit-chat. This location outside the home complies with the Amish objection to interconnecting their homes into a network that includes non-Amish homes, as would be the case with both electrical and telephone wires. The Amish find this a reasonable method of accepting an increasingly useful technology without violating church regulations.

The poultry house on the right (at mile 11.2) has a capacity of 57,000 layers.

BUCK TO STRASBURG

Turn right onto Route 372 east (Buck Road) at mile 12.5.

For nearly 3 miles to Quarryville we will pass through variable land uses and topography. New housing developments, individual houses, farmsteads, small orchards, croplands, wooded areas, and poultry and dairy operations use a variable surface that is underlain

At mile 12.5, a left turn leads to a variety of opportunities for fishing and other outdoor recreational activities, for visiting an environmental preserve and nature center, or for observing facilities that wrest electricity from the Susquehanna River. In appropriate seasons many species of migratory birds use these waters as temporary stopovers along the Atlantic Flyway. The entrance to *Muddy Run Recreational Park* is 3.8 miles from here; just beyond that is a sign with directions to various *Lake Aldred Recreational Area* facilities; and at 6.8 miles the bridge across the river offers a panoramic view of the *Susquehanna Gorge* and *Holtwood Dam*. The power companies that own and operate these facilities also provide maps and brochures at their information centers. No admission fee is charged but there are fees for camping.

Horse-and-carriage parking area at the Quarryville, Pennsylvania, post office. Photograph by Joseph W. Glass.

by the last of the schists and the first of the quartzites and limestones we will traverse.

The three poultry houses (mile 13.6) on the left have a capacity of 90,000 layers which produce an average of 65,000 eggs each day.

Enter *Quarryville* (mile 15.7) and observe the main intersection, the housing and its relationship to sidewalks, and the general appearance of the town for comparison with Strasburg, the culturally different next small town.

Continue straight ahead at the traffic signal in the main intersection; Route 222 north connects here.

At mile 17.3, the bridge crosses an old Pennsylvania Railroad line, now abandoned by Conrail. The county government is investigating the possibility of purchasing this right-of-way for use as a linear park for hiking and biking.

For the next 2 miles we will be riding near the line of contact between quartzite bedrock on our left and limestone on the right.

One-room Amish school. Photograph by Joseph W. Glass.

Surface and land-use differences are obvious. The largest of the farms between here and the railroad off to the right is 71 acres.

At mile 18.0, on the right is *Beiler's Harness & Shoe Repair,* another Amish-operated and farm-located business.

Beiler is one of eight common surnames in the Lancaster Amish community. In order of their frequency people named Stoltzfus, King, Fisher, Beiler, Esh, Lapp, Zook, and Glick make up about 80 percent of the Amish population. More than a quarter are named Stoltzfus, and the first four names account for more than half the community. Since they seek no converts, their endogamous practice of marrying only church members has closed their surname and gene pools for more than two centuries.

At mile 19.3, turn left onto May Post Office Road. For nearly 6 miles this road crosses the western end of *Mine Ridge.* Composed of Precambrian gneiss and Lower Cambrian quartzite, the ridge is not generous to farmers and much of it is wooded. One of the mines from which its name is derived served as the world's major source of nickel during part of the nineteenth century.

Split farm. The larger portions of the barn and house nearer the main road were constructed in 1825. The barn and house further from the road were built recently to accommodate the brothers' separate families and farms. Photograph by Joseph W. Glass.

On the right along Furnace Road is an *Amish school* (mile 20.1). One-room schools containing eight grades are operated by the Old Order Amish as part of their effort to keep their children within the influence of Amish society, separated from exposure to non-Amish activities and peer pressures in public schools. These buildings are all about the same size, possess a bell on the roof, and contain a pair of outhouses in the schoolyard. Land for new schools is donated by Amish farm families.

All students live close enough to walk, and many are siblings or other close relatives. Discipline is usually no problem, and the basic program of studies satisfies both state requirements and what the Amish perceive to be their needs.

At mile 20.6, there is an *Amish farm* on each side of the road owned by brothers whose father bought a 100-acre farm and divided it between them. The original farm contained the stuccoed stone farmhouse on the right and the stone barn across the road, both of which contain datestones inscribed 1825. Even these were divided, requiring one brother to build a new house and the other to build a new barn.

Fifty acres is close to the minimum from which an Amish farmer can make a living—and farms this small can't be split among their sons. Although farm division can't continue indefinitely, it is a strategy the Amish have been using to provide sons with farms and often requires the construction of a full set of farm buildings.

On the right at mile 21.2 is *Mt. Eden Lutheran Church.* This and other rural churches are identified to dispel any notion that Lancaster County is inhabited only by Amish farmers.

To the left on White Oak Road (mile 22.2) is the *Strasburg Pallet Co.,* a major consumer of timber from farm woodlots. To the right is *White Oak Campground,* one of more than thirty campgrounds in the county, a partial indicator of the importance of tourism.

Zook's quilts (mile 23.4) illustrates an Amish cottage industry that is riding the crest of a popularity wave.

Notice how closely the *Amish school* at mile 24.4 resembles the other one we saw.

Meandering *Little Beaver Creek* (mile 24.6) has cut through this final ridge before we enter the Lancaster Plain.

STRASBURG TO MINE RIDGE, 2.1 MILES

At the square in Strasburg (mile 26.1) turn right onto combined Routes 741 east and 896 south (East Main Street). A culturally Pennsylvanian town, *Strasburg* differs from Quarryville in several respects. One is the square we are entering from the south. Despite some recent modifications, it is still easy to see that this square is actually a rectangle at a crossroads through which the east–west street has been widened for a short distance.

Strasburg residents take considerable pride in the history and beauty of their town. Two blocks of South Decatur Street and about 0.5 mile of Main Street on both sides of the square have been declared a *Historic District.* The shiny oval plaques on many

Country road worn in the center of each lane by the steel horseshoes of the Amish horses. Photograph by Joseph W. Glass.

houses are awarded by the Strasburg Heritage Society to buildings in the Historic District which can be documented as pre-1925 construction in which architectural integrity has been maintained. Each plaque is inscribed with the construction date of the building to which it is attached.

Before leaving the square you might be interested to learn that the *Creamery,* across from where we entered the square, bakes its own cones and makes ice cream that is hard to beat. In the same building is a bed-and-breakfast (B&B) inn.

Bear right at the Y at mile 26.5 and follow Route 896 (Georgetown Road).

On the left at mile 27.0 can be seen some of outdoor exhibits and the main building of the *Railroad Museum.*

As we leave Strasburg we can see two unique Amish contributions to the cultural landscape. In this and other heavily populated Amish areas, thousands of steel horseshoes land repeatedly with considerable force from their 1,000-pound wearers on the narrow

At mile 26.5, a double treat awaits railroad buffs just a quarter mile ahead on Route 741, the left option at the Y. The *Strasburg Rail Road,* a stock company chartered in 1832, offers train rides in vintage cars pulled by steam locomotives. Across the road are the outdoor and indoor exhibits of the Railroad Museum of Pennsylvania. Separate operations charging separate admissions, both are first rate. In winter the train operates only on weekends and the museum is closed Mondays.

central strip of each lane in the roadway. The wear they cause on the road surface and the repairs that wear necessitates are often prominent. The second contribution is horse manure, which is often concentrated in the same middle portion of each lane.

At mile 27.4 and elsewhere along our route, tobacco can be seen growing in fields from mid-June until near Labor Day and then drying as it hangs in special sheds such as this for several months after the harvest. Hinges near the top of alternate vertical side boards permit those boards to be opened outward to improve air circulation for more uniform drying. This tobacco shed provides a close view of the hinged vertical siding, as do the sheds at mile 27.7.

Michael's Bakery (mile 28.1) turns out breads, rolls, and sticky buns par excellence.

MINE RIDGE TO LINCOLN HIGHWAY, 4.6 MILES

The rise at mile 28.2 along the north side of Mine Ridge offers an overview of the gentle terrain in the *Lancaster Plain.* It is underlain by various limestones and dolomites that have produced deep, rich soils. Values per acre here average near the high end of the county's price range. Our route will cross this terrain for the next several miles. The farms we see in front of us range in size from the largest at 128 acres to several being less than half of that, but there is little wasteland. Dairying is typical with most fields planted in feed crops.

At mile 29.1 turn left onto Esbenshade Road, pass a bed and breakfast at mile 29.3, and cross route 741 (Strasburg Road) at mile 30.2. At mile 30.5 is the main line of the Strasburg Rail Road.

Esbenshade Turkey Farm claims to be "America's oldest." Founded in 1858 by the great-grandfather of the present owner, this sixty-acre farm is one of Pennsylvania's Century Farms. They grow, dress, and market 7,000 turkeys each year for Thanksgiving and Christmas dinners. Another Ebenshade operation is the green building that houses 80,000 laying chickens (mile 30.7)

Back this lane (mile 30.9) and around the barn is a farmhouse whose owners operate their dairy farm plus a bed and breakfast for tourists. B&B's are becoming more common as tourism increases.

The mailbox at mile 31.1 reveals that this is where Elam M. Beiler lives and just ahead is the Jonas E. Fisher farm. These are both common Amish surnames. Their first names are also among those more commonly given by Amish than by mainstream Americans. Although the biblical pool of these first names is large, there are enough Amish that many bear identical first and last names.

Propane tanks (mile 31.3) are obvious here at the Fisher farm. Propane is used for lighting and space heaters as well as for water heaters, gas stoves, and gas refrigerators. Unlike wires from the power or telephone company which, if connected to Amish homes, could tempt them into undesirable activities and would connect them into networks they prefer to avoid, propane is totally practical and the absence of a permanent connecting link retains a sense of separation. It is, however, another example of Amish selectivity in their use of modern technology.

Turn left onto Cherry Hill Road (mile 31.8). At about mile 32.0 is 40 degrees north latitude, the northern limit of the territory disputed by Maryland and Pennsylvania.

Turn right onto Paradise Lane. *Paradise Mennonite Church* will be on your left. Mennonites are not Amish. Amish are the followers of Jacob Amman, who broke away from the Mennonites in 1693 because they regarded Mennonites as not being strict enough about certain things.

Turn left onto Singer Road (mile 32.7). Turn right onto Route 30, the Lincoln Highway (mile 32.8). This highway was built originally in 1792 to 1794 by a stock company as the *Lancaster Turnpike* to Philadelphia. Constructed with a stone base according to MacAdam's design, its success in attracting stagecoach, Conestoga wagon, and other traffic inspired a rash of turnpike construction in the young nation.

PARADISE TO INTERCOURSE, 4.7 MILES

Turn left onto Leacock Road and drive past the front of the Post Office (mile 33.0).

Beside the Pequea Creek is another B&B (mile 33.2).

Gordonville Book Store (mile 33.3) is owned and operated by Amish but open to the public.

The railroad tracks at mile 33.7 are part of what was once the *Pennsylvania Railroad's Main Line* between New York and Chicago.

The fifty-foot windmill (mile 34.0) in the field to the right pumps water into the thirty-five-foot tank beside it. The height of the tank and the elevation difference are enough to move the water downslope to the farmstead with adequate pressure for all household and barn needs.

Still another *Amish school* (mile 34.3) serves this neighborhood.

Leacock Coleman Center (mile 34.5) is another Amish business established on a farm property. Many of the products sold here are particularly useful to the Amish. Coleman lanterns, for example, are standard Amish house and barn lighting, but this store sells a wide range of Coleman products to the public, including tents and canoes.

Harvest View Produce (mile 34.9) is a roadside stand selling home-grown vegetables and is a very typical and long-standing enterprise for farmers just about everywhere. *Leacock Woodcraft,* back the lane on the left, is operated by an Amish family who manufactures fine-quality solid-oak furniture. Their showroom is open to the public.

Smoker's Custom Butchering (mile 35.0) is Amish but operated only in the farm off-season from October to early April. The "Horses Only" sign at the hitching rail indicates that it is patronized by Amish and non-Amish alike.

Old Leacock Presbyterian Church (mile 35.0) indicates that Scots-Irish were here, too, first worshipping in a log church on this site in 1724.

Turn right onto Route 340, the *Old Philadelphia Pike* (mile 35.2). Governor Thomas Penn ordered the construction of this road as a "King's Highway" to connect Lancaster with Philadelphia shortly after Lancaster County was established in 1729.

In the 2 miles between here and Intercourse, all farm families are Amish.

Entering *Intercourse,* drive carefully. Drivers and pedestrians are especially unpredictable along the main street. Intercourse is close to the historic core of Amish settlement in Lancaster County. In contrast to scattering themselves far and wide around the country as individual families, the establishment of a relatively compact settlement pattern by the Amish has contributed in various ways to their survival as a religious group. They have expanded outward from this area east of Lancaster to its south as we have seen, and north as we will see. The village is now basically tourist oriented but once served primarily as a commercial center for the surrounding farmers. For those seriously interested in the Amish, *The People's Place* is legitimate (mile 37.4 on the left). There is no charge to browse in their book shop but there are admissions for the film and museum.

At mile 37.6, bear left at the Y and continue on Route 340.

Perhaps you remember Zimmerman's—mile 37.7 on the left— from a scene in the 1985 movie *Witness.* Among the customers in its first-floor grocery store and small upstairs department store are Amish who, as you can see, tie their horses at the hitching rail.

Some people wonder whether the Amish use banks. After you see the hitching rail and perhaps some horse manure in front of the bank a few doors beyond Zimmerman's, the answer will be obvious.

HOLLANDER ROAD TO HARRISBURG PIKE, 25.6 MILES

Turn left onto North Hollander Road (mile 37.9) before passing the motel. For nearly 14 miles between here and our turn onto Quarry Road (mile 51.7), we will pass no farms larger than eighty-seven acres.

At the three-way intersection at mile 39.0, left turn, remaining on North Hollander Road.

Eli Wood Shop (mile 39.3) uses no electricity. All their woodworking tools are powered by hydraulics or compressed air. The showroom is open to the public.

On the hill (mile 39.7) to the left is another elevated windmill–water tank combination utilizing gravity to provide adequate water pressure. We'll see a few more of these in the next few miles and a couple will be much closer to the buildings they serve.

At mile 40.5, turn hard right onto Peters Road. This road is part of a route between the Susquehanna and Philadelphia that was established by Peter Bizellion, a French fur trader. As early as 1717, it was already commonly known as Old Peter's Road.

At mile 41.7, turn left onto South Custer Road. After the turn, look right for another windmill and water tank on a higher elevation than the farm they serve. On the left farther ahead is a recently built, modern-looking home of a non-farming Amish family. According to the sign on the right, they are the Smuckers, one of the minor Amish names. A home this size appears to be too small to be used for worship services, but that is misleading. Young Amish couples who build these modern houses are expected to include a full basement in which services can be held. The small frame building on the right between the fences is another telephone booth.

At the next three-way intersections (miles 42.4, 42.6, and 42.7) stay left, remaining on South Custer Road.

Amos Blank's farmstead is at mile 43.7. Blank is another minor Amish name.

Part of *New Holland* is ahead (mile 44.0) but we'll just skirt the edge of town. Despite the name of this town, the Pennsylvania Dutch heritage is not Holland "Dutch" but Germanic "Deutsch."

Tyson Foods, Inc. bought Weaver's (mile 44.2), a locally owned firm that developed this plant. Many county chickens are processed here into frozen chicken products.

Turn left onto Orlan Road (mile 44.4); then in half a mile, right onto Hollander Road, and left onto George C. Delp Road. This is the home of *New Holland farm machinery* and this road is owned by the company, but we can drive through its grounds to see the various buildings and finished machinery stored outside. With humble beginnings serving local farmers, New Holland has experienced enormous growth and several changes in corporate ownership. Its products are now used around the world. For plant tours, inquire at the building next to the Post Office on Hollander Road.

The railroad tracks at mile 45.9 are used frequently—stop and look. Turn left onto Route 23 (West Main Street) (mile 46.0). Along this main highway between New Holland and Lancaster are many non-farm residences that date from pre-automobile days. Some are in the linear villages but most are not. The same is true along the main roads between Lancaster and other outlying towns. Many of these houses are a consequence of the trolley lines that were constructed more than a century ago. These fanned out from Lancaster like spokes of a wheel connecting the smaller towns to the city and with one another through it. People who could not have done so otherwise were then able to establish their non-farm residences along the trolley line connecting links and work some distance from home. The New Holland line ran along the south side of this road.

About a half-mile along Brethren Church Road on the right is the *Leola Produce Auction* (mile 48.8) to which 1,100 local vegetable growers brought their harvests for wholesale auction in 1990. Buyers are attracted from much of Megalopolis by the fresh produce marketed as "Lancaster County Brand Vegetables." Increasing numbers of local farmers have been finding it economically worthwhile to set aside one to ten (or even more) acres of their farms for labor-intensive vegetable production. The auction operates six days each week from mid-July to mid-September and somewhat less frequently during the rest of the season between late April and late November.

Turn right onto Quarry Road (mile 51.7). (This is called Bushong Road on the Leola 7½-minute USGS Map.) Over the next 10 miles or so, our road alternates between passing through suburbia and open farmland. Here and in a couple of other places along our route, our road actually separates the built from the sown. Although nowhere does our road serve as a boundary between different political units, it does serve here and in other places as the boundary between different land-use zoning classifications within a political unit.

At mile 52.9 is another *Amish school.*

The *Conestoga River* (mile 54.0) is the source of the name given to the famous type of covered wagon which was built in its valley. The *limestone mill* here was constructed in 1857 and originally harnessed the Conestoga to turn its waterwheel. More than 300 water-powered mills once played an essential role in the county's economy and development. They ground flour into grain, sawed wood, pressed flaxseed into linseed oil, crushed apples for cider, and converted other raw materials into useful products. Only a few remain and many of those have been adapted to other uses.

We cross the bridge over Route 222 at mile 54.7. Just ahead is an unmarked road angling left. Be prepared to turn forty-five degrees left onto a road without a name sign (its actual name is Bushong Road) at mile 54.8.

Cross Route 272 (Oregon Pike) onto Route 722 (Oregon Road) (mile 55.1).

At mile 55.3 is one of the remaining mills adapted as an office building.

Cross Route 501, leaving Route 722 temporarily (mile 57.8), and bear right onto East Petersburg Road to rejoin Route 722.

At the one-lane bridge (mile 59.0), yield to oncoming traffic. Cross the Fruitville Pike (mile 59.5) and enter East Petersburg. Route 722 is also called State Street here. Cross Route 72 (Main Street). Remain on State Street (Route 722); cross Route 741 (Lemon Street); and cross the bridge over Route 283. Lancaster is to the east, Harrisburg west.

At mile 55.1, *Landis Valley Farm Museum* lies 3.2 miles to the left along Route 272. Simply called "the farm museum" by locals, it offers indoor and outdoor exhibits, craft demonstrations, and interpretations of eighteenth- and nineteenth-century Pennsylvania German daily rural life. Admission fee except for the bookstore. Closed Mondays.

At mile 55.1, *Ephrata Cloister* is 6.4 miles to the right along Route 272 in Ephrata. The ten Germanic medieval-style buildings that survive were used by an eighteenth-century communal society of religious celibates, who became well known for their art and music as well as their printing and publishing. These buildings now contain exhibits and interpretations of their austere society and are open to the public. Admission fee except for the gift shop and bookstore. Routes to both of these are well-marked by blue and yellow "Pennsylvania Trail of History" signs.

Your *Kellogg's Corn Flakes* may have been produced in this state-of-the-art plant (mile 63.0). Some locally grown grains are used in the cereals made here, but most come from elsewhere.

Turn right onto Harrisburg Pike (mile 63.5) and immediately prepare to turn left onto Centerville Road.

CENTERVILLE ROAD TO THE SUSQUEHANNA RIVER, 14.6 MILES

Most of the land along the next 4 miles of *Centerville Road* was in farms until the 1940s when development began slowly and then picked up momentum. Before that, some non-farm residences existed along two-lane rural roads that had no traffic signals, but there were no businesses among them. It's very different now. Much of the development is very recent and some is still in process. Beyond those 4 miles (after mile 68.0), we'll be in farm country once again. Bear left at the curve at mile 64.4, but be wary of oncoming traffic turning across your lane. Cross Route 23 (Marietta Pike) at mile 65.5.

Cross the bridge over Route 30 (mile 66.0) (Lancaster is east, York is west) and turn right onto Route 462 (Columbia Avenue) at mile 66.9. The land to our left was productive farmland until a few years ago. It had contained a beautiful 1809 Pennsylvania barn that was demolished to provide a bit more space.

Turn left at mile 65.5 onto Route 23 for a 4.0-mile trip to *Wheatland,* the home of President James Buchanan from 1848 until his death there in 1868. The house is well appointed with many of Buchanan's and other period furnishings. Open April 1 to November 30, admission fee.

Turn left onto Weaver Road (mile 67.1). Until we cross Route 462 again in about 8 miles we'll be in *Manor Township.* This name was derived from William Penn's Manor of the Conestoga, which he reserved for his own family.

The brick barn (mile 67.8) on the left is the first we've seen. They are more common elsewhere, especially in the lower Cumberland Valley about 75 miles west of here. The log house was moved here in pieces from its original site.

Turn left onto Donnerville Road (mile 68.0). The land on both sides to the top of the grade is usually planted in potatoes. At the three-way intersection (mile 68.5), bear left around the curve and stay on Donnerville Road.

Mile 69.2 is an awkward intersection. Turn ninety degrees right, then ninety degrees left. Stay on Donnerville Road. Could the new houses at mile 69.4 be the beginning of the end for farmland around here?

Turn right onto Route 999 (Blue Rock Road) (mile 69.8). In the next 2 miles we'll be passing through productive farmland that is used primarily to grow feed for the cattle on the dairy farms we'll see, but tobacco has long been a cash crop here also.

The collection of *limestone buildings* at mile 70.4 beside the Little Conestoga Creek includes a pair of houses, a barn, and a mill. In the nineteenth century a post office, called *Windom,* was housed in the mill.

To our right at mile 70.9 on the near side of the brick farmhouse is a white tobacco shed with sections of its horizontally arranged siding hinged to maximize air flow for drying tobacco. Beyond the farmhouse is a good example of a south-facing *Pennsylvania barn.*

Pennsylvania barn and silo. Photograph by Joseph W. Glass.

At mile 71.6, turn right onto Central Manor Road. Ahead in the woods on the left are the 126 small cabins, auditorium, dining hall, and other buildings of the *Central Manor Camp-Meeting Association.* The religious camp-meetings held here every summer since 1892 are now non-denominational. Several of the farms just past the woods are strictly cash-grain and hay producers.

As we cross Habecker Church Road (mile 72.7), the name of our road changes to Franklin Road. Mennonites worship at *Habecker Church,* which is the small brick building beside the cemetery a half-mile to the right. Just past this intersection we begin an ascent that offers a panoramic view of this lush countryside as far as Lancaster to the east and into York County on the west. Enjoy, but be careful—there's no room to park and little room to pull over on the ascent or at the top.

At mile 73.1, turn right onto Seitz Road, and at mile 74.2, turn right onto Prospect Road.

CAREFUL! There is a one-lane railroad underpass at mile 74.4.

A right turn at the end of this ramp leads to *Three Mile Island.* The visitor's center is 19.7 miles north along Route 441 directly opposite the four much-photographed cooling towers. Free.

A left turn at the ramp's end leads to more than 6,000 timepieces of all sorts on display at the *Watch and Clock Museum* in Columbia. Go left 0.4 mile on 441, which becomes Third Street past the bridge, then turn left onto Poplar Street for two blocks. The museum is on the corner of Fifth and Poplar streets. Admission fee.

Both the *mill* (mile 74.3) on the left and—a little farther on—the *lime kiln* on the right have suffered greatly from neglect.

At the three-way intersection at mile 74.6 turn right to stay on Prospect Road. *St. Joseph's Convent* is operated by the Adorers of the Blood of Christ order of Catholic nuns. Founded in 1926, the nuns also operated an academy for ninth to twelfth grade girls here from 1941 until 1991.

Cross Route 462 (Columbia Avenue), cross the bridge, and turn left onto Route 30 west. For either side trip above, exit the ramp at mile 78.6 for Route 441.

The Susquehanna River (mile 78.8) is the end of our guided field trip. Route 30 continues west to York and on beyond to Gettysburg. On this side of York Route 30 intersects I-83, south to Baltimore and north to Harrisburg.

Safe journey!

Suggestions for Visitors to Lancaster County

PLEASE RESPECT AMISH RELIGIOUS BELIEF: DO NOT PHOTOGRAPH AMISH PEOPLE.

Having seen the movie *Witness,* many people question this request. Yet, even though a great many Amish were portrayed in that movie, not a single one was a real-life Amish person. All were professional actors and actresses.

At the core of Amish religious beliefs and practices is their literal interpretation of the Bible. When the First Commandment states: "Thou shalt not make any graven image or any likeness of anything . . ." (Exodus 20:4), the Amish regard that as a clear prohibition of photographs. Pure and simply, being photographed is against their religion. To violate their religious beliefs is discourteous and inconsiderate, at the very least.

Obtain a current copy of the annual Lancaster County tourist brochure before your visit. This includes maps, lists of attractions, and a calendar of events for the entire year as well as other useful information about lodging, restaurants, and shops. Free from: Pennsylvania Dutch Convention and Visitors Bureau, 501 Greenfield Road, Lancaster, Pennsylvania 17601, tel. (717) 299-8901.

Consider participating in the free farm tour sponsored by the Lancaster County Farmers Association each year on the weekend before Thanksgiving. Nine or ten different farmers open their farms to the public on both Saturday and Sunday afternoons. Although not normally listed in the annual brochure, information can be obtained from the Visitors Bureau after Labor Day.

◁ Day Eight

BEYOND THE BELTWAY—SUBURBAN DOWNTOWNS IN NORTHERN VIRGINIA

by John B. Fieser, *U.S. Department of Commerce;*
Truman A. Hartshorn, *Georgia State University;*
Peter O. Muller, *University of Miami, Coral Gables*

How have the suburbs recently transformed the American city? How can we make sense of the massive growth and development of suburban business activity since 1980? In this excursion the traveler will experience several quintessential types of suburban centers that now characterize the American metropolis. Our field trip offers an opportunity to understand the economic, geographical, and sociopolitical processes that have created these landscapes and view them at different stages in their development.

Tysons Corner is a testament to the spirit and success of unbridled private-sector entrepreneurial initiative in creating a new suburban downtown from scratch. Reston suggests another philosophy—that of the master-planned new town. The much younger and less developed Dulles Corridor is not yet as structured as either of the previous two centers, but provides insights and challenges of its own as an emerging commercial market. Fair Lakes illustrates yet another perspective; created by a single developer, this center has evolved with a flexible master plan that has benefited from the

Beyond the Beltway

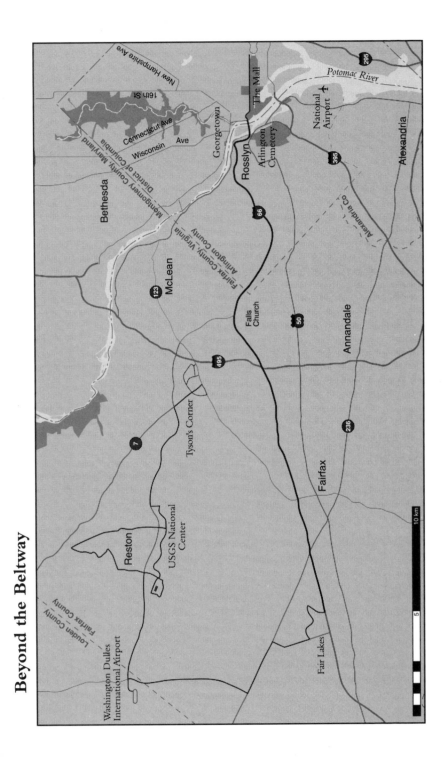

lessons learned from older projects in the region and elsewhere in the country.

Before we discuss the similarities and differences of each of these centers in greater detail, it is useful to place them in perspective. It is also useful to address our first question concerning the contribution of the suburbs to the restructuring of the American city, whether it be Washington, D.C., Los Angeles, or Atlanta. Let us first focus on the suburban transformation.

Metropolitan Restructuring

In the 1990s the polycentric city has unmistakably taken the place of the pre–World War II, single-centered urban region. A growing majority of the residents of metropolitan America now live and work beyond the central city line; more than one half of metropolitan voters in the United States reside in the suburbs. Two of three office employees find their work there. This phenomenal growth of the suburbs has occurred in response to the convergence of three overarching processes that have totally reshaped the form of the American city since 1970.

The first and most significant of these forces of change is the automobile and its servant, the interstate highway, whether it be a beltway, originally envisioned as a bypass highway, or a radial freeway leading to and from the old downtown. The automobile not only expanded the scale and scope of the city; it also assisted the transformation of the suburbs from single-purpose residential communities into full-fledged employment, shopping, and cultural centers offering a complete range of urban services.

The second force that nurtured and propelled suburban growth has been the burgeoning service economy associated with the maturation of the information age. The rapid growth of the office function and the expansion of producer services have outpaced the capacity of any one center in the city to house the metropolitan white-collar labor market. Producer services include legal, finance, accounting, insurance, and computer-service employment. These activities account for the largest source of demand by firms for office space, far outpacing the demand for headquarters space. Many corporations have expanded their demand for producer services in recent years: They hired out specific tasks to other firms as they grew, tasks became more specialized, and competitive pressures intensified. The office, in fact, has now become the factory of the information age.

The third and final linchpin influencing the phenomenal growth of the suburbs has been the robust private-sector–based entrepreneurial spirit that has characterized cities in the post–World War II era. This investment activity was promoted by the liberal availability of mortgage finance funds, favorable tax policies, and a prevailing laissez-faire market that welcomed this growth. Most of this expansion occurred in growing regional service centers that attracted white-collar employment expansion as opposed to traditional manufacturing cities, which did not benefit as much from the information-age boom.

The most visible and significant manifestation of this process of change during the last two decades of the twentieth century has been the emergence of the so-called suburban downtown. Suburban downtowns now rival and often surpass their central-city downtown forebears in terms of the quantity of corporate headquarters, office employment, and retail sales. These centers typically emerge at the intersections of beltways and radial highways, which give such nodes the same accessibility advantages formerly associated with the central-city downtown.

Nowhere in the eastern United States can the convergence of these three processes be more vividly seen on the landscape than in suburban Washington, D.C., especially in the Virginia suburbs. We visit four submarkets in Fairfax County that are superb examples of the impact of the automobile, the information age, and private-sector initiative in reshaping the city beyond the beltway. In each case suburban downtowns now exist or appear to be emerging in these areas as focal points for the surrounding urban realms they dominate. Together they form the basis of the polycentric city.

Suburban Downtowns

The suburban downtown may be the most significant and perhaps most lasting contribution to urban form of the twentieth-century American city. Earlier in the century, the downtown office tower was conspicuous on the landscape, as was the suburban regional mall in the 1960s. But today, it is the emerging suburban downtown that is capturing publicity. It is such a new phenomenon that little consensus exists as to how it should be defined or even what it should be called. For our purposes a suburban downtown includes the following minimal criteria:

□ A regional shopping center of 1 million square feet;
□ Three or more high-rise office buildings housing at least one Fortune 1,000 corporate headquarters or regional headquarters;
□ Office space of 5 million or more square feet;
□ Two or more major chain hotels with 400 or more rooms each; and
□ An employment base of 50,000 or more.

Others have called the suburban downtown a nucleation, an urban village, or a suburban activity center (Hartshorn and Muller, 1989). Geographer-journalist and *Washington Post* editor Joel Garreau, in his best-selling book on the topic, labels these forms edge cities. Garreau identifies sixteen of these edge cities around the Washington area, including eight in the Virginia suburbs.

The origins of most suburban downtowns can be traced to shopping centers or office parks that have become more attractive for additional growth as surrounding residential areas and markets have matured. Hartshorn and Muller developed a five-stage process model that describes the sequence of growth these centers typically experience:

□ Stage 1 Bedroom community
□ Stage 2 Independence
□ Stage 3 Catalytic growth
□ Stage 4 High-rise/high-technology
□ Stage 5 Mature town center

The Washington D.C. Market

The Washington metropolitan area, which numbers just under 4 million residents, has experienced several transformations in recent years. It is one of the most affluent and best-educated markets in the country and experienced steady growth during most of the present century. The 1990–1991 recession is a notable exception to that steady growth.

The growing federal government labor force traditionally provided the backbone for overall growth in and around Washington, but a phase-shift in employment shares in recent years now means that the private sector influences this labor market more directly today. As recently as the early 1970s, one in four jobs was supported by the federal payroll, whereas the number is one in six jobs today in the Washington market. This declining federal presence is a major reason the market is more susceptible to economic cycles today than in the past.

The burgeoning private-sector market in Washington in the 1980s yielded a demand for commercial office space in excess of 12 million square feet per year. Most of this growth occurred in Maryland and Virginia beyond the Capital Beltway. By 1990, the labor force grew to 2.2 million, a remarkable 37 percent increase over comparable 1980 figures. Suburban growth outside the District of Columbia has been more free-wheeling in the Virginia suburbs than in Maryland because of the stronger presence of planning and growth controls in Maryland. A larger share of development has also occurred at or near Metrorail stations in Maryland than in Virginia. Furthermore, federal investment in Maryland's suburbs occurred earlier than in comparable communities in Virginia. The National Institutes of Health in Bethesda, the National Institute of Standards and Technology in Gaithersburg, and the Food and Drug Administration in Rockville are cases in point. Dulles International Airport and the Dulles Access Road, completed in the early 1960s, represent the exception for Virginia. Built in a rural area of Loudoun County on Fairfax County's western flank, this complex was several decades ahead of its time as an international airport and economic-development generator.

Despite fast access to the city via the Dulles Access Road and Interstate 66, little development occurred along the Dulles Corridor to the west of Reston until the 1980s. Today, however, Dulles Airport facilities are functionally inadequate because the demand for additional capacity accelerated following airline deregulation in the early 1980s. Moreover, a land boom came to the immediate vicinity in the late 1980s just before the 1990–1991 recession slowed development to a snail's pace.

Development of Fairfax County

By any standard, the growth of Fairfax County in the past sixty years has been phenomenal, transforming the area from a rural agrarian economy to the leading edge of growth and development in the Washington region. Fairfax County became an important bedroom residential community for the central Washington labor market during the New Deal years, and the residential base of the county grew fourfold between 1930 and 1950. The first major shopping centers came to the county in the late 1950s, and Fairfax County tripled its population to 261,000 between 1950 and 1960.

The completion of the Capital Beltway in 1964 signaled a new era for development in the county. Zoning for more industrial acreage occurred first, followed by the demand for more office-based facilities and retail services. Many defense and high-technology firms also set up facilities in the area, some new to the region and others relocating from sites within the Beltway. The Tysons Corner area benefited enormously from these tenants, including Flow General (1963), Honeywell (1967), MITRE (1969), TRW (1970), Engineering Science (1972), PRC (1974), SDC (1975), BDM (1977), and Boeing (1979). The population of Fairfax County expanded to 454,000 by 1970 as a result of this employment growth in jobs and improved accessibility.

By the end of the 1980s, not only did the county boast many corporate headquarters and associated office functions, but it had become a high-technology powerhouse. Fully one third of its employment base is now high technology in nature, and the county houses about 700 firms focused on research and development, electronics, data processing, and consulting. Fairfax County's reputation as a high-tech corridor received additional support when the state of Virginia established the Center for Innovative Technology (CIT) in Dulles/Herndon (1984); the Software Productivity Consortium decided to co-locate with CIT (1986); and NASA selected Reston for the Jet Propulsion Laboratory/Manned Space Station Program (1987). Today, over half of the Fairfax population resides and works in the county—a far cry from its bedroom-community status of just a few years ago. More than half of the county's residents over twenty-five years of age are college graduates and are well prepared to participate in the local labor markets, which "are now fueled largely by the three C's—corporations, computers, and communication" (Bolan and Smart, 1991).

TYSONS CORNER

Tysons Corner's name derives from a rural crossroads near Vienna on the long-traveled Leesburg Pike (Virginia Route 7). At one time a gas station distinguished this intersection. But present-day Tysons Corner is a product of the accessibility provided by the Capital Beltway (I-495), the Dulles Access Road/Toll Road, and State Routes 7 (Leesburg Pike) and 123 (Chain Bridge Road). Once these transportation arteries were in place, speculators and property owners began assembling larger parcels for development. In the meantime commercial-strip development began along Routes 7 and 123, including automobile dealerships, gas stations, car repair services, hardware stores, and the like. Remnants of these earlier functions still remain, but most were gradually replaced in the 1970s and 1980s with more specialized office, hotel, and commercial functions, including specialty shopping complexes and upscale restaurants. Route 7 still serves as the main street of Tysons Corner.

Tysons Corner regional mall, built in 1968, ushered in a new stage of development for the area. In recognition of the rapid urbanization of the county, the first master plan for Fairfax was completed in 1974. Interestingly enough, Tysons Corner is not itself an incorporated community, nor does it have its own postal (zip) code. Rather, it is an unincorporated part of Fairfax County lying in three magisterial districts: Dranesville, Centreville, and Providence. In many metropolitan areas in the United States today, counties instead of municipalities provide the local governmental services in the suburbs—as is the case with Fairfax.

The residential base in the immediate vicinity of Tysons Corner remains relatively small, but within a fifteen-minute commute a large market exists. About 35,000 people live within a 2-mile radius of the center (five-minute commute), and 61,000 within 4 miles (ten-minute commute). The majority of the close-in residents occupy rental and condominium units. Some new luxury apartments have been constructed in recent years and many single-family units have succumbed to development pressure. An excellent county park system buffers many high-quality single-family residential areas from commercial uses. Examples include Scott Run, Stream Valley Park, Westgate Park, Raglan Road Park, and Freedom Hill Park.

The original regional mall at Tysons Corner, now called Tysons Corner Center, houses 1.9 million square feet of retail space and about 10,000 parking spaces on eighty-two acres. An extensive mall renovation completed in 1988 included the opening of its fourth and fifth anchor stores, Nordstrom and Lord & Taylor. This renovation also involved a $13 million private investment in road improvements. The original mall has now been loosely ringed by a collection of office-building complexes, hotels, and related services including restaurants, banks, and athletic clubs.

Learning from the past, the more recently developed Corporate Office Center at Tysons II opened in 1988 as an integrated mixed-use center incorporating retail, office, and hotel space in a unified setting. It is a more pedestrian-friendly and aesthetically pleasing center in terms of architectural design than its predecessor. The three-level Galleria Mall that anchors this center offers 1 million square feet of retail space including three department stores: Macy's, Saks Fifth Avenue, and Neiman Marcus. A luxury hotel (the Ritz Carlton) and an office tower complete the first phase of the project, which anticipates adding 300 townhouses, several more office towers, and a second hotel in the future.

The Tysons II shopping mall, with upscale Saks Fifth Avenue in the center of the photograph and Neiman Marcus in the foreground. Photograph by John B. Fieser.

Visitors to Tysons will also want to visit Fairfax Square, a small, upscale, mixed-use office/retail complex on eleven acres on Route 7 across from Tysons Corner Center, completed in 1990 and 1991. This facility features a rich finish of granite and gray reflective glass with retail uses at ground level capped by office space in a series of three buildings. Distinctive roof lines with peaked dormer windows distinguish the structures, which frame a courtyard paved with granite cobblestones. The prestige of the center is magnified by the presence of several premier retail boutiques including Hermes of Paris, Gucci America, Tiffany & Company, and La Cicogna, in addition to several high-cachet restaurants.

Aside from the retail function, the big story in Tysons today is the robust office market. It is now one of the leading office centers in the nation and the largest suburban office center on the East

*Tysons Corner office buildings, surrounded by their large parking lots.
Photograph by John B. Fieser.*

Coast, with over 20 million square feet of space. Office buildings
have sprouted all about this urban complex, separated by seas of
parking lots. This creates increasing difficulties in traffic movement not only at rush hour, but during the noon hour as local
employees, and others attracted to the center, seek a restaurant.
The visual impact of this scattered development and lack of architectural coordination is striking.

It is difficult to gain a sense of place in Tysons Corner due to the
complexity of development. No visual hierarchy seems readily
apparent. No gateways or formal entrances exist. Traffic improvements, structured parking, and more pedestrian amenities are being
incorporated, but make no mistake, the automobile rules at Tysons.
The nearest Metro stations to Tysons, at West Falls Church and
Dunn Loring, are more than 3 miles away, and only limited bus

service is available. A locally sponsored public-private partnership organization, TYTRAN, was established in 1981 to develop a shuttle-bus service for the Tysons area, but it did not attract significant ridership. The organization still runs a shuttle to the West Falls Church Metro station and serves a coordinating function among the many property owners, focusing on delivering such other necessary services as the first corporately sponsored child-care center in the area.

RESTON

Reston is a study in contrast to the unbridled growth ethic characteristic of Tysons Corner. It is sedate, ordered, and proper in the classic sense. There are gateways from the highway and curvilinear streets with wooded, earth berms screening clusters of residences, which themselves face inward with their backs to the street and away from the noise of traffic. Retail centers serve each of the villages and employment nodes are separate from the rest. There are lakes, schools, and recreation areas all carefully tied together. Even the names contribute to the feeling—Sunrise Valley Drive, Sunset Hills Road, South Lakes Drive. And most recently, a new Town Center has emerged to give a truly urban feeling to an otherwise relaxed community nestled in the woods.

Reston was planned this way from the beginning. This is hardly a place we would associate with the two leading oil companies, but indeed they developed the place—first Gulf, then more recently Mobil. Robert Simon, Jr., whose family owned Carnegie Hall in New York, was the visionary behind the master plan for Reston. As he set about acquiring Reston in 1961, Simon envisioned a community where housing could be clustered and open space preserved, thereby creating an urban feeling in a rural setting. He sought the best advice of planners and architects in drawing up plans for the infrastructure and design of a planned community on the 7,000-acre Sunset Hills estate he had purchased. But by 1967 his work, but not the plan, came to a halt in the face of potential bankruptcy due to the high front-end costs of building a city. Gulf Oil, previously a partner in the venture, came to the rescue. Later, in 1978, Mobil Oil purchased the remaining undeveloped land to

Reston's carefully planned Lake Anne Center, now close to thirty years old. Photograph by John B. Fieser.

see the community through its next stage of growth. Today, Mobil is still actively developing the community through its Reston Land Company subsidiary.

By 1962, appropriate zoning changes had been secured from Fairfax County and the first two residential communities in Reston began taking shape, complete with homeowners' associations to take responsibility for the care of the public space. Lake Anne Village, a townhouse community named for Simon's wife, sprang up around an artificial lake north of the Dulles Access Road. Simultaneously, Hunters Woods Village, a detached single-family housing complex, rose to the south. The first residents moved into Lake Anne in 1964 and the first golf course opened at about the same time.

At the dedication ceremony for Reston in 1966, Secretary of the Interior Stewart Udall announced that the U.S. Geological Survey (USGS) would build its new headquarters facility in Reston. Concurrently with that announcement, the fifth cluster of townhouses opened. By that time the county was clearly on its way to national prominence as both a prestigious residential and employment center.

Reston homes became instantly successful with their pastoral setting and the lure of expanding cultural and recreational programs to potential residents. Theater groups, music camps, nature programs, art programs, and sporting clubs helped create a prestigious reputation for the maturing quality of life in Reston. The residential population grew to 6,800 by 1970 and tripled to over 20,000 in 1973.

In Reston today there are about 18,500 occupied housing units and a population of about 55,000 living in five residential villages. The mix of units is approximately one-third detached, one-third attached, and one-third multifamily, with the last group split equally between rental and condominium units. Housing prices have appreciated steadily over the years. Smaller single-family units originally built for $120,000 to $140,000 now bring over $200,000, larger single-family estate homes bring $600,000 or more, and cluster homes sell in the $200,000 to $400,000 range.

Accelerated growth in the Reston business community began in 1984 with the opening of the expanded Dulles Toll Road that paralleled the original Dulles Access Road built in the 1960s. By

Selected Reston Business Centers

Name/Size	Representative firms
The Branches (25-acre office park)	Apple Computer, American College of Radiology
Campus Commons (Corporate and R&D space in four buildings of 500,000 square feet)	USAA Eastern Regional Headquarters, First American Data Service
Cascades Executive Center (15-acre office park)	The Connection Newspapers
Center of Educational Associations (27-acre wooded campus)	Headquarters for several educational associations
Commerce Executive Park (27-acre office park)	Centel, Federal Express, Allstate Insurance, Eastern Regional Hdqtrs.
Isaac Newton Square (33-acre office/R&D facility)	NOVA USA telecommunications, National Park Service
Lake Fairfax Business Center (82-acre office park)	Grumman, Federal Home Loan Mortgage Corp.
The Newspaper Center	American Newspapers Publishers Association and 14 other newspaper organizations
Park Ridge Center (46-acre office park)	NASA, Fairfield Aerospace, Siemens, Boeing Computer Services
The Summit at Reston	U.S. Sprint East Coast Hdqtrs., DynCorp International Hdqtrs.
U.S. Geological Survey (1,000,000-square-foot facility)	America's largest earth science and water resource agency

Source: *Reston Business,* Reston Land Corporation, Reston , Va., 1991.

vastly improving accessibility along this expressway corridor, the new superhighway stimulated a dramatic boom in Reston as an employment center. In 1982 the area had 3 million square feet of office space; the total jumped to over 12 million square feet by the end of the 1980s. Much of this office capacity was built in an office-park setting along the boulevards paralleling each side of the Dulles Access Road. The office-park setting was overwhelmingly preferred by the developers. The table lists major business clusters in Reston.

Reston is now Virginia's second largest business center, after Tysons. In recent years, over 500,000 square feet of office space have been absorbed annually. Over 2,000 firms in Reston employ a labor force of more than 34,000. A *Fortune 500* firm, LaFarge, now lists a Reston headquarters address. High-technology firms, professional association offices, and regional offices characterize most of the local office market. Several prominent office functions moved into the impressive new Town Center office towers when they opened in 1990, ushering in a newly mature phase of development for the Reston market.

RESTON TOWN CENTER

The last piece in the original Reston plan developed by Simon became a reality in 1990 with the opening of the Town Center. The first phase of this urban core is a mixed-use center on twenty acres, including twin eleven-story office buildings that face Fountain Plaza, an open courtyard that serves as a civic center with its outdoor artwork, public seating, and ice-skating rink in winter. Occupants of Town Center offices include Rolls-Royce, Host International, Molson Breweries USA, and Learning Tree International. A 500-room Hyatt Regency hotel flanks the space along with a traditional row of specialty retail shops and restaurants. A distinct feature of the Town Center is its grid-street pattern, a marked contrast to the curvilinear roads elsewhere in Reston. The pedestrian spine along Market Street is unusually lively for an outdoor retail center without a traditional department-store anchor. In its place, a multi-screen movie theater and an international market draw in customers, as do upscale restaurants.

Town Center, only two years old, and Reston's new commercial core.
Photograph by John B. Fieser.

A recent report states that "at completion, the Urban Core is planned to contain a total of 2.15 million square feet of office space, 315,000 square feet of retail area, 1,200 hotel rooms, and 600 units of housing" (Urban Land Institute, Project Reference File, Reston Town Center, 1991). Other cultural facilities in the center include a library, art gallery, government center, child-care facility, and an adjacent hospital.

DULLES CORRIDOR

The Dulles Access Road and State Route 28 corridors to the west of Reston in the vicinity of Dulles International Airport experienced a commercial awakening during the growth boom that overtook the area in the 1980s. Several large, upscale, mixed-use facilities were envisioned, but those that have reached completion stand alone as islands of development in an otherwise predominantly rural environment. That is not to say that property has not been assembled into larger tracts and the infrastructure for development does not exist. In fact, many kilometers of frontage roads and highway improvements have materialized.

A prime example of a landscape in transition that became frozen in time occurs in the Dulles Corner complex. A large AT&T office tower and Hyatt hotel sit in one corner of an otherwise vacant mixed-use complex. This is a classic example of development stalled by the recession of the early 1990s. The grass stubble and the names of the roads suggest a bygone rural era—Frying Pan Road and Horse Pen Road—but one that has not yet succumbed to the urbanization process as far as a skyline is concerned.

A public-private partnership in the form of a special tax district funded the widening of Route 28 in this area in the late 1980s to six lanes, but projected tax revenues and traffic volumes have not materialized because development has ceased. The local landowner share of the bill, originally set at 80 percent to be paid back over thirty years as a special tax, appears to be in jeopardy.

The boom times of the 1980s produced overly optimistic estimates of tax revenues that are not materializing in the recession of the 1990s. Officials say millions of taxpayer

The AT&T complex at Dulles Corner, overlooking Dulles International Airport. Photograph by John B. Fieser.

dollars may have to be used to make the $11 million annual debt payments. The money would come from the state's annual highway construction budget for Northern Virginia, a move that could delay or shelve other road projects. (Anderson, 1991)

Commercial real-estate values are dropping faster in western Fairfax County than in the rest of the county, adding to the problem because the tax is based on the assessed value of projects. Even steeper real-estate declines are anticipated in the Loudoun County (western) portion of the 14,000-acre tax district that straddles Route 28.

Several speculative "see-through" buildings along the corridor—so named for their high vacancy rates—speak volumes for the weakness of the office market in the area. Nonetheless, there are some success stories in this market, especially for high technology, back offices, and warehousing facilities.

The Dulles Corridor is also known for its dramatic architecture and not just for the famous swooping roof line of the main Dulles terminal, designed by the architectural firm of Eero Saarinen & Associates. The "black wedge" building on the north side of the Dulles Access Road when approaching the airport is most striking. Officially known as the Center for Innovative Technology, this structure looks as if it were just dropped from the sky.

Other remnants of the "old" Virginia economy still exist along Route 28 as well. The Sully Plantation Park with its split-rail fence and traditional buildings recalls a bygone era that may not be so old after all. Loudoun County to the west, for example, still boasts many horse farms.

Another major issue facing planners and citizens in this part of Fairfax County revolves around the "down-zoning" of property along Route 28. The Fairfax County Board of Supervisors passed a down-zoning ordinance for the area in 1989 and the bill was upheld in the Virginia Supreme Court in 1991, but some former "slow-growth" commissioners, including the board chairperson, were also defeated in 1991. Developers, of course, have been unhappy with the development restrictions, and a reversal of pol-

The Dulles Corridor's Center for Innovative Technology, typical of striking suburban architecture that quickly become local landmarks. Photograph by John B. Fieser.

icy may occur in the future, but that was a moot point as 1992 began because of market conditions and the oversupply of existing office space in the market.

FAIR LAKES

The fourth and final commercial core we visit is the Fair Lakes center. This property was purchased in 1978 and zoning was approved by the county for its development in 1984. In order to eliminate land debt, about 500 acres of the original 1,100-acre purchase was sold at the beginning of the development process. A major sale ($25 million) to TRW for a Washington-area headquarters office building financed the infrastructure for the planned community. To date, the complex is about 60 percent developed, with 1.8 million square feet of office space, a 316-room Hyatt hotel, and 1,200 residential units.

The lakes in this development assist the retention of drainage and runoff within the complex. A filtration system cleanses the runoff, which is minimized by the heavily landscaped and wooded nature of the project. Only 25 percent of the area will be developed, and a balance between office and residential space must be maintained to minimize negative transportation and environmental impacts.

This complex is a part of a much larger 5,600-acre Fairfax Center Special Development District,

> formed by a public-private partnership to avoid the uncontrolled sprawl affecting high-growth areas of the Washington, D.C. region. A baseline zoning level was established for all parcels in the area. To build above the baseline, a developer has to make a contribution for off-site roads and provide amenities such as open space, landscaping, lighting, plazas, and parks to mitigate the affects of additional growth. (Urban Land Institute, *Deals on Wheels,* 1991)

The plan also identified a cash contribution amenity improvement level for each parcel and a road contribution level for each type of use—residential, office retail, and hotel. This sophisticated approach has worked well and contributed to the prestige of the community.

Itinerary

As we leave Metro Center in the heart of Washington, D.C. (mile 0), we proceed to Tenth Street and drive down Constitution Avenue toward the Potomac River. We cross the Potomac River on the Theodore Roosevelt Bridge; then we will proceed west on I-66 (Custis Memorial Parkway). Notice the wall of high-rise office buildings on the left in *Rosslyn*. The gleaming rounded front of the *USA Today* communications building and its next-door twin symbolizes the strength of the office market on this side of the Potomac in Virginia, which is not subject to the building height restrictions of the District of Columbia. This commercial center is part of Arlington County, which was originally a part of the District, but was ceded back to Virginia as surplus property in 1846. Georgetown and Georgetown University are directly across the Potomac. Georgetown and Alexandria, Virginia, long predate the planned city of Washington.

Proceeding west on I-66 (mile 4), the freeway climbs through a series of marine terraces formed during interglacial periods. Upon entering Fairfax County just west of Falls Church, about 7 miles beyond the Roosevelt Bridge, we are on the gently rolling Piedmont itself. In Tysons Corner we skirt Gantt Hill, which rises approximately 155 meters (510 feet) above sea level. Farther west, in the vicinity of Dulles Airport, the elevation of the Piedmont drops to about 90 meters (300 feet). We again climb to about 120 meters (400 feet) in the Fair Lakes vicinity. At our first stop at Tysons Corner we can look northeast across the landscape to the Maryland suburbs, viewing the skyline profile to the north of Washington across the unseen Potomac Valley.

Our westward route on I-66 carries us on the old right-of-way of the now-defunct Washington and Old Dominion (W&OD) Railway (1859 to 1968), on the alignment of the old Lee Highway (U.S. 29/211), on old Arlington Street segments, and through

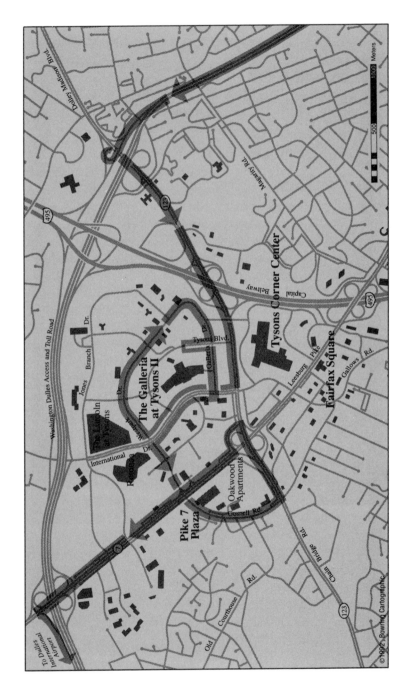

former vacant land. Most of the railway right-of-way also now serves as the greater part of a heavily used 45-mile paved trail/bicycle path that extends to exurban Purcellville, Virginia, on the western fringe of the urban region near the Blue Ridge Mountains. We will later cross the trail/bicycle path several times in Reston.

The Metrorail line to Vienna (Orange line) emerges from a tunnel at Ballston (mile 7) and then follows an alignment down the median of the I-66 expressway. As we pass by, we can glimpse two stations in this area, East Falls Church and West Falls Church (mile 11). Beyond the latter point the expressway and rail line both curve to the southwest while we swing to the northwest toward Tysons Corner.

On this leg of the trip we leave I-66 and take the Dulles Access Road to Chain Bridge Road, which passes under the Capital Beltway. Just outside the Beltway (mile 14), Tysons Corner Center lies to the left and Tyson II to the right. Note that we are suddenly in a very specialized commercial area. There is no formal gateway or ceremonial entrance to Tysons Corner. Turning right on International Drive, we circle around Tysons II (mile 16) to our first stop.

Our stop is by the Neiman Marcus parking deck. We leave the vehicle and proceed upstairs to the top level to view the complex. Note the distant skyline of the Maryland suburbs to the east. Whereas the District's Washington Monument is obscured to the right, to the left are development clusters at Friendship Heights, Bethesda, Rockville, and beyond as one looks northward. The famous Bethesda Naval Medical Center Tower is just visible to the left (north) of the Bethesda cluster. The Saks Fifth Avenue department store anchors the far end of the Tysons II mall. Office towers of Tysons Corner to the north and west envelop the Gantt Hill area. Returning to our vehicle, we proceed around to Westpark Drive, where we turn left. The Rotunda apartments are to the right. Note the dominance of surface parking lots in the Tysons complex. Circling the NADA office tower, we have a good view of strip development along State Route 7, including hotels, automobile dealerships, and service stations. This is where the old and new Tysons meet. Low-rise functions are being replaced by high-rise ones. Crossing Route 7 (Leesburg Pike), we see some evidence of residential buyouts on the right. Back on Chain Bridge Road we see unorthodox suburban commercial architecture on the left. Proceeding northwest on Leesburg Pike, we enter the Dulles Toll Road (mile 20) (outer lanes, which parallel the original Dulles Access Highway inner lanes).

This gently rolling suburban landscape is vintage Fairfax County. It is filled with middle- and upper-middle-income residential communities. Amenities in the area include parks, country clubs, the trail/bicycle path previously discussed, and most notably world-famous *Wolf Trap Park* for the performing arts. This complex includes an outdoor performing arts pavilion seating over 3,000 people under a roof and another 4,000 on adjacent lawns. This dramatically styled facility built of wood is the premier summer theater and concert facility in the Baltimore-Washington-Richmond segment of the megalopolis conurbation. We proceed to the Hunter Mill Road exit at the eastern edge of Reston.

Turning left, we cross the Dulles Access Road/Tollway (mile 24), and then turn right on Sunrise Valley Drive, which parallels the expressway corridor. To the north (between the Dulles Corridor and Sunrise Valley Drive) several campus-like office parks blanket the landscape. To the south is the South Lakes Village community, which has been built up around Lake Thoreau and Lake Audubon. Hunters Woods Village is also in this *South Reston* region. South Reston is largely built-out today, with about 3,000 single-family homes, 3,700 townhomes, and 3,600 multifamily units, a mix that parallels that of Reston as a whole. Several schools and convenience retail centers serve this area, along with the eighteen-hole Reston Golf Course and a community center with an indoor pool, arts-and-crafts studios, and a fully equipped theater. Note the contrast between the restrained form and design of Reston and the more free-wheeling development of Tysons Corner.

The first office-park complex on the right, *Park Ridge Center,* sets the tone for what is to come in high technology and white-collar employment facilities in Reston. This forty-six-acre office park includes four buildings with 500,000 square feet of space, and two more buildings are planned. This complex is a veritable global Who's Who of aerospace and computer firms. Primary tenants include NASA, the European Space Agency, the National Space Development Agency of Japan, Fairchild Aerospace, Siemens, Boeing Computer Services, and Horizon Data Corporation.

Among the other important business communities we pass on this boulevard is *The Branches,* a twenty-five-acre wooded office park that houses many more high-technology firms and national association headquarters including Spot Image, Inc., Upjohn Healthcare Services, Inc., the American Medical Students Association, the American College of Radiology, and the National Pharmaceutical Council.

There are too many separate business centers along this corridor to mention individually, but the essential pattern to be aware of is the clustering of related firms, whether it be educational associations, newspaper organizations, research and development facilities, high technology, aerospace, defense, or computer firms. Together these firms provide a distinctive niche for the Reston labor force in the Washington metropolis.

After crossing Reston Avenue we enter the *U.S. Geological Survey* (USGS) campus (mile 28). This 1 million-square-foot sprawling office complex houses North America's largest earth-sciences and water-resources information agency, the United States' largest civilian mapping agency, and the largest earth-sciences library in the western hemisphere. At its Reston headquarters USGS employs 2,500 persons. This facility was the first major employer to locate in Reston (the announcement of the decision to locate here was made in 1965). The architects for the striking building were Skidmore, Owings, and Merrill. Most of the land for the 100-acre site was donated by developer Robert Simon, Jr., who also promised at the time to build inexpensive housing for USGS employees in Reston.

After leaving the USGS campus, we turn left onto Reston Avenue and right onto Sunrise Valley Road, retracing our route to Wiehle Avenue, where we turn left to cross the Toll Road/Access Road. We then cross Sunset Hills Road and the W&OD Railroad trail/bikeway, passing *Isaac Newton Square* on the left. This was the first industrial/commercial complex in Reston, dating back to the mid-1960s. These two-story sprawling business park buildings are slated for replacement by mid-rise buildings in the future.

We now approach the *Lake Anne Village* residential community and pass over the dam of the lake of the same name. This was Reston's first community and remains its best known and most picturesque. The retail center that we pass on the left was built as a part of the complex and is relatively isolated, lacking exposure to the major access street, Baron Cameron Avenue. This has limited its success, a situation rectified in Reston's more recently built retail villages, which offer more direct street exposure. Crossing Baron Cameron Avenue, we enter the newest of Reston's villages, *North Point* (mile 33). We pass the Reston Visitors' Center on the right, a good source of current literature on the community.

As we proceed north on North Village Road, we see narrower streets and large homes which can only be accessed by feeder roads and which have reverse frontages to the street that give a cozier, more private feeling to this community. A wetlands mitigation project is under way in this area of emerging homes and community facilities that include pools, schools, and a picnic pavilion.

Using Wiehle and Baron Cameron avenues, we turn left on Reston Avenue. Note Hechinger's home improvement store on the right. After passing Reston's hospital complex on the right, we turn right into the *Town Center* (mile 37). This is our second stop. Take a short walk through this exciting pedestrian-friendly commercial center. The Town Center of Reston is now the mixed-use hub and focal point for the immediate region, complete with a 514-room Hyatt Regency Hotel, 500,000 square feet of office space, and 245,000 square feet of retail space, anchored by a multiscreen theater and international food market. The grand opening of the Town Center took place in October 1990.

The spine of the area is *Market Street,* an automobile and pedestrian corridor flanked by twin office buildings facing Fountain Square and an open entertainment space used for concerts in the summer and ice skating in the winter. The headquarters of Rolls Royce USA and Molson Breweries are here, along with the offices of the Reston Land Corporation, developers of Reston. Eventually this present-day twenty acres of development will become an eighty-five-acre Urban Core. Flexible zoning will allow for more office, hotel, and high-rise residential uses in the future as the market matures. The grid-iron street pattern of this commercial center contrasts strongly with the curvilinear pattern used throughout residential Reston. A very expensive finish occurs on all surfaces in the Town Center whether it be sidewalks, fountains, street furniture, ornamentation, or lobby spaces. This quality of appointments is rare in any community today.

Return to Reston Avenue and then take the Dulles Access Road heading west toward Dulles Airport. The Herndon community is to the right, northwest of Reston. Much commercial development has taken place along the highway, including the offices of the Center of Innovative Technology located in a highly visible, dark-glass-encased, wedge-shaped building on the right. This is the beginning of the Dulles Corridor complex.

We complete a loop through the *Dulles Airport* terminal area (mile 44). Note the huge parking lot in front of the complex. Much more parking is unseen beyond. The main terminal building is woefully inadequate for the air-passenger volume it now handles. Its intriguing roofline makes it one of the most striking and distinctive terminals in the world. It will be extended soon, as envisioned by its designer. In the meantime, facilities have been expanded in the midfield area.

Note that we crossed into Loudoun County when we entered the airport property. The county line cuts diagonally across the airport property with the bulk of the airport located in Loudoun County. Leaving the airport we proceed south on State Route 28 (Sully Road). This highway forms the eastern boundary of Dulles Airport, hence the lack of development on the west side to our right. To the east (left) development occurs sporadically, as is typical in a corridor on the leading edge of development. Nevertheless, the infrastructure is in place to handle more expansion once the recession that began in 1990 is over. A good case in point is the mixed-use Dulles Corner complex on the left. We drive through this facility by turning left on Frying Pan Road and left again on Horse Pen Road (mile 48). Only the far north end of the area has been developed to date, even though utilities are in place. Currently, the complex contains only a Hyatt hotel and an AT&T office cluster. Buildings caught under constructon by the recession have been completed, but no further construction is under way.

Returning to State Route 28 we proceed south to U.S. Route 50 (Lee-Jackson Memorial Highway). Note *Sully Plantation* to the left. The *Washington Redskins NFL football team training facility* is also to the left, farther back. The back-office and research-and-development nature of this corridor is illustrated by the EDS facility and the Grumman, NEC, GTE, and Hallmark buildings. Farther south on Route 28, development becomes less intense and warehouse/business park uses become more dominant.

Turning east (left) on Route 50, we enter the Chantilly community. Strip commercial development oriented to automobile access characterizes this area. It is like Tysons Corner Route 7 was twenty years ago. Turning right on Stringfellow Road, we proceed south to the Fair Lakes entrance passing Chantilly High School on the left along with its many temporary classrooms in mobile-home-type trailers.

Turning left on Fair Lakes Parkway, we enter *Fair Lakes* (mile 59), a master-planned mixed-use community that emerged during the 1980s growth boom. It represents the best thinking of planners in recent years in terms of protecting the environment; preserving open space; encouraging dense development that will minimize sprawl; and using joint public–private participation in the provision of infrastructure, including roads, utilities, and recreational facilities. Note the broad expanse of the parkways and the positioning of buildings with deep setbacks in a wooded setting, occasionally interrupted by scenic lakes and open space.

We then turn right on Fairfax County Parkway and east on Interstate 66. After about a mile, we pass *Fair Oaks Mall* on the left, which is wedged into the apex formed by the intersection of I-66 and U.S. Route 50. Fair Oaks Mall is one of the two major regional shopping centers serving most of Fairfax County. Of course, Tysons Corner is the other.

We are now on I-66 proceeding eastward back to Washington with Fair Oaks Mall to our left. We pass by the Vienna Metrorail station (mile 62) in the center of the expressway near the Nutley Street interchange. This station is the western terminus of the radial Washington Metrorail system's Orange line. The rail line runs down the median of the interstate highway until going underground at Ballston. We pass the Dunn Loring station (mile 70) just before crossing the I-495 Capital Beltway and soon approach the West Falls Church Station where we veered off to the north on our outbound trip. We now retrace our outbound route, heading back to the Potomac River into Washington D.C. and ending back at Metro Center (mile 82).

Geomorphology of the Maryland Piedmont

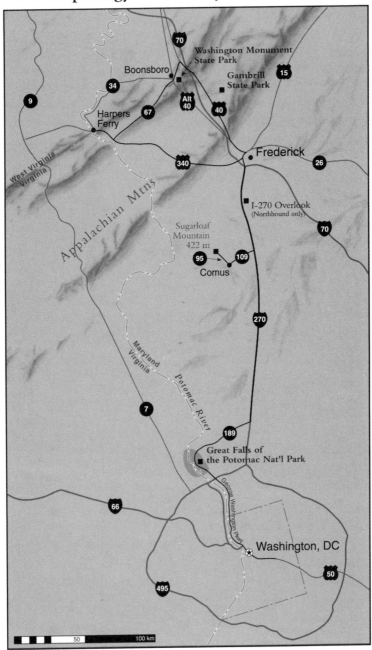

◿ Day Nine

SCENIC GEOMORPHOLOGY OF MARYLAND'S PIEDMONT AND BLUE RIDGE

by Harold A. Winters, *Michigan State University*

Those not familiar with this area's overall topography and geology should read the sections on "The Terrain" and "Important River Characteristics" in Day Six entitled "Geography and the Civil War—The Eastern Theater and Gettysburg." The sites described below are organized for a day trip from Washington, D.C., but their order may be rearranged without disadvantage for the convenience of a traveler starting out or finishing at another place. The objective of this excursion is, on the basis of observations at several especially scenic sites, to provide a comprehensive understanding of the terrain in Maryland's Piedmont and Blue Ridge Mountains.

Great Falls Park and the Potomac River Gorge

Proceed to *Great Falls Park* on the Virginia (south) side of the *Potomac River* about 18 kilometers (11 miles) northwest of downtown *Washington, D.C.* At the Visitor Center obtain a copy of the National Park Service's Official Map and Guide. More detailed walking-trail logs for numerous features on both sides of the river

Block diagram of the Washington-Baltimore region showing physiographic provinces and geographic and geologic features.

plus useful information on the geology and forests of the area are contained in U.S. Geological Survey Bulletin 1471 (1980) by Reed et al. entitled *The River and the Rocks*. From the Visitor Center, walk about 300 meters south along the river-bluff trail to the *second* overlook.

The land east of the Blue Ridge Mountains in Maryland may be divided into two distinctly different physiographic provinces: the Atlantic Coastal Plain to the east and the Piedmont to the west. The higher stream-dissected Piedmont consists of rolling hills underlain by ancient, relatively strong, crystalline rocks that reveal several phases of intense crustal deformation and igneous activity. In contrast, the Atlantic Coastal Plain is underlain by undeformed

Drowned ice-age
channel now filled
with silt and clay

younger and weaker strata that dip gently toward the sea. Altogether these form a great wedge of eastward-thickening sediments that was originally derived from erosion on the Piedmont and Appalachian Mountains. In addition to its scenic beauty and historical importance, the gorge before you is significant for two reasons. First, it is an important component in the boundary relationship between the Atlantic Coastal Plain and the Piedmont. Second, it clearly reveals some primary aspects of the area's bedrock geology.

The highly fractured yet relatively strong igneous (granite and lamprophyre) and metamorphic (schist, metagraywacke, and amphibolite) rocks here are typical for much of the eastern Piedmont. Mineral composition in the schists and the presence of granite make it evident that these rocks formed deep within the Earth's crust. Radiometric dating and regional relationships indicate that the ages for the formations range from about 365 million to more than 550 million years.

About 300 million years ago internal forces lifted the area above sea level. Since then, persistent weathering and erosion have tended to level the land as it was pushed upward. As a result, rocks that were formerly tens of kilometers beneath the surface are now exposed at many places in the Piedmont, their presence providing a basis for estimating the amount of uplift and erosion that has occurred here in the last 300 million years. Such vast degradation of the land must also have resulted in a great amount of deposition that is at least partially revealed in thick sequences of sedimentary rocks both to the west in the Appalachians and to the east beneath the Atlantic Coastal Plain.

The removal of weathered material from the Piedmont has been achieved largely by running water that transported material by solution, suspension, and movement of bed load. It is estimated that the river transports about 1 million metric tons of dissolved material and approximately 1.5 million metric tons of clastics through this gorge annually. Comparison of these figures with the size of the river's drainage basin upstream from the falls indicates that each year an average of 80 metric tons of material is removed per square kilometer, although this measure is by no means uniform across the area.

Since the break-up of Pangaea and the separation that led to the formation of the Atlantic Ocean, the drainage of the eastern United States evolved to form a number of southeast-flowing streams, with the Potomac River one of the largest. Its headwaters far to the west, this river has cut large water gaps through the Blue Ridge at both *Harpers Ferry* (described elsewhere in this chapter) and *Point of Rocks*. It then continues southeastward to traverse all of the Piedmont and cross onto rocks of the Atlantic Coastal Plain at the *Arlington Memorial Bridge*.

In its final approach to the lower surface of the Atlantic Coastal Plain and sea level, the stream's gradient becomes greater than at any other place on the Piedmont. Narrowing abruptly as it enters *Mather Gorge* and dropping about 12 meters (40 feet) in less than 200 meters (650 feet), the average velocity increases markedly.

Furthermore, the rate of flow and associated turbulence becomes even greater with the increased volume that accompanies flooding, which is a common annual event. During these high-water stages the river is especially effective at removing and transporting more and larger material while also scouring the fractured bedrock through abrasion by transported clastics.

As a measure of volume variability, the stream's average annual flow is about 350,000 liters per second, but this figure may be less than 40,000 during a dry summer and more than 40 million during a larger flood. The record floods of 1936, 1942, and 1972 inundated the parking lot and Visitor Center area here, and it is not uncommon for water to rise within 5 meters (16 feet) of this overlook. A nearby monument shows the highest water level for record floods (photographers may wish to position themselves so that both the distant falls and the nearby flood-marking monument appear in the same picture). Another less quantitative but quite vivid measure of flood levels and their effects is the height of the boundary between the vegetated and bare-bedrock areas adjacent to the river.

Thus, the combination and interaction of ancient rock, complex structures, tectonic uplift, long-term weathering, deep erosion, and stream processes have produced a zone of falls and rapids that has gradually migrated upstream to its present position, known as the Fall Line (or Fall Zone). Similar conditions exist at equivalent positions along a number of larger streams traversing the Piedmont. Although especially obvious along the Delaware, Susquehanna, Rappahannock, and James rivers, there is no better example of such geomorphic relationships than here at the Great Falls of the Potomac River.

Sugarloaf Mountain

Here, three high, easily accessible overlooks provide a marvelous panorama of the surrounding Maryland Piedmont and Catoctin Mountain to the west, which is an eastern range of the Blue Ridge. To get to the area take Exit 22 off I-270, proceed south on Maryland 109 (Old Hundred Road) about 5 kilometers (3 miles) to

Comus. In Comus turn right (west) and follow Comus Road about 3 kilometers (2 miles) to enter the *Sugarloaf Mountain Natural Area*. Follow the one-way winding blacktop road, and if time permits stop at the East View Overlook; otherwise proceed to the West View Overlook parking lot which is about 100 meters (330 feet) below Sugarloaf's summit. Here one may walk to the West View Overlook near the southwest corner of the parking lot or hike to the summit viewpoint for a higher but similar westward view.

To get to the summit area follow either the shorter but much steeper "Yellow" trail or take the longer but more gradual "Blue" pathway to a junction with the "Red" trail; then follow the red-marked trail to the overlook. Both trails start near the concession stand at the south end of the parking lot, and many hikers combine them for a more diverse experience.

Sugarloaf Mountain is a combination conservation/recreation area owned by a private organization, Stronghold, Inc. The area is open to the public at no charge 365 days a year from sunrise to sunset. Do not pick plants or disturb wildlife. Blemishing and removing rocks are prohibited. Fires, overnight camping, and alcohol are not permitted on the property.

The most common trees of the area are oaks belonging to the red and white groups, and more than 500 species of plants have been identified here. Deer are abundant, and birds include the pileated woodpecker, great horned owl, wild turkey, and red-shouldered hawk. Be observant when hiking because this area is inhabited by the *poisonous timber rattlesnake* and *copperhead*.

Sugarloaf's summit, 391 meters (1,282 feet), is about 250 to 275 meters (800 to 900 feet) higher than the surrounding upland surface of the Piedmont. Rather than a product of localized tectonics, the feature is an erosional remnant composed of quartzite that is much more resistant than the surrounding rocks. Often referred to as a "monadnock" in the past, it remains as a splendid example of lithologic and structural influences on landform development within an area that has experienced long-term weathering and erosion.

Although the structure of the "mountain" has been interpreted differently, overall relationships suggest that it is a complex north-east-plunging anticlinorium made up of many folds of varying magnitude including a large syncline in this southern section. The age of the Sugarloaf Mountain Quartzite is also somewhat controversial. Some believe that the formation was deposited during the Late Precambrian while other have concluded that it is Lower Cambrian. Furthermore, it has been proposed that it may be the equivalent to the Weverton Formation (described in a following section on *Gambrill State Park*) about 16 kilometers (10 miles) to the west, but differences in stratigraphy make such a correlation tenuous on the basis of present knowledge. Regardless of these questions, there is general agreement that the sand that formed this rock was originally deposited between 550 million and 850 million years ago with most favoring a younger rather than older age estimate.

It is important to note, however, that the topography here is very young in geological terms. This feature and all of the surrounding landscape, including the Blue Ridge Mountains to the west, are no older than Miocene, evolving through erosion with details established largely within the last five million years.

Rounded and smoothed surfaces, openings along fractures in the rock, and an abundance of large and small angular quartzite blocks forming talus (scree) provide clear evidence for past degradation of this extremely resistant rock. The widespread occurrence of slow-growing lichen on fallen rocks and large old trees soundly rooted on talus indicates that mass wasting is certainly not rapid at present. Yet freshly-broken rock is abundant in the area. All of these relationships suggest that rock shattering was accelerated by more severe climatic conditions induced by Pleistocene glacial events that deposited drift less than 200 kilometers (125 miles) to the north.

The remaining overlook is located along the descending section of the one-way road. It offers a fine view toward the south with the Potomac River about 7 kilometers (4 miles) away.

Scenic Overlook at I-270 Mile 28.5 (Northbound Only)

This easily accessible viewpoint of the *Frederick Lowland* vividly illustrates the difference between the eastern and western parts of the Piedmont in this part of Maryland. In fact the topographic variation is so great that some consider the Frederick Lowland a distinct physiographic unit.

The bedrock of the lowland is also quite different than that beneath the Piedmont to the south and east. Instead of a complex array of Late Precambrian and Lower Cambrian metasedimentary rocks (mainly gneiss, schist, metaconglomerate, quartzite, phyllite, and slate), the formations underlying the Frederick Lowland consist almost wholly of the Upper Cambrian Frederick Limestone, the Cambro-Ordovician Grove Limestone, and much younger Triassic Formations of the Newark Group. Collectively the two limestones along with the Triassic sediments are relatively weak, which accounts in large part for the lower elevation of the land's surface.

The presence and preservation of these less resistant rocks are largely the result of major movements along ancient high-angle faults that are located along both the west and east border of the lowland, with the latter in the foreground of this overlook. Relative movement along these faults, which occurred periodically over a long time-span, lowered the intervening rocks to produce a large and complex graben structure.

It is important to note, however, that the present-day lowland is not the direct result of the faulting, for that took place more than 150 million years ago. Instead, the Frederick Lowland is the end product of recent weathering and erosion on weaker rocks that were faulted into their present position long, long ago. Thus, although linear bluffs, such as those at this overlook, exist along the fault zones marking the boundaries of the graben, their presence is not the result of crustal subsidence. Instead the escarpments are the result of differential erosion that has, at some places, exhumed long-inactive tectonic structures.

Triassic Redbeds and Fanglomerate in Frederick, Maryland

Proceed to the parking lot behind the *Pier One Imports* retail store on the south side of U.S. 40, about 3 kilometers (2 miles) west of

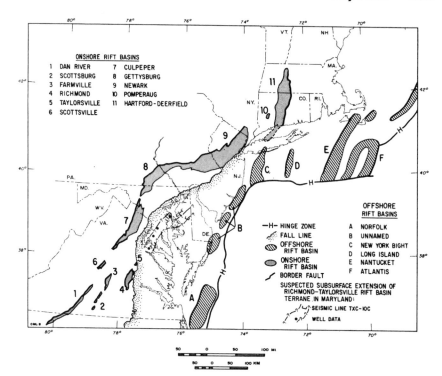

Map of the Middle Atlantic area showing distribution of exposed rift basins, buried rift-basin rocks in Maryland, and off-shore rift basins. Source: H. J. Hansen, Geology 16 *(1988): 779–782.*

downtown *Frederick*. Here are two outcrops to be examined: one at the southwest corner of the parking lot at the rear of the store and the second in the landscaped area at the front of the establishment. Be sure to ask the store manager for permission to examine the exposures, and make sure that no one hammers on the rocks or tramples the plantings.

To appreciate the significance of these outcrops it is important to know that some of the faulting related to the Frederick Lowland took place during the Triassic Period, an episode lasting from about 245 million to 208 million years ago. At that time this part of ancestral North America was above sea level and in the tropics. The faulting, associated with the break-up of Pangaea, produced numerous rift valleys (linear, down-faulted lowlands). One of the largest of these extended southwestward from what is now northern New Jersey through this part of Maryland.

Numerous streams transported weathered terrestrial sediment from adjacent uplands into the rift valley; these then accumulated on the much older Grove and Frederick limestone discussed previously. The bulk of the Triassic sediment is clay and silt derived almost wholly from the east; this was deposited as mud in flood plains, swamps, and lakes within the lowland. Through time these fine-textured sediments were compacted into shale and siltstone known as "red beds" because of their distinct color, which is also revealed in the area's soil.

At some places sand and gravel were also deposited in the form of coalescing alluvial fans. Derived from the west and extending a short distance eastward, these sediments are limited in extent but impressive where exposed. This type of deposit is known as fanglomerate, a term that combines lithologic and topographic characteristics.

Both types of Triassic rock may be seen in outcrops near Pier One Imports. The "red beds," consisting of shale and siltstone, crop out on the southwest side of the parking lot to the rear of the building. These strata are known to dip gently westward and provide evidence for modest post-depositional tectonic movement that most likely occurred during Late Triassic–Early Jurassic time.

The fanglomerate is well exposed at a lower level in front of the store. Here larger clasts are embedded in a matrix of red calcareous sandy silt. Angular and sub-rounded limestone pebbles derived form the Grove and Frederick limestone are abundant, their shapes indicating that they did not travel far before being deposited. Etching can be seen on some of the pebbles, and lapies (a general term for solution grooves, commonly separated by knifelike ridges) exist along the contact with the overlying "red beds," both evidence for solution of calcareous matter. When quarried, cut, and polished, this becomes an impressive decorative stone. Known as "Potomac Marble," it has been used in many eastern buildings including the *Library of Congress.*

Gambrill State Park and Catoctin Mountain

This park is about 5 kilometers (3 miles) west of *Frederick*. Access is northbound from U.S. 40 via Gambrill State Park Road. Follow the road to the top of the ridge, make a sharp left (south) turn, and proceed to the turn-around-loop parking area. Walk to the west overlook.

The Blue Ridge Mountains of Maryland are by no means uniform in terms of rock type, structure, and topography. Commencing about 10 kilometers (6 miles) north of *Gambrill State Park* the range consists of a massive upland, 8 to 16 kilometers (5 to 10 miles) wide, that extends northward into Pennsylvania. In that area the overall structure is an anticlinorium with numerous tectonic complexities; as a result a wide variety of rocks are exposed. Aside from two rugged passes, one east of Waynesboro, another east of Chambersburg, this part of the Blue Ridge is high and rough enough to present a formidable barrier to east-west movement.

About 20 kilometers (12 miles) to the south of this location, along Maryland's southern boundary marked by the Potomac River, the Blue Ridge consists of three prominent north-south-trending ridges. The two to the west, known as *South Mountain* and *Elk Ridge,* are separated by the relatively narrow *Pleasant Valley.* The third ridge, *Catoctin Mountain,* lies about 10 kilometers (6 miles) to the east across the southern continuation of the *Middletown Valley.* All three of these ridges have water gaps eroded by the southeast-flowing Potomac River, openings that have long facilitated east-west transportation and communication.

Movement across the Blue Ridge is less obstructed here than at most other places, favoring the establishment of the westward-trending National Road (now *Alternate 40*) early in this country's history.

The overall geologic structure related to Catoctin Mountain, South Mountain, and the Middletown Valley is that of a large, asymmetrical, overturned anticline. Over millions of years the crest of that huge fold has been eroded away to expose a central area of relatively weak Precambrian metabasalt, gneiss, and granodiorite. These rocks have been removed to a lower level than adjacent layers of more resistant quartzite that underlie the flanking ridges, Catoctin and South Mountains. Intriguingly, these relationships produce a lowland directly over an anticline, which is a classic example of an inverse relationship between rock structure and topography. The ridges east and west of the Middletown Valley are composed of overlying and younger rocks of the Chilhowee Group, most notably the especially strong quartzitic Weverton Formation. These resistant rocks, generally believed to have formed during the Early Cambrian but possibly of latest Precambrian age, are well exposed here at the west overlook.

South Mountain on the horizon to the west (the next site on this itinerary) and Catoctin Mountain with its Gambrill State Park are both composed of the same formation; and because the rock is so resistant, it forms two homoclinal ridges associated with the limbs of a large but deeply eroded anticline. Here on the east flank of the anticline, strata of the Weverton Formation are right-side-up and dip twenty to thirty degrees east. Where viewed as an east-west profile, slightly gentler slopes extend eastward to Frederick while the steeper inclines are westward toward the Middletown Valley.

The altitude at the park is about 450 meters above sea level (1,500 feet), or about 340 meters (100 feet) higher than the Frederick Lowland and 280 meters (900 feet) above the Middletown Valley. North of Gambrill State Park maximum elevations of Catoctin Mountain increase to 500 to 550 meters above sea level (1,600 to 1,800 feet), but southward these decrease markedly as the ridge gradually loses all prominence south of the Potomac River.

Washington Monument State Park and South Mountain

Access to this park is via Washington Monument Road, which extends north from Alternate U.S. 40; the junction is about 3 kilometers (2 miles) east of *Boonsboro, Maryland*. Drive upward to the end-of-the-road parking lot and hike the short, gradually winding trail to the observation tower.

South Mountain, which here forms the western part of the Blue Ridge Province, is a homoclinal limb of a large but deeply eroded anticline that is centered on the *Middletown Valley.* The ridge is supported by resistant Weverton Quartzite (likely Early Cambrian but possibly Late Precambrian) that, on the basis of graded bedding and cross-bedding, is known to be overturned and dipping about forty degrees to the east. The immediately younger Harpers Formation, which is for the most part a phyllite, crops out downslope to the west while older Precambrian metavolcanics are exposed in the lowland immediately east of the ridge. In combination with the structural characteristics of the Weverton Formation apparent on *Catoctin Mountain* at *Gambrill State Park,* relationships clearly demonstrate that the topography of the Blue Ridge is relatively simple, consisting of two narrow homoclinal ridges (Catoctin and South mountains) separated by a wide anticlinal valley (Middletown Valley).

There are a number of block fields in the central Appalachians that have been attributed to accelerated periglacial activity during glacial phases of the Pleistocene. The overall form of these angular boulder diamictons varies with differences in geologic structure, rock type, and morphologic position. Here the block field below the tower consists of Weverton Quartzite that has accumulated on the west-facing scarp of the east-dipping Weverton Formation. Altogether, the general absence of tree deformation induced by mass movements, the advanced and widespread lichen growth, scattered weathering pits on certain rock surfaces, and the thick accumulation of overlying organic matter at some places indicate that this block field has been stable for a long period of time. Geomorphic and paleobiological evidence suggests that during the Late Wisconsin glacial maxima the mean annual temperature here was between zero and two degrees Celsius, and the timberline was at about 500 meters (1,640 feet), only 100 to 150 meters (35 to 500 feet) higher than the undulating ridge crest near the observation tower. On all of these bases it is concluded that this and other block fields in the central Appalachians are relics of Pleistocene glacial conditions. If this interpretation is correct their presence also provides a basis for estimating the amount of climatic change that has occurred at this site since the block field formed.

One interesting characteristic of this block field is that it accumulated near the ridge summit, and the source area of the angular boulder is very limited in extent. These two factors indicate that the blocks moved only a short distance to reach their present location.

The land to the west, which is within the Valley and Ridge Physiographic Province, differs markedly from the Blue Ridge. The rocks there consist of a great thickness of weak and strong Paleozoic sedimentary strata that, because of tectonic compression, have been deformed into an assemblage of northeast-southwest-trending folds. Over many millions of years erosion has lowered the land to form valleys on less resistant rocks while ridges remain where the stronger sediments exist.

The wide lowland to the west is the *Hagerstown Valley* (a section of the Great Valley). It is underlain mainly by Cambrian and Ordovician limestone along with some dolomite and shale. These formations are relatively weak and extensive, thus accounting for both the existence and the size of the valley. The resulting terrain and soil are quite suitable for crops, making this an important agricultural area.

Farther west, 35 kilometers (22 miles) distant, are much stronger Silurian rocks that support the easternmost of many ridges within this province. With steep slopes and infertile soils, these numerous, high, linear, and forested barriers tend to separate and isolate the many fertile valleys. The result is an especially close relationship between bedrock geology, geomorphology, historical geography, and types of land use within the Valley and Ridge Province.

Harpers Ferry and the Water Gaps of the Potomac River

The overall drainage history of the Potomac River and its major tributaries is presented in Day Three of this volume and for purposes of brevity will not be repeated here. What is important at

Harpers Ferry is that the river has succeeded in cutting a major water gap through two closely-spaced western ranges of the Blue Ridge. (About 15 kilometers [10 miles] downstream the Potomac has eroded another water gap in *Catoctin Mountain,* a ridge at the eastern margin of the province.) The result is a spectacular set of geologic exposures within one of the most impressive topographic scenes in this part of the Blue Ridge.

In the vicinity of Harpers Ferry the western part of the Blue Ridge consists of two parallel, north-south-trending ridges, both interrupted by the gap occupied by the Potomac River. One of these, *South Mountain,* extends southward and is known as *Short Hill Mountain* south of the Potomac River; this ridge gradually becomes lower and dies out 16 kilometers (10 miles) south of the water gap. The second and westernmost of the two ridges, known as *Blue Ridge,* extends north to become *Elk Ridge* north of the Potomac River; and about 16 kilometers (10 miles) north of the water gap this ridge also disappears. Thus the water-gap bisection of the two ridges produces four components with each going by a distinct name even though they are, more or less, associated with the same topographic system.

The gradual termination of both ridges at equal distances either north or south of the water gap at Harpers Ferry is of interest because a slight change in the course of the river would enable it to completely avoid one or the other of the ridges.

Although a detailed and authoritative account of the area's geology has been presented by Ernst Cloos (see *The Geology of the South Mountain Anticlinorium, Maryland,* Johns Hopkins University Studies in Geology, No. 16, Pt. I, 1950, Johns Hopkins University Press), interpretation of the geologic structure of the ridges as revealed by rocks exposed extensively within the water gap has been the subject of interest and controversy for decades. Field study along the water-gap cliffs and on river islands and falls indicates that Elk Ridge and its southward continuation, Blue Ridge, are both supported largely by rocks of the resistant Weverton Formation that are associated with the west limb of a large and overturned fold. However, rather than a simple flexure, the structure consists of a com-

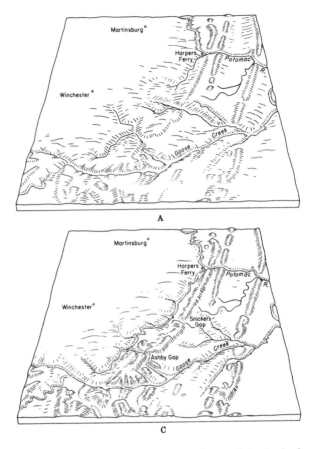

Diagrams showing progressive stream piracies resulting in the formation of Snickers, Ashby, and Manassas wind gaps. Source: William J. Wayne.

plex anticlinorium made up of innumerable folds of greatly varying magnitude.

On the north side of the river at the west portal of the railway tunnel, the Weverton Formation is overturned and dips steeply toward the east. The adjacent and slightly younger Harpers Phyllite crops out immediately to the west with numerous exposures in Harpers Ferry (especially accessible and observable in stairs carved directly into the rock that lead to *Jefferson Rock* in the village) and

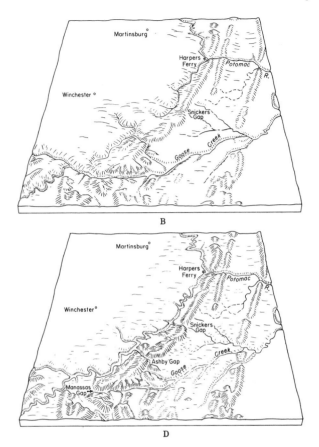

along both the Potomac and Shenandoah rivers immediately above confluence. Furthermore, downstream (east) in the gap just west of the U.S. 340 bridge over the Potomac River, older Precambrian rock including greenstone and gneiss crops out. Thus the formations become younger toward the west, indicating that the crest of the anticlinorium must be somewhere to the east.

Curiously, the same general pattern of outcrops (youngest rocks to the west) is repeated in water-gap exposures associated with the South Mountain/Short Hill ridges which are immediately to the east of Elk Ridge/Blue Ridge. This strati-

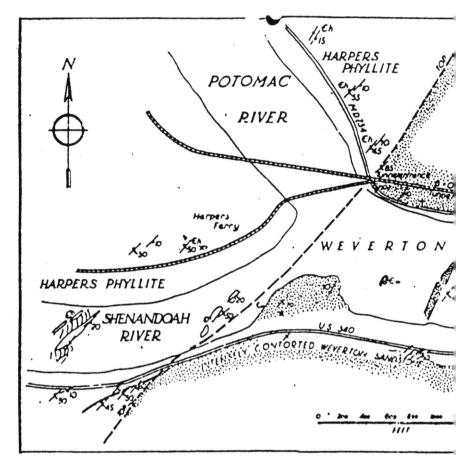

Geological features at Harpers Ferry water gap. Source: H. Cloos, Bulletin of the Geological Society of America *(1950).*

graphic repetition suggests to some that high-angle faulting is also involved, while others have invoked a less well accepted notion of thrust faulting.

Either way, lithology, structure, and stratigraphy all indicate that orogenic activity occurred here during the Precambrian and Paleozoic eras. Since the early phase of the Mesozoic, however, this region has remained tectonically stable, affected only by epeiro-

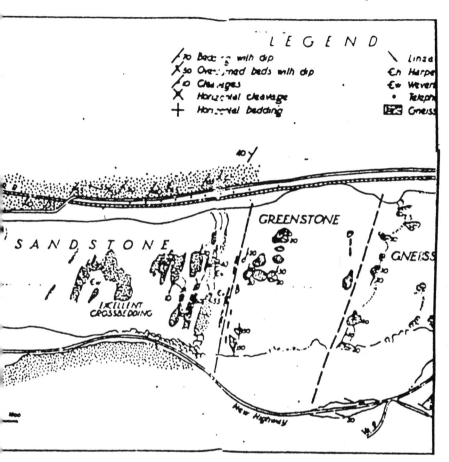

genic crustal movement. On this basis it is clear that the landscape of the water gap and surrounding areas is wholly the product of late-geologic degradation of ancient rocks and structures.

This last deduction reasserts the most important message of this chapter. The varied and marvelous scenic geomorphology of Maryland's Blue Ridge Mountains, Piedmont, and Valley and Ridge Province is not the direct product of dramatic geologic upheaval. To the contrary, it is the slowly-evolving and ever-changing product of long-term geomorphic degradation of bedrock that has remained passive for more than 200 million years. This means that the present terrain of Maryland has been preceded by a great array of evolving landscapes. The extension of this conclusion is obvious, certain, and profound: The scenic geomorphology of today will certainly evolve into something different in the future.

PART THREE

Resources

△ Hints to the Traveler

An easy way to see Washington is to take a guided tour-mobile of Washington and its environs. This is an excellent way to get oriented to the city, especially to the Mall and downtown area, but also to the Virginia sites across the Potomac River, such as Arlington National Cemetery. These guided trips are available from sites throughout the Mall area, and one price includes transportation and sightseeing.

ACCOMMODATIONS

As is the case with any large city in the United States or abroad, you can pay handsomely for a four-star hotel and for less prestigious, but well-located hotels and motels in the downtown area. Therefore, it is wise to consider where you want to stay and how much you want to spend well before coming to Washington. Reservations are always recommended, given the regular business and tourist travel.

Discounts are usually available at most hotels and motels, if you inquire. These include senior citizen discounts, corporate discounts, group rates, weekend rates, and the like.

CLOTHING

In the travel business, Washington, D.C., is often referred to as a "blue collar" tourist town, because so many of the museums are free and families can have a fairly inexpensive visit. As a result, casual attire is acceptable just about anywhere, but fine restaurants have their own dress code, so it is wise to inquire about appropriate dinner attire when making dinner reservations.

Also, even during the hot and humid summer, it is wise to bring along a light sweater, for air conditioning can be cool indoors. A waterproof or windproof outer jacket is also recommended during any time of the year, for precipitation can occur throughout the year. In winter, of course, you will need warm clothes. Essential are good, comfortable walking shoes, for you will do a lot of walking in the Mall and downtown area.

MAPS

The maps that appear in this field guide are useful for general orientation and for planning purposes, but less useful for details. So be sure to pick up city maps and a good road atlas either at visitor centers or at bookstores. There are excellent map stores, conveniently located in the downtown area, which are listed in the Yellow Pages of the telephone directory.

RESTAURANTS

Numerous lists and directories will guide you to any of a wide variety of restaurants at a wide variety of prices. Sholl's Colonial Cafeteria (1990 K Street, N.W.) is a Washington institution renowned for inexpensive if utilitarian dining.

SAFETY

Washington, D.C., like any large city in the United States, has its full share of crime. In general, however, most of the high-crime areas (areas in which drug use is a serious problem) are away from the typical tourist centers. Still, one must use common sense, no matter where you are.

TRANSPORTATION

Washington, D.C., is well-served by Amtrak, and there is no finer way to arrive in the nation's capital than through beautiful, renovated Union Station near the Capitol building. Washington is also served by three airports: National, which is the closest to the city and easily reached by taxi and Metro; Dulles, about forty-five minutes to the west in the former Virginia countryside, which is reached by taxi and limousine service; and BWI (Baltimore–Washington International), about fifty minutes to the northeast of the city (actually only fifteen minutes from Baltimore), which is served by taxi, limousine service, and by rail (some Amtrak trains stop here). Both Dulles and BWI are international airports, with excellent connections to cities overseas. Currently, BWI is a hub for USAir, and Dulles is a hub for United, though all major airlines serve the national capital region's three airports.

Public transportation is also excellent, especially with respect to the D.C. subway system, known as Metro. The Metro is clean, convenient, safe, and easy to use. You are encouraged to use it. It suspends operations, however, between midnight and 6:00 a.m. Taxi cabs are available throughout the region, and most drivers are friendly, courteous, and excellent conversationalists (if you ask questions). Fares are charged according to the number of zones traversed. Metro bus service goes just about everywhere in the area. The routes complement Metro subway routes. You can get a bus transfer when you get on the Metro.

WEATHER

Washington, D.C., is a four-season climate. During some years, of course, it seems as if winter runs right into summer with only a short reprieve of spring-like weather. And winters can be mild or harsh, depending on the year. But there are almost always two certainties with respect to the region's weather. First, there is high heat and humidity from about June 1 through September 15. Second, during this period, there is a 30 percent chance of afternoon or evening thundershowers.

Many travelers wish to plan their visit to Washington so they can see the cherry trees in bloom at the Tidal Basin. The Cherry Blossom Festival is held annually during the first week of April, but this does not guarantee that the blossoms will peak then. Some years the blossoms appear as early as the last week or ten days of March, and often a strong wind or rain will diminish the length of the peak season.

△ Suggested Readings

FIELD GUIDES

Two favorite guides to Washington are *Washington On Foot: 23 Walking Tours (with Maps) of Washington, D.C., and Old Town Alexandria,* edited by John J. Protopappas and Alvin R. McNeal (Smithsonian Institution Press, 1992, new revised edition); and *Washington, D.C.: A Traveler's Guide to the District of Columbia and Nearby Attractions,* which is Handbook 102 of the National Park Service (U.S. Department of the Interior, 1989). Also useful is *The Smithsonian Guide to Historic America,* a series of twelve volumes organized by regions. For our purposes, see Volume I, *Virginia and the Capital Region,* by Henry Wiencek (Stewart, Tabori, and Chang, 1989), and Volume III, *The Mid-Atlantic States,* by Michael S. Durham (Stewart, Tabori, and Chang, 1989). For those who are interested in the trees of Washington and who want to explore some of the city's natural history, see *City of Trees: The Complete Field Guide to the Trees of Washington, D.C.,* revised edition, by Melanie Choukas-Bradley and Polly Alexander (The Johns Hopkins University Press, 1987). Another "old reliable" field guide is *Maryland: A New Guide to the Old Line State,* compiled and edited by Edward C. Panenfouse *et alia* (The Johns Hopkins University Press, 1976). For those who are interested in physical geography, see *Roadside Geology of Virginia,* by Keith Frye (Mountain Press, 1986).

STATE HISTORIES

A model in state histories is *Maryland: A Middle Temperament, 1634–1980,* by Robert J. Brugger (The Johns Hopkins University Press, 1988). Also useful are four volumes that appeared in the States and the Nation Series: *West Virginia: A History,* by John Alexander Williams (Norton, 1976); *Virginia: A History,* by Louis D. Rubin, Jr. (Norton, 1977); *Pennsylvania,* by Thomas C. Cochran (Norton, 1978); and *Maryland,* by Carl Bode (Norton, 1978).

REGIONAL BOOKS AND NATURAL HISTORY

Most bookstores in the area will have an excellent section of regional books from which to select, but here are some of the classics: *Tobacco Coast: A Maritime History of Chesapeake Bay in the Colonial Era,* by Arthur Pierce Middleton (The Johns Hopkins University Press, 1984); *Maryland Lost and Found: People and Places from Chesapeake to Appalachia,* by Eugene L. Meyer (The Johns Hopkins University Press, 1986); *The Potomac,* by Frederick Gutheim (The Johns Hopkins University Press, 1986; Holt, Rinehart, and Winston, 1949); *Bay Country,* by Tom Horton (The Johns Hopkins University Press, 1987); *The Bay,* by Gilbert C. Klingel (The Johns Hopkins University Press, 1984; Dodd, Mead, 1951); *Spring in Washington,* by Louis J. Halle (The Johns Hopkins University Press, 1988); and *The Transformation of Virginia, 1740–1790,* by Rhys Isaac (Norton, 1988; University of North Carolina Press, 1982). Also of interest are *Life in the Chesapeake Bay,* by Alice Jane Lippson and Robert L. Lippson (The Johns Hopkins University Press, 1984); *Chesapeake Country,* by Lucien Niemeyer and Eugene L. Meyer (Abbeyville Press, 1990); *Maryland Time Exposures, 1840–1940,* by Marion E. Warren and Mame Warren (The Johns Hopkins University Press, 1984); *Baltimore: When She Was What She Used to Be, 1850–1930,* by Marion E. Warren and Mame Warren (The Johns Hopkins University Press, 1983); and *Tidewater by Steamboat: A Sage of the Chesapeake,* by David C. Holly (The Johns Hopkins University Press, 1991).

DAY ONE (L'ENFANT'S WASHINGTON)

Carr, Martha S. 1950. *The District of Columbia, Its Rocks and Their Geologic History.* Geological Survey Bulletin 967. Washington, D.C.: Government Printing Office.

Ehrenberg, Ralph. 1979. "Mapping the Nation's Capital: The Surveyor's Office, 1791–1818." *The Quarterly Journal of the Library of Congress* 36:279–319.

Friis, Herman R. 1968. *Geographical Reconnaissance of the Potomac River Tidewater Fringe of Virginia from Arlington Memorial Bridge to Mount Vernon.* Washington, D.C.: Association of American Geographers.

Gales, Joseph. 1834–1836. *Annals of the Congress of the United States.* Washington, D.C.

Hawkins, Don Alexander. 1991. "The Landscape of the Federal City a 1792 Walking Tour." *Washington History* 3:11–33.

Henrikson, Alan K. 1983. "A Small, Cosy Town, Global in Scope: Washington, D.C." *Ekistics: The Science and Study of Human Settlements* 50:123–145.

Hodges, Allan A., editor. 1976. *Washington on Foot: A City Planner's Guide to the Nation's Capital.* Washington, D.C.: American Institute of Planners.

Jennings, J. L. Sibley, Jr. 1979. "Artistry As Design." *The Quarterly Journal of the Library of Congress* 36:225–278.

L'Enfant, Pierre Charles. 1791. "Plan of the City, intended for the Permanent Seat of the Government of the United States." Computer-assisted reproduction produced by the U.S. Geological Survey for the Library of Congress from the original manuscript plan. Washington, D.C.: Library of Congress.

McNeil, Priscilla W. 1991. "Rock Creek Hundred." *Washington History* 3:34–51.

Merrens, Harry Roy. 1957. "The Locating of the Federal Capital of the United States." M.A. Thesis, University of Maryland.

Nine Geographical Field Trips in the Washington, D.C. Area. 1968. Washington, D.C.: Association of American Geographers.

Schuyler, David. 1986. *The New Urban Landscape: The Redefinition of City Form in Nineteenth-Century America*. Baltimore and London: The Johns Hopkins University Press.

Scott, Pamela. 1991. "L'Enfant's Washington Described." *Washington History* 3:76–95.

Stephenson, Richard W. 1979. "The Delineation of a Grand Plan." *The Quarterly Journal of the Library of Congress* 36:207–224.

Washington City and Capital. 1937. Federal Writers' Project, Works Progress Administration, American Guide Series. Washington, D.C.: Government Printing Office.

Williams, Garnett P. 1977. *Washington, D.C.'s Vanishing Springs and Waterways*. Geological Survey Circular 752. Washington, D.C.: Government Printing Office.

DAY TWO (SHAW AND LEDROIT PARK)

Fitzpatrick, Sandra and Maria R. Goodwin. 1990. *The Guide to Black Washington: Places and Events of Historical and Cultural Significance in the Nation's Capital*. New York: Hippocrene Books.

Green, Constance McLaughlin. 1962. *Washington: Village and Capital, 1800–1878*. Princeton, New Jersey: Princeton University Press.

Green, Constance McLaughlin. 1963. *Washington: Capital City, 1879–1950*. Princeton, New Jersey: Princeton University Press.

Smith, Cathryn Schneider, ed. 1988. *Washington at Home: An Illustrated History of Neighborhoods in the Nation's Capital*. Columbia Historical Society, Northridge, California: Windsor Publications.

DAY THREE (GEORGE WASHINGTON'S POTOMAC)

Garrett, Wilbur E. 1987. "George Washington's Patomack Canal." *National Geographic* 171 (June):716–753.

Grim, Ronald E. 1971. "The Origins and Early Development of the Virginia Fall Line Towns." Master's thesis, Department of Geography, University of Maryland.

Gutheim, Frederick A. 1949. *The Potomac.* New York: Rinehart.

Hahn, Thomas F. 1976. *George Washington's Canal at Great Falls, Virginia.* Shepardstown, W.Va.: American Canal and Transportation Center.

————. 1984. *The Chesapeake and Ohio Canal: Pathway to the Nation's Capital.* Metuchen, N.J.: Scarecrow Press.

Mitchell, Beth. 1987. *Fairfax County Virginia in 1760: An Interpretive Historical Map.* Fairfax, Va.: Office of Comprehensive Planning.

Mount Vernon: A Handbook. 1985. Mount Vernon, Va.: Mount Vernon Ladies' Association of the Union.

O'Mara, James. 1983. *An Historical Geography of Urban System Development: Tidewater Virginia in the 18th Century.* Geographical Monographs no. 13. Downsview, Ont.: York University, Atkinson College, Department of Geography.

Reed, John C., Jr., et al. 1980. *The River and the Rocks: The Geological Story of Great Falls and the Potomac River Gorge.* U.S. Geological Survey Bulletin no. 1471. Washington, D.C.: GPO.

Reps, John W. 1972. *Tidewater Towns: City Planning in Colonial Virginia and Maryland.* Charlottesville, Va.: University Press of Virginia for Colonial Williamsburg Foundation.

Stephenson, Richard W. 1981. *The Cartography of Northern Virginia: Facsimile Reproductions of Maps Dating from 1608 to 1915.* Fairfax, Va.: Office of Comprehensive Planning, History and Archaeology Section.

DAY FOUR (COLONIAL VIRGINIA)

Billings, Warren M. n.d. *Jamestown and the Founding of the Nation.* Gettysburg, Pennsylvania: Thomas Publications.

Billings, Warren M., ed. 1975. *The Old Dominion in the Seventeenth Century: A Documentary History of Virginia, 1606–1689.* Chapel Hill, North Carolina: The University of North Carolina Press.

Blouet, Brian W. 1990. "Welcome to Williamsburg." *Journal of Geography* 89, no. 5:194–196.

Bridenbaugh, Carl. 1980. *Jamestown 1544–1699.* New York: Oxford University Press.

Earle, Carville V. 1979. In ed. Thad W. Tate and David L. Ammerman, *The Chesapeake in the Seventeenth Century,* New York: W. W. Norton and Company.

Farmer, Charles J. 1988. "Persistence of Country Trade: The Failure of Towns to Develop in Southside Virginia during the Eighteenth Century." *Journal of Historical Geography* 14, no. 4:331–341.

Gottmann, Jean. 1969. *Virginia in Our Century.* Charlottesville, Virginia: University Press of Virginia.

Hale, John S. 1978. *A Historical Atlas of Colonial Virginia.* Verona, Virginia: Old Dominion Publications.

Hatch, Charles E. 1957. *The First Seventeen Years: Virginia, 1607–1624.* Charlottesville, Virginia: University Press of Virginia.

Isaac, Rhys. 1987. *Worlds of Experience: Communities in Colonial Virginia.* Williamsburg, Virginia: Colonial Williamsburg Foundation.

Kocker, A. Lawrence and Howard Dearstyne. 1976. *Colonial Williamsburg: Its Buildings and Gardens.* 2nd ed. Williamsburg, Virginia: Colonial Williamsburg Foundation.

Olmert, Michael. 1985. *Official Guide to Colonial Williamsburg.* Williamsburg, Virginia: Colonial Williamsburg Foundation.

O'Mara, James. 1982. "Town Founding in Seventeenth-Century North America: Jamestown in Virginia." *Journal of Historical Geography* 8, no. 1.

Taylor, E.G.R. 1935. *The Original Writings and Correspondence of the Two Richard Hakluyts.* Second series, no. 76. 2 vols. London: Hakluyt Society.

DAY FIVE (SOUTHERN MARYLAND)

Barth, John. 1960. *The Sot-Weed Factor.* New York: Doubleday.

Carr, Lois Green, et al. 1991. *Robert Cole's World: Agriculture and Society in Early Maryland.* Chapel Hill: University of North Carolina Press.

Heimann, Robert A. 1960. *Tobacco and Americans.* New York: McGraw-Hill.

Kulikoff, Allan. 1986. *Tobacco and Slaves: The Development of Southern Cultures in the Chesapeake, 1680–1800.* Chapel Hill: University of North Carolina Press.

Main, Gloria L. 1982. *Tobacco Colony: Life in Early Maryland, 1650–1720.* Princeton, N.J.: Princeton University Press.

Michener, James A. 1978. *Chesapeake.* New York: Random House.

Miller, Henry M., et al. 1986. *Discovering Maryland's First City.* St. Mary's City: Archaeology Series no. 2.

Percy, David O. 1919. *The Production of Tobacco along the Colonial Potomac.* Accokeek, Md.: The National Colonial Farm, Research Report no. 1.

DAY SIX (CIVIL WAR)

Bigelow, John. 1910. *The Campaign at Chancellorsville.* New Haven, Connecticut.

Bloom, Arthur L. 1991. *Geomorphology: A Systematic Analysis of Late Cenozoic Landforms.* 2nd ed. Englewood Cliffs, New Jersey: Prentice Hall.

Brown, Andrew. 1961. "Geology and the Gettysburg Campaign." *Geotimes* 6, no. 1:8–12, 40–41.

Fenneman, Nevin M. 1938. *Physiography of the Eastern United States.* New York: McGraw-Hill Book Co.

Freeman, Douglas Southall. 1946. *Lee's Lieutenants.* New York: Charles Scribner's Sons.

Fuller, J.F.C. 1958. *The Generalship of Ulysses S. Grant.* Bloomington: Indiana University Press.

King, Philip B. 1977. *The Evolution of North America.* Princeton, New Jersey: Princeton University Press.

Lobeck, A. K. 1939. *Geomorphology.* New York: McGraw-Hill Book Co.

McPherson, James M. 1988. *Battle Cry of Freedom.* New York: Ballantine Books.

Morisawa, Marie. 1968. *Streams.* New York: McGraw-Hill Book Co.

Murfin, James. V. 1965. *The Gleam of Bayonets.* New York: Thomas Yoseloff.

Ritter, Dale F. 1978. *Process Geomorphology.* Dubuque, Iowa. Wm. C. Brown Co.

Scientific American. 1983. Vol. 249, no. 3:114–142.

Stackpole, Edward J. 1957. *The Fredericksburg Campaign.* Harrisburg, Pennsylvania: Military Services Publishing Company.

Stewart, George R. 1959. *Pickett's Charge.* Boston: Houghton Mifflin Co.

Tanner, Robert G. 1976. *Stonewall in the Valley.* New York: Doubleday and Company.

Thornbury, William D. 1965. *Regional Geomorphology of the United States.* New York: John Wiley and Sons.

————. 1969. *Principles of Geomorphology.* 2nd ed. New York: John Wiley and Sons.

Vandiver, Frank E. 1957. *Mighty Stonewall.* New York: McGraw-Hill Book Co.

DAY SEVEN (AMISH COUNTRY)

The use of U.S. Geological Survey 7½-minute topographic maps will enhance this trip. The nine sheets traversed by this field trip are identified alphabetically and are numbered in the sequence of their use on the trip:

Columbia East, Pennsylvania	(10)
Columbia West, Pennsylvania	(11)
Conowingo Dam, Maryland and Pennsylvania	(1)
Gap, Pennsylvania	(4)
Lancaster, Pennsylvania	(9)
Leola, Pennsylvania	(6) & (8)
New Holland, Pennsylvania	(7)
Quarryville, Pennsylvania	(3) & (5)
Wakefield, Pennsylvania	(2)

Glass, Joseph W. 1986. *The Pennsylvania Culture Region: A View from the Barn.* Ann Arbor, Michigan: UMI Research Press.

Hostetler, John A. 1980. *Amish Society.* 3rd. ed. Baltimore and London: The Johns Hopkins University Press.

Hostetler, John A., editor. 1989. *Amish Roots: A Treasury of History, Wisdom, and Lore.* Baltimore and London: The Johns Hopkins University Press.

Kraybill, Donald R. 1989. *The Riddle of Amish Culture.* Baltimore and London: The Johns Hopkins University Press.

Zelinsky, Wilbur. "The Pennsylvania Town: An Overdue Geographical Account." *Geographical Review* 67:127–147.

DAY EIGHT (BEYOND THE BELTWAY)

Anderson, John Ward. 1991. "Money Trouble Ahead on Route 28?" *Washington Post.* December 2, pp. C1, C4.

Bolan, Lewis, and Eric Smart. 1991. "Metropolitan Washington: A Real Estate Market and Religion in Flux." *Urban Land* 11:4–15.

Cervero, Robert. 1986. *Suburban Gridlock.* New Brunswick: Rutgers University, Center for Urban Policy.

––––––. 1989. *America's Suburban Centers. The Land Use–Transportation Link.* London: Unwin Hyman.

Garreau, Joel. 1991. *Edge City: Life on the New Frontier.* New York: Doubleday.

Hartshorn, Truman A. 1992. *Interpreting the City: An Urban Geography.* 2nd ed. New York: John Wiley and Sons.

Hartshorn, Truman A. and Peter O. Muller. 1989. "Suburban Downtowns and the Transformation of Metropolitan Atlanta's Business Landscape." *Urban Geography* 10, no. 4:375–395.

––––––. 1992. "The Suburban Downtown and Urban Economic Development Today." In *Sources of Metropolitan Growth,* ed. Edwin S. Mills and John F. McDonald. New Brunswick: Rutgers University, Center for Urban Policy Research.

Knox, Paul L. 1991. "The Restless Urban Landscape: Economic and Socio-Cultural Change and the Transformation of Washington, D.C." *Annals of the Association of American Geographers.* 81:181–209.

"L'Enfant's Legacy: A Survey of Washington, D.C." *The Economist* April 16, 1988.

Muller, Peter O. 1981. *Contemporary Suburban America*. Englewood Cliffs, N.J.: Prentice-Hall.

———. 1989. "The Transformation of Bedroom Suburbia into Outer City: An Overview of Metropolitan Structural Change Since 1947." In *Suburbia Revisited,* ed. B. M. Kelly. New York: Greenwood Press.

Netherton, Nan. 1989. *Reston: A New Town in the Old Dominion*. Norfolk, Virginia: The Donning Company/Publishers.

Real Estate Corporation. 1991. "Washington, D.C. Metropolitan Area." In ULI Market Profiles. Washington, D.C.: Urban Land Institute.

Reston Land Corporation. 1991. *Reston Neighborhoods*. Reston, Virginia.

Urban Land Institute. 1991. *Deals on Wheels (Mobile Workshops)*. 1991 Fall Meeting, Washington, D.C.

———. 1991. *Project Reference File* 21, no. 11. Reston Town Center, Reston, Virginia.

DAY NINE (GEOMORPHOLOGY)

Bloom, Arthur L. 1991. *Geomorphology: A Systematic Analysis of Late Cenozoic Landforms*. 2nd ed. Englewood Cliffs, New Jersey: Prentice-Hall.

Fenneman, Nevin M. 1938. *Physiography of the Eastern United States*. New York: McGraw-Hill Book Co.

King, Philip B. 1977. *The Evolution of North America*. Princeton, New Jersey: Princeton University Press.

Ritter, Dale F. 1978. *Process Geomorphology*. Dubuque, Iowa: Wm. C. Brown Co.

Thornbury, William D. 1965. *Regional Geomorphology of the United States*. New York: John Wiley and Sons.

———. 1969. *Principles of Geomorphology*. 2nd ed. New York: John Wiley and Sons.

△ Index